POSTCARD HISTORY SERIES

Santa Rosa California

IN VINTAGE POSTCARDS

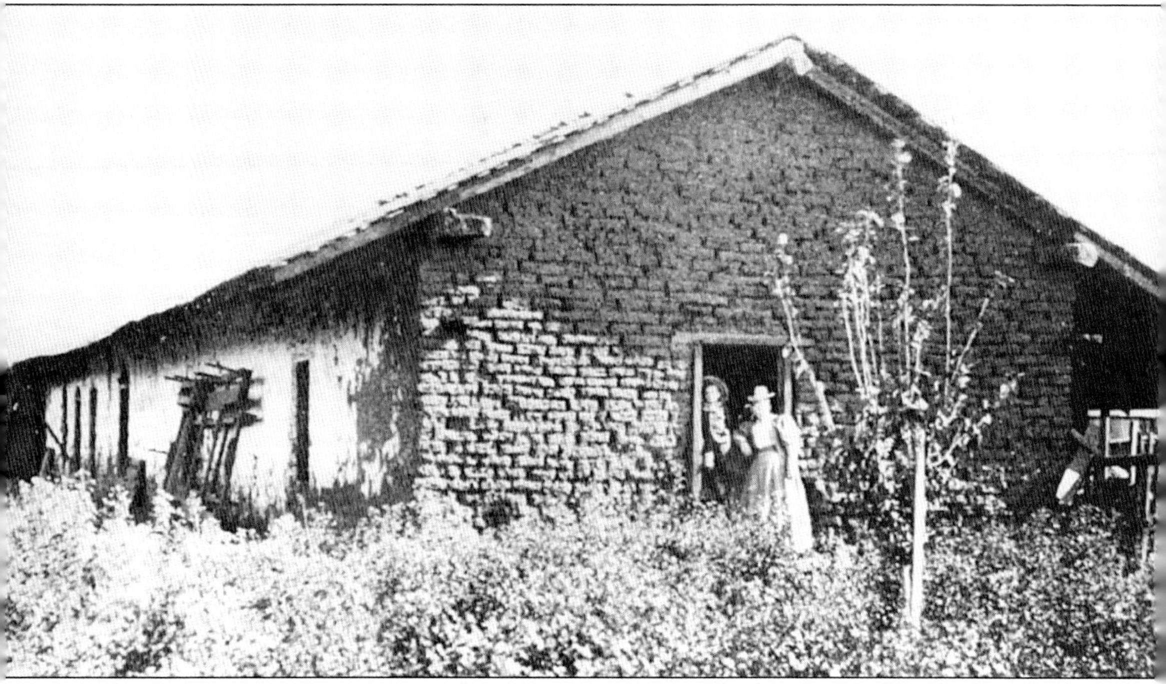

THE CARRILLO ADOBE, C. 1890. The Carrillo Adobe was the first non-Indian dwelling in the Santa Rosa area. Its history is long and wide, and deserves special recognition in this book. In 1837, Doña Maria Ignacia López de Carrillo, mother-in-law to General Mariano Vallejo, built the adobe on 8,800 acres along Santa Rosa Creek. On a current map those boundaries would be approximately as follows: northeast to slightly east of the Maria Carrillo High School campus at Montecito Avenue and Calistoga Road, northwest to Guerneville Road at Stony Point Road, southwest to Stony Point Road at Hearn Avenue, and southeast to Hoen Avenue ending at Annadel State Park.

By the 1850s the adobe housed a store, an inn, and a post office. Later, from 1860 to 1950, the building was owned and operated by the Feodor Hahman family. In the mid-1940s a wing of the adobe collapsed. Six years later the remainder of the building and the surrounding 17 acres became the property of the Roman Catholic Diocese of San Francisco. In 1960, the control of the land passed to the Diocese of Santa Rosa.

Most of the efforts in the past have failed to arrest the building's decay or indeed to resolve its future. There is hope that the Friends of the Carrillo Adobe, together with the cooperation of the Diocese, can move forward quickly with plans to save this treasure from complete annihilation.

POSTCARD HISTORY SERIES

Santa Rosa California in Vintage Postcards

Bob and Kay Voliva

ARCADIA PUBLISHING

ISBN 978-0-7385-0233-5

Published by Arcadia Publishing
Charleston, South Carolina

Printed in the United States of America

Library of Congress Catalog Card Number: 99065992

For all general information contact Arcadia Publishing at:
Telephone 843-853-2070
Fax 843-853-0044
E-Mail: sales@arcadiapublishing.com
For customer service and orders:
Toll-Free 1-888-313-2665

Visit us on the Internet at www.arcadiapublishing.com

Postcards and photocards scanned by John Peck Graphic Services, Rohnert Park, California.

Dedicated to Local Historians Everywhere!

Contents

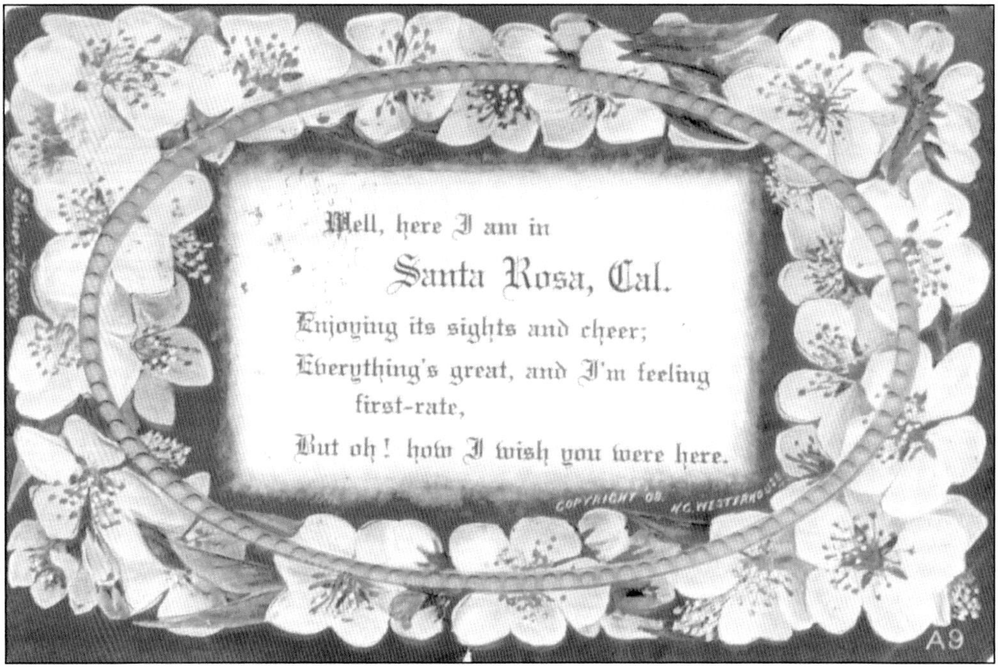

A Typical Novelty Card.

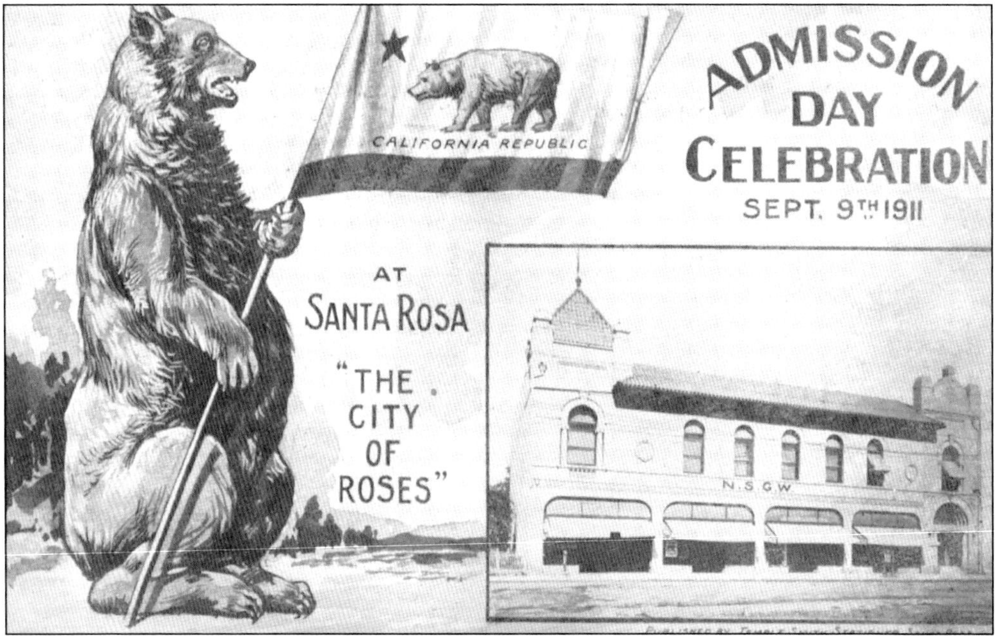

Admission Day Celebration, 1911.

ACKNOWLEDGMENTS

In addition to our own postcard collection, we wish to thank the following people who graciously loaned us their postcards and memories for use in this book:

Al and Stella Aloise
Sherman and Phoebe Boivin
John and Nanci Burton
Earl Carrillo
Donna Carrillo Endicott
Dennis and Martha Keegan
Luther Burbank Home & Gardens, Lynne Collins
Mary Ann Mariani
Bill Montgomery
Maury and Theresa Nelson
John Schmale
Don and Susan Silverek
Temple and June Smith
Sonoma County Historical Society, Harry Lapham
Sonoma County Library, Audrey Herman
Sonoma County Museum, Evangeline Tai
Frank Sternad

INTRODUCTION

Why do we need a visual history of Santa Rosa? Both of us are non-natives who migrated to California in the mid-1970s from the Midwest—an area interested in its history and with many of its historic buildings and landmarks still remaining. As history buffs and collectors of local memorabilia, we became more interested in old Santa Rosa. Where was this building located? What happened to the courthouse? How did Railroad Square develop? It was hard to visualize the changes that had occurred.

After reading the excellent two-volume history of Santa Rosa currently on the market, we began to understand the changes over the last one hundred years and some of the reasons for them. Three major factors have influenced the course of Santa Rosa's appearance.

The Great Earthquake of 1906 had a tremendous impact on the face of the town. In that few minutes before dawn on April 18, 1906, almost all of the major structures in the downtown commercial area were destroyed. The town was rebuilt, but a pre-1906 brick structure is a rare item today.

The next major event was the construction of Highway 101, completed in the late 1940s. The proposed route for the new highway would have followed Fulton Road, several miles west of Santa Rosa. Fearing travelers would bypass downtown and the resulting loss of business, city fathers successfully lobbied to change the route to more closely follow the old Redwood Highway. Unfortunately, the new multi-lane highway effectively split Santa Rosa in two.

The last important influence, and probably the most dramatic for the appearance of Santa Rosa, was the general desire for urban renewal in the late 1960s and early 1970s. Santa Rosa lost its courthouse and plaza, many landmark buildings on the plaza were removed, streets were rerouted or eliminated, and several square blocks downtown were incorporated into the Santa Rosa Plaza shopping mall.

It is not the purpose of this book to judge these changes or to rewrite the already mentioned history of Santa Rosa. We merely want to give the reader a tool to look at our past heritage. How can we see into the past? Reading about what used to be here is wonderful, but it is hard to see it in your mind. There are probably hundreds, maybe thousands, of personal photographs out there, but most are in private hands and therefore hard to access. The picture postcard provides us with a great window back to a time period we want to discover.

Postcards have been collected for many years. A visit to any antique shop will turn up a vintage postcard album. People purchased the cards to remember a place or an event. Whether they were mailed to someone or kept unused, most people had a tendency to save them. Due to the fact that people retained them, and because there was a vast number of cards produced, all of us are left with a valuable and accessible picture of the past.

On May 1, 1873, Congress authorized the Post Office Department to sell small postal cards at 1¢ each for short written communication. Within six months, over 60 million cards had been sold. Enterprising companies soon found they could print pictures and advertising on the government-printed cards. Pictorial cards were printed in Europe by the late 1870s and quickly found their way to the United States. At the Columbian Exposition held in Chicago in 1893, visitors purchased hundreds of thousands of pictorial souvenir postcards. Even though the post office now charged 2¢ to mail a picture postcard, the rage was on.

The postcard was quickly becoming the most popular form of written communication. On May 19, 1898, the government lowered the cost to mail a card to 1¢. In 1906, Rural Free Delivery allowed mail delivery to the entire United States population. Prior to 1907, a picture postcard could only contain a written message on the picture side, the back being reserved exclusively for the address. On March 1, 1907, the post office changed the regulations to allow written messages on a divided back card. By the end of the fiscal year, June 30, 1908, the post office had handled 667,777,798 postcards.

In the following pages you will see us refer to both postcards and photocards. The first term describes the commercially printed postcard that was available in a wide variety of subjects and styles. The photocard is a very different form and provides us with a personal view of a range of subjects. In 1888, Eastman (Kodak) introduced a simple box camera that was affordable to everyone. It was sealed with enough film for one hundred photographs and had to be sent to Kodak for development. With the developed photographs, one would also receive a new camera, ready to take more pictures.

By the turn of the century, Kodak had refined the developing process for local professional photographers and the amateur home photographer. Soon, preprinted postcard paper was available, and everyone could make their own postcards. By 1910, most people owned a camera, and no subject remained uncaptured by the amateur camera lens. Many scenes and subjects that would have been lost forever were retained for our enjoyment today.

The preparation for this view of Santa Rosa's past has been enjoyable and interesting. We found ourselves becoming detectives. Not only did we have to search out local collectors to access their cards, but identifying and locating buildings proved to be a greater challenge. Buildings have been torn down or drastically remodeled. Names have changed and streets no longer exist. We spent hours going through old city directories and telephone books and driving through streets and alleys where we had never gone before. Oh, what an adventure! Following this text, we have included a section of a map of Santa Rosa showing the downtown area *c.* 1935. This might aid the reader in locating some buildings, places, and streets shown in the postcards.

One of the most pleasant parts of the research process was the opportunity to meet with many local residents who opened their homes and their collections to us. We hope that you, the reader, will get as much pleasure out of this short look at Santa Rosa's past as we did in writing it. In the period covered by these postcards, 1890 to 1950, Santa Rosa's population grew from 10,000 to 25,000 people. In the last 50 years the population has grown to over 140,000 people, and the changes to Santa Rosa that came with that increase were dramatic. We hope you will be able to use this book to gain a feeling of how things were in a much smaller and quieter time.

—Bob and Kay Voliva

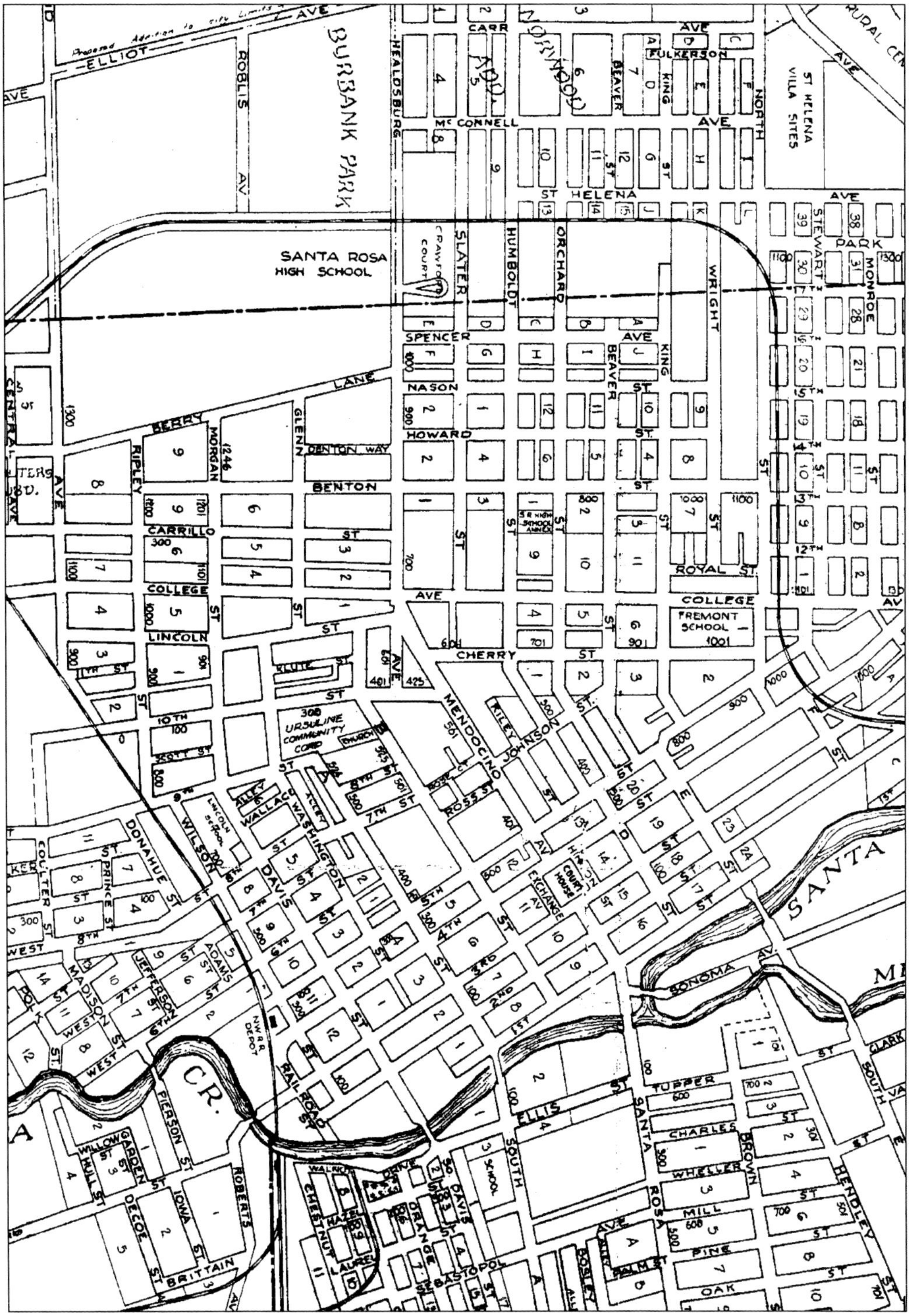

Map of Santa Rosa, c. 1935. (Published by Thomas Bros. of San Francisco.)

One

Rose Carnivals, Festivals, and Parades

The Rose Carnival or Festival has been Santa Rosa's premier event since its inception before the turn of the century. The festival events are always anticipated with great enthusiasm each year. Why a Rose Carnival? Luther Burbank stated it best when he was asked what his favorite flower was: "I have no favorite flower except, of course, the rose."

The first Rose Carnival was held in May of 1894. Until that year there had always been a number of celebrations, dances, and parades sponsored by various groups but nothing on an annual basis. Thomas P. Keegan, the Father of the Rose Carnival, was the leading promoter of an annual celebration for the entire city. In 1896, rain spoiled the parade and the city fathers decided to hold a Chrysanthemum Festival in the fall of 1897. In 1898, the Rose Festival had returned and by the turn of the century it was a well-established event.

Although considered a yearly event, there have been some gaps in its operation. No official celebrations were held in 1906 due to the earthquake, nor between 1918 and 1932 due to World War One and Luther Burbank's death. General economic conditions stopped the festivities, and World War II caused some missed years, but since the late 1950s there have been few cancellations.The Rose Parade is distinctive to Santa Rosa, and as you will see from the following real photo postcards, it was quite the event—with floats, flowers, crowning the queens, and many onlookers enjoying the fun.

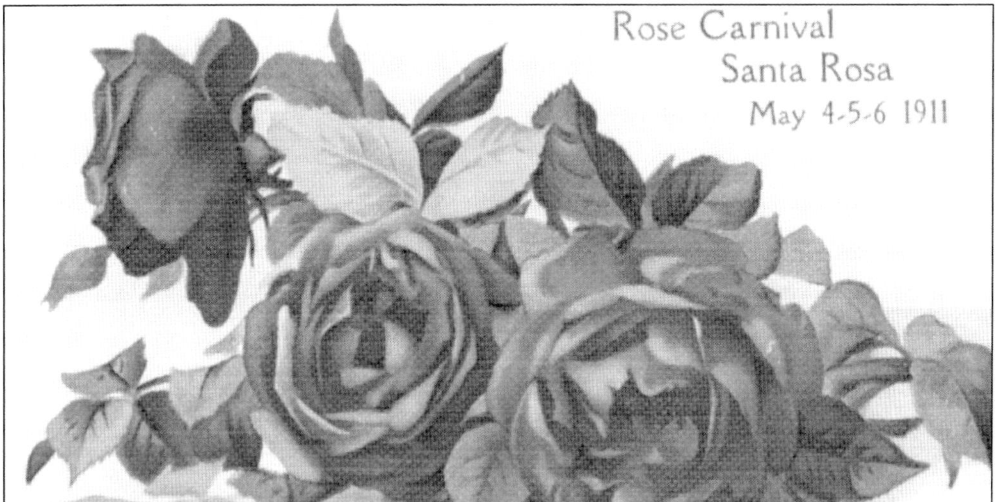

Rose Carnival, 1911. This postcard is typical of those produced each year to advertise Santa Rosa's Rose Carnival.

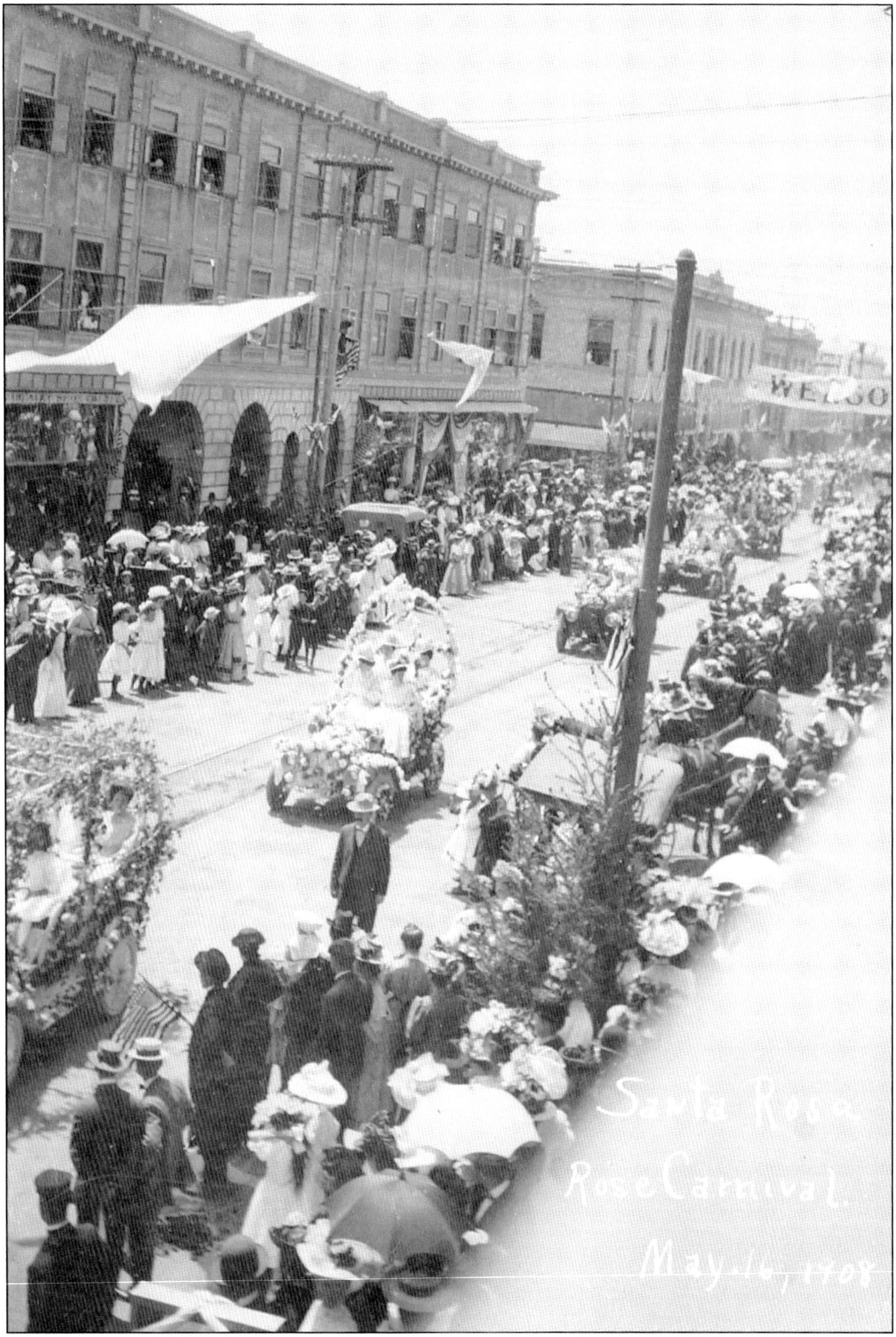

Rose Carnival, 1908. The parade of decorated automobiles is shown passing the rear of the fire station in the 500 block of Fourth Street.

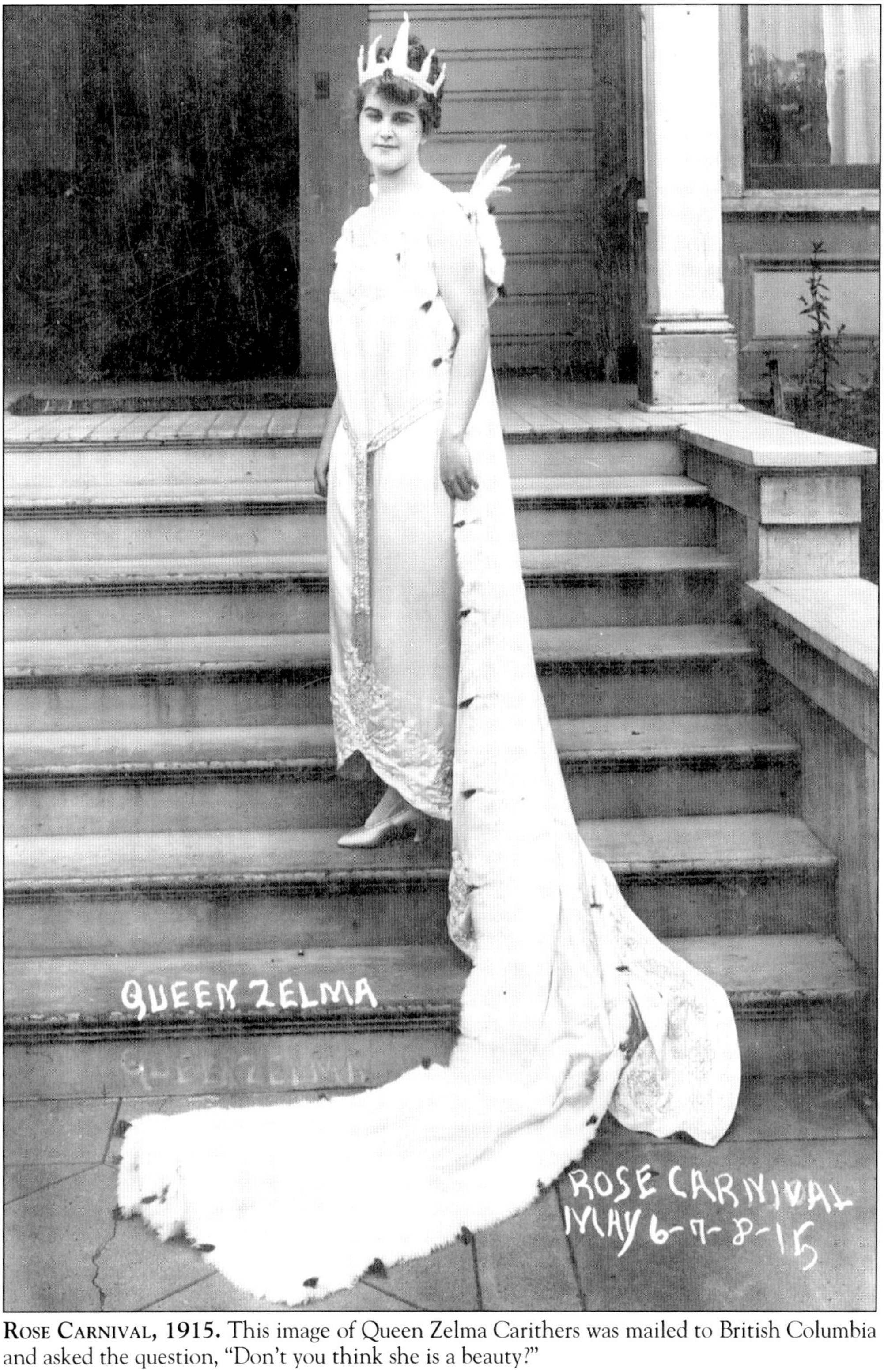

Rose Carnival, 1915. This image of Queen Zelma Carithers was mailed to British Columbia and asked the question, "Don't you think she is a beauty?"

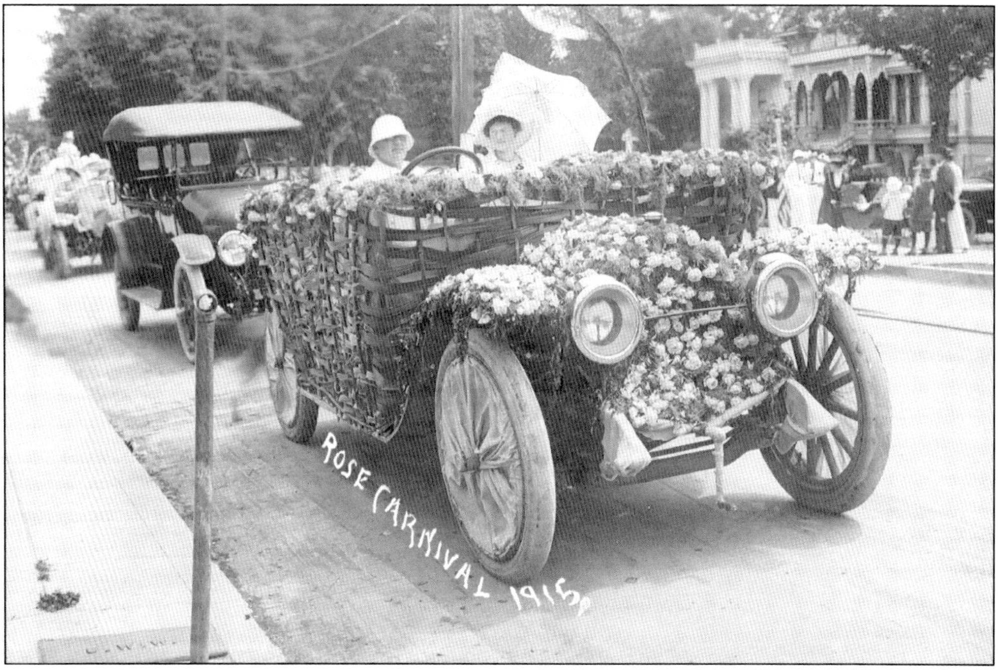

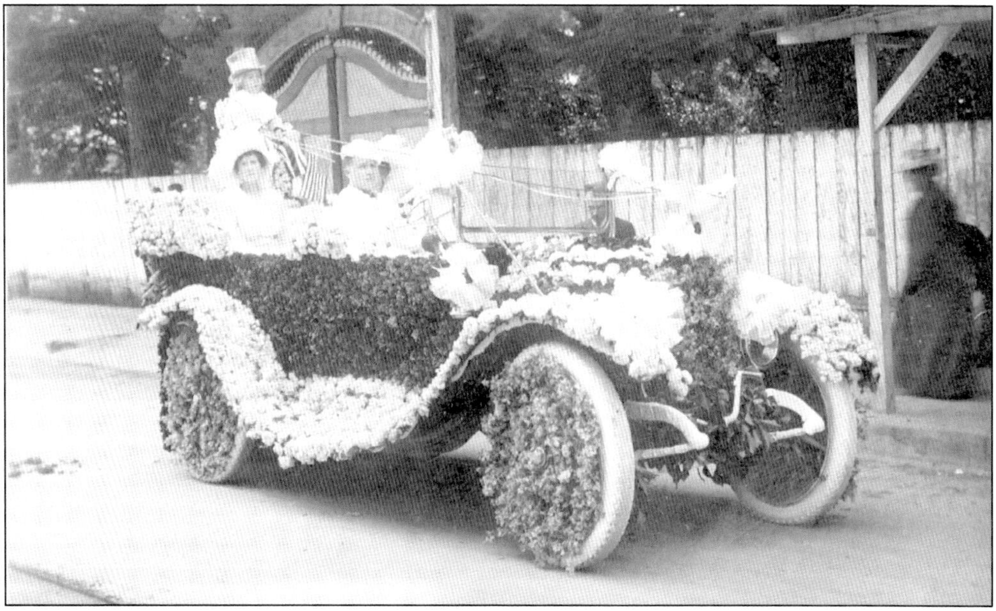

ROSE CARNIVALS, C. 1915. Automobiles decorated with fresh greens and flowers were popular and favorite attractions.

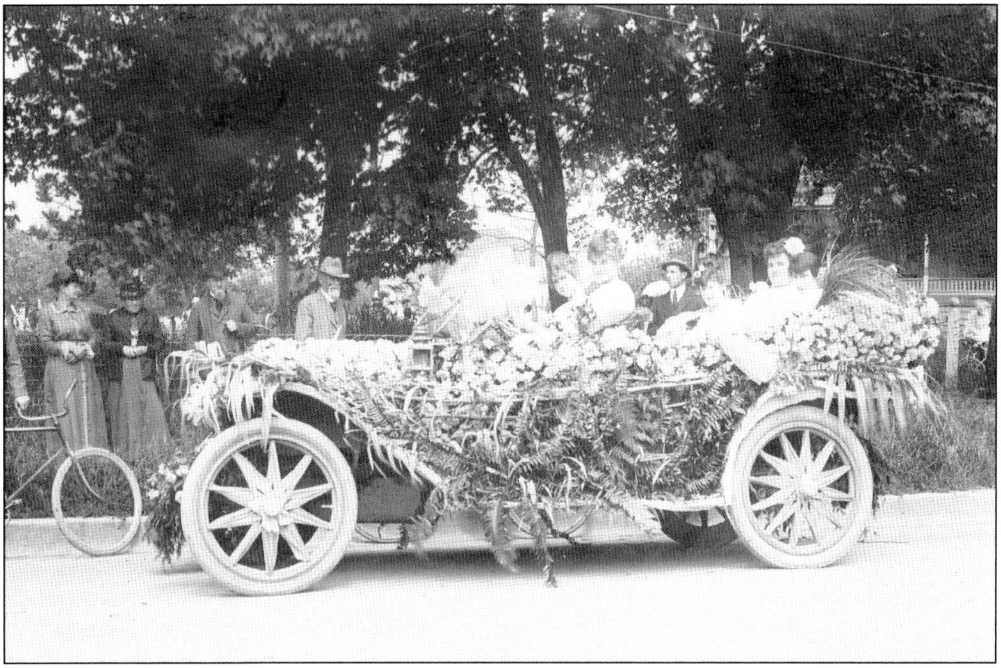

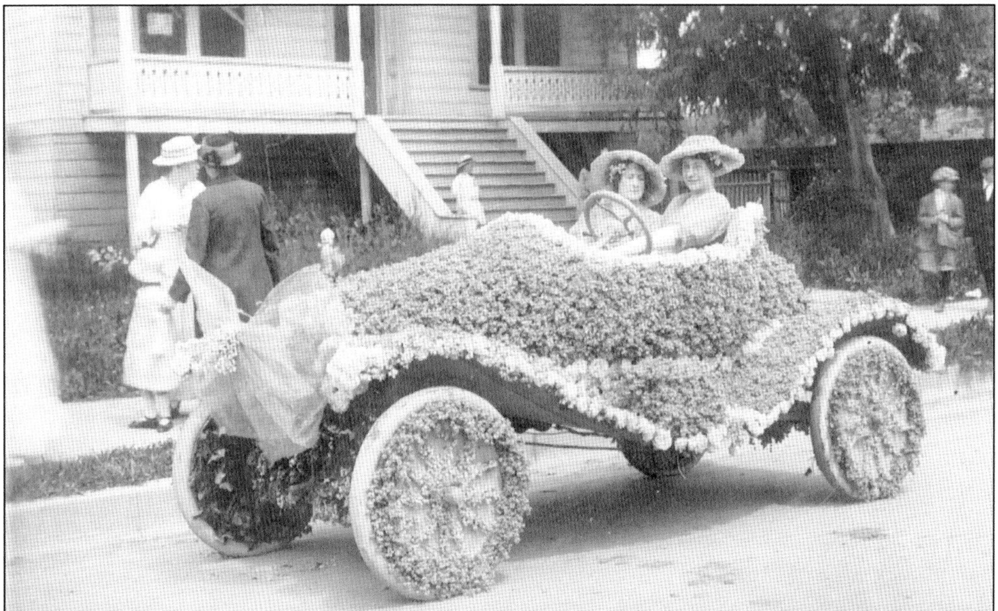

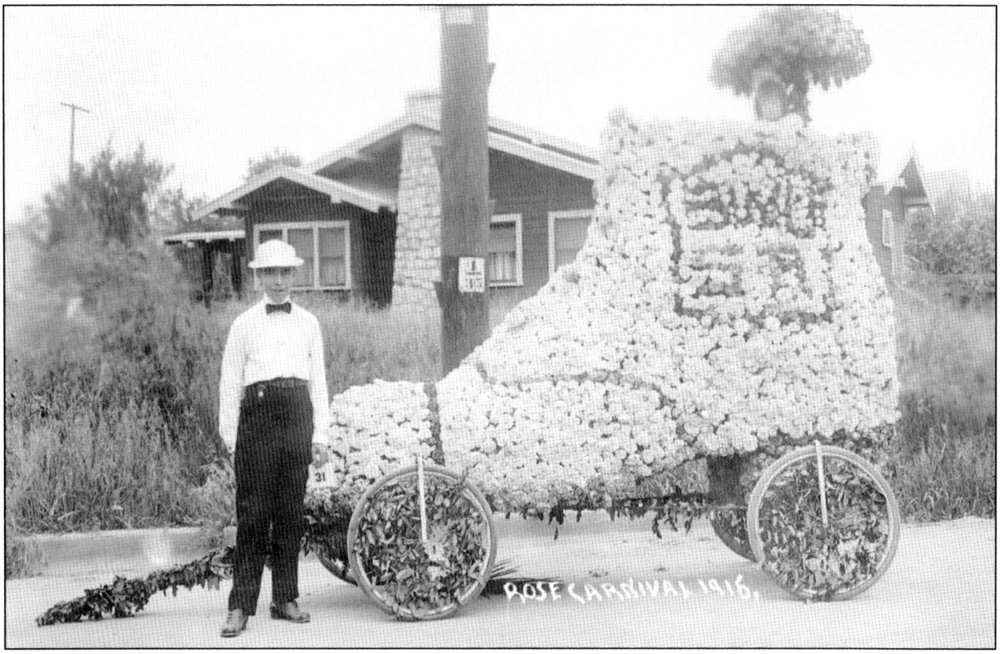

Boot Float Entry. Both photos depict the Boot and Shoe Workers Union, Santa Rosa Local Company No. 446, but in different years. The float in the top photo entered the parade in 1916 and the one below entered later. Santa Rosa had a strong leather tanning and manufacturing industry.

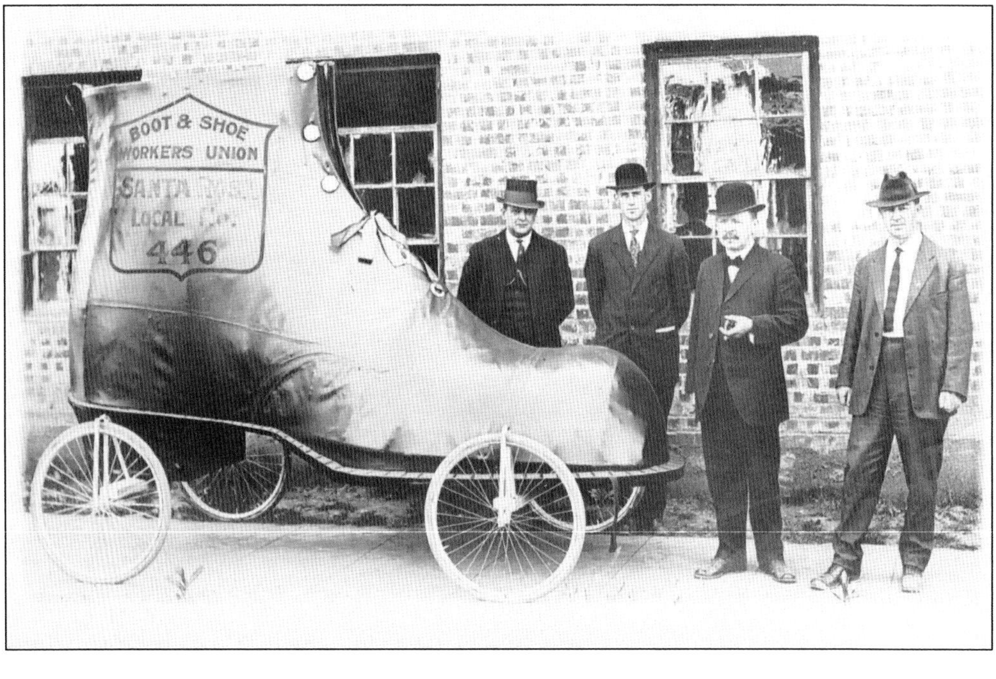

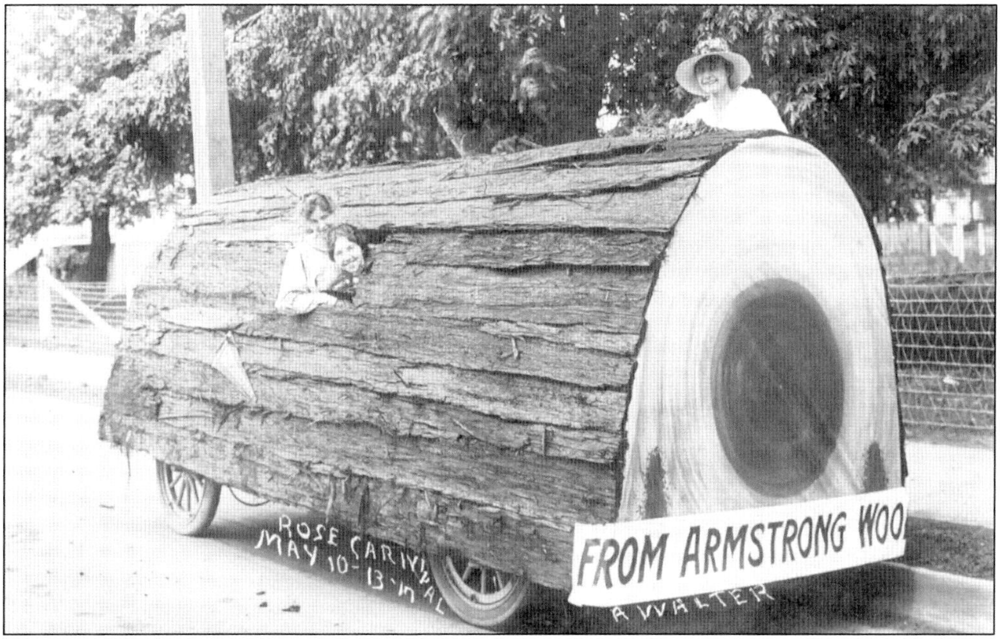

ROSE CARNIVAL, 1917. This clever entry came from Armstrong Woods, a state park that features more than 800 acres of the tallest and oldest redwood trees in Northern California.

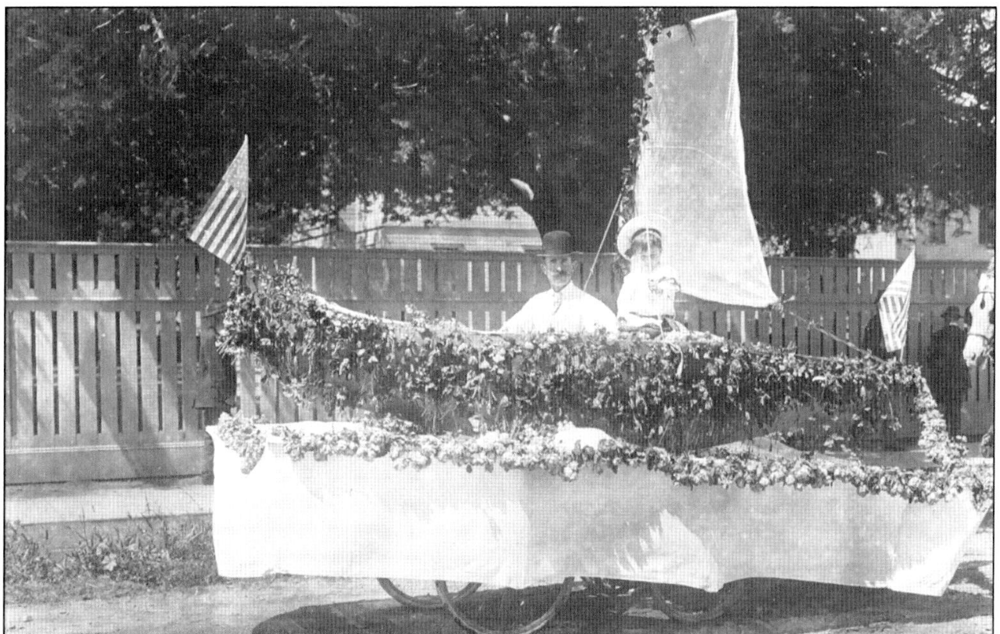

ROSE CARNIVAL, C. 1910. Nautical themes were popular entries.

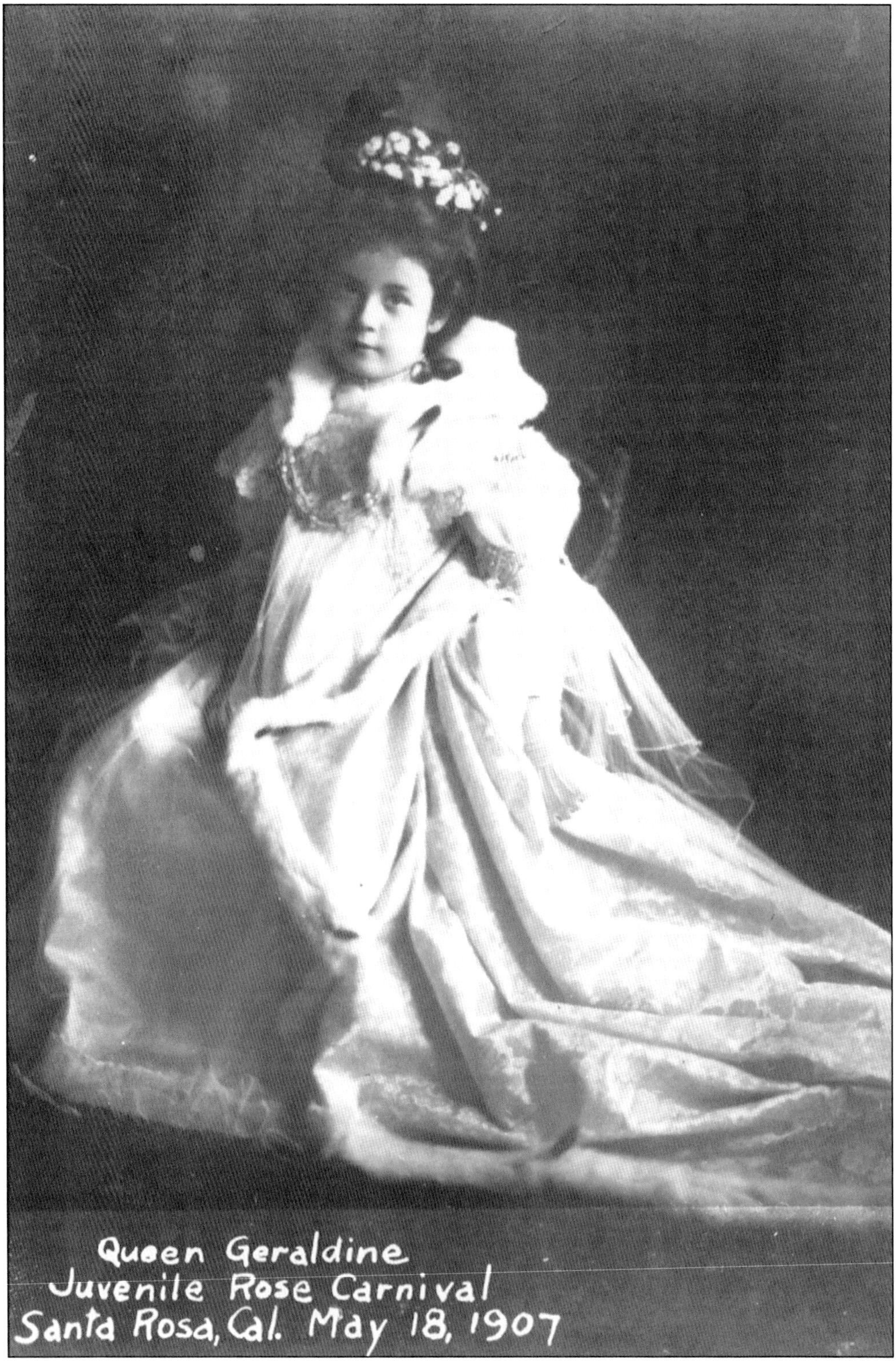

JUVENILE ROSE CARNIVAL QUEEN GERALDINE GRACE, 1907.

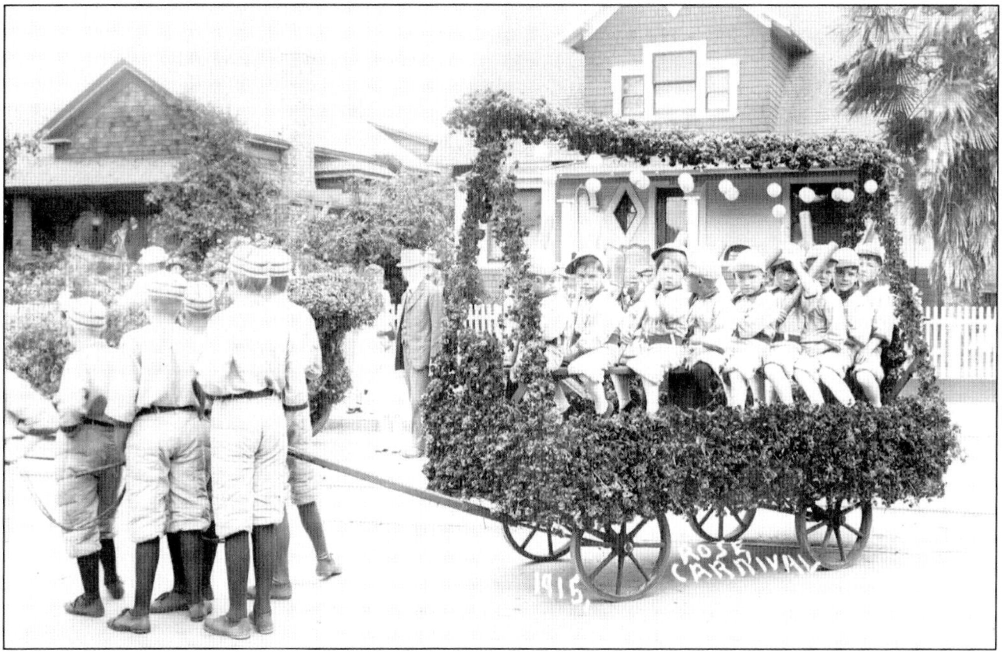

ROSE CARNIVAL, 1915. A "pee-wee" baseball team gets a pull from the big sluggers!

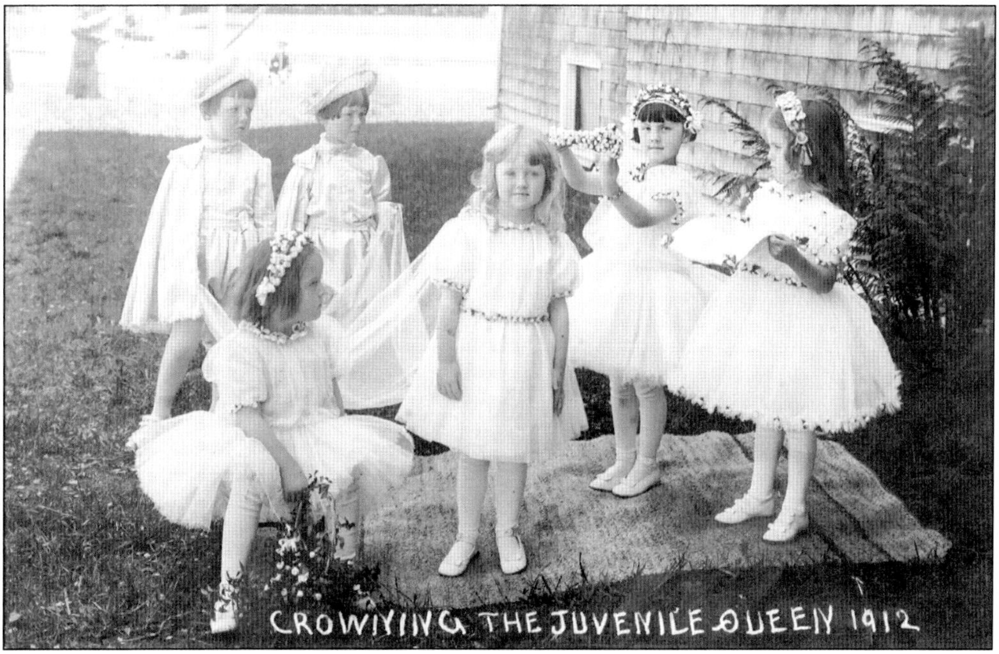

JUVENILE QUEEN ESTHER JUNE VAUGHAN AND HER COURT, 1912.

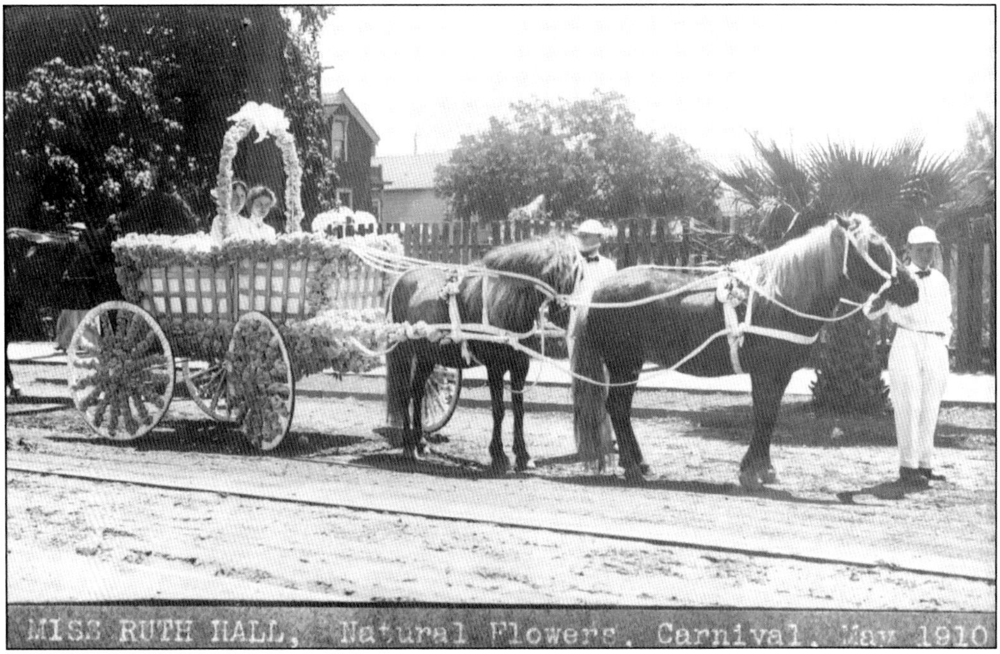

FLOWER BASKET FLOAT, 1910. Local librarian Ruth Hall is seated in the basket of this beautiful horse-drawn entry.

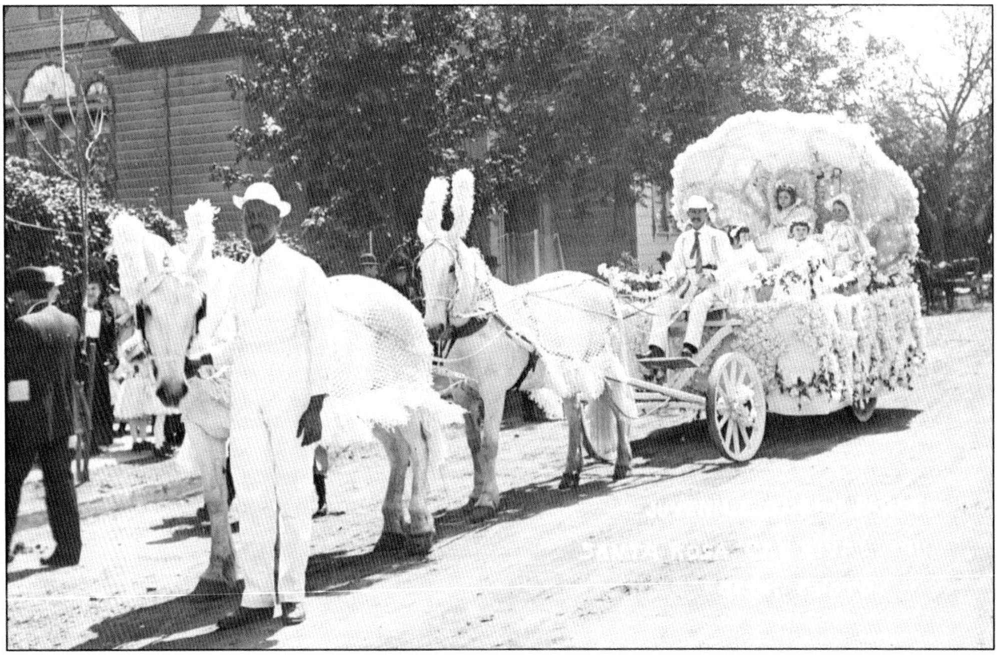

JUVENILE QUEEN ENTRY, 1911. This year's Juvenile Queen and her court ride under this spectacular floral umbrella.

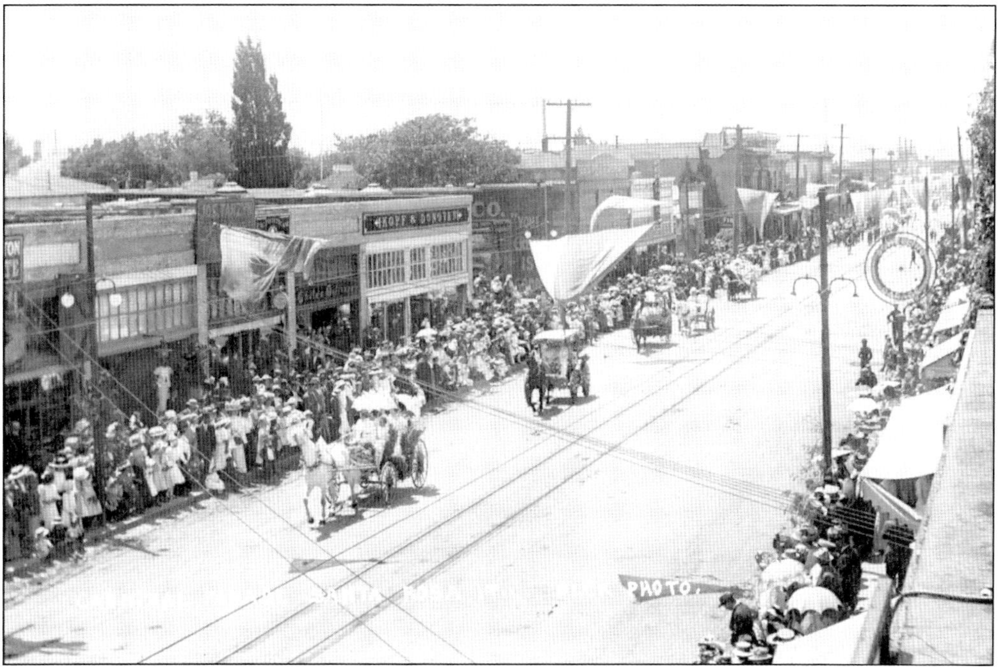

ROSE CARNIVAL, 1911. This grand parade moves down Fourth Street.

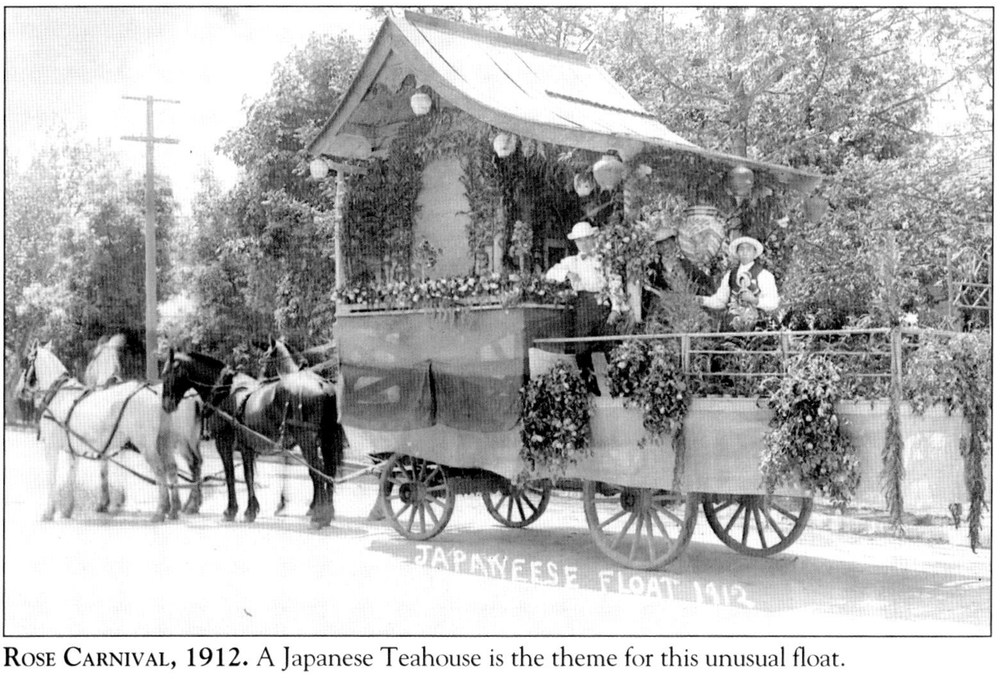

ROSE CARNIVAL, 1912. A Japanese Teahouse is the theme for this unusual float.

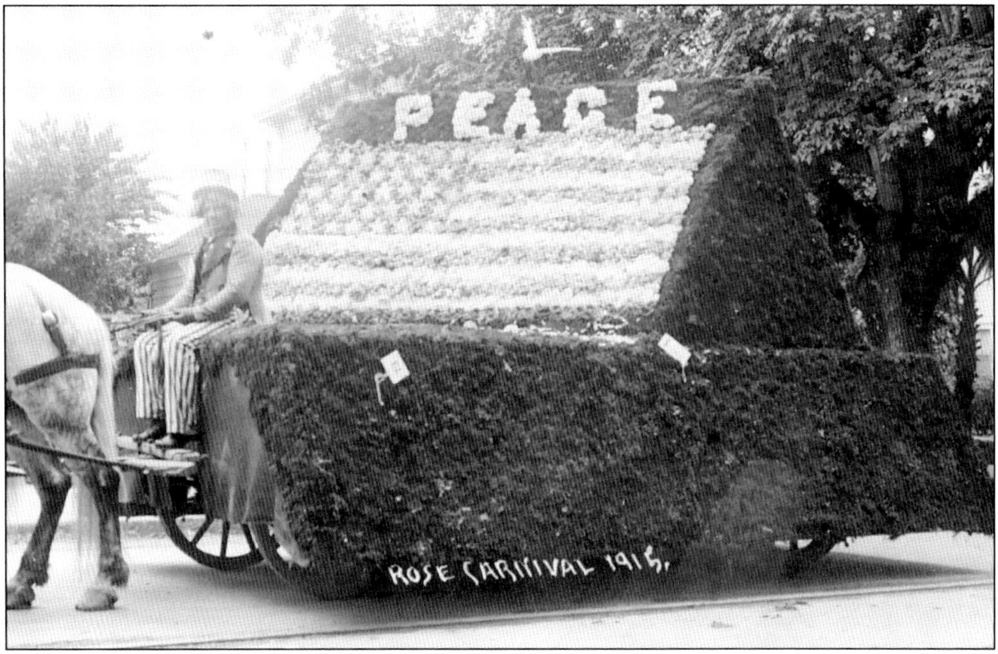

UNCLE SAM, 1915. Uncle Sam drives this patriotic horse-drawn peace float.

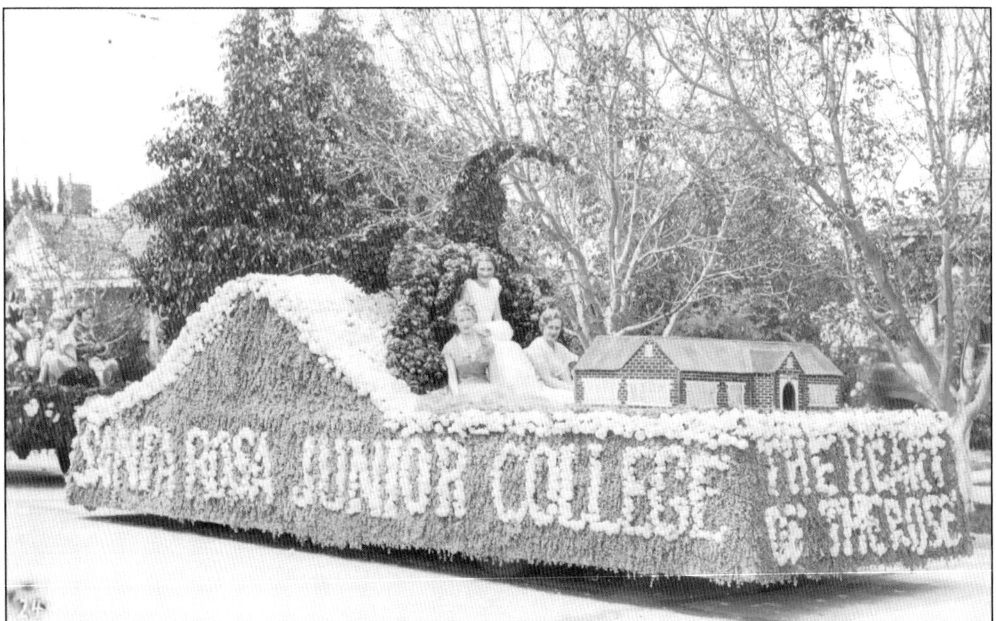

SANTA ROSA JUNIOR COLLEGE, 1936. The "Heart of the Rose" was the title of this entry by the Junior College.

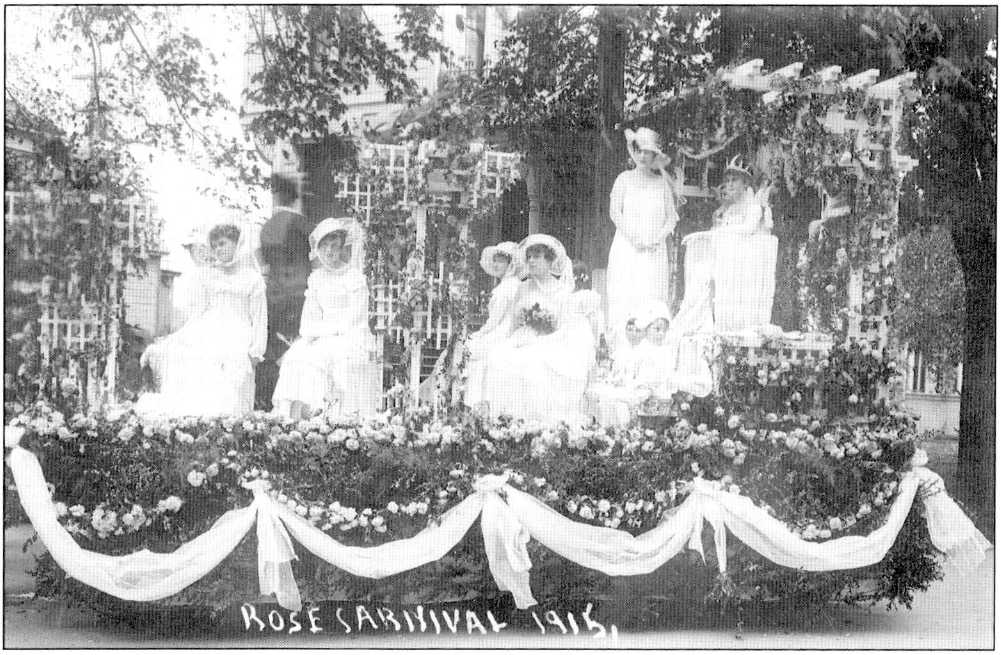

QUEEN'S FLOAT, 1915. Queen Zelma Carithers and her court pose on her float.

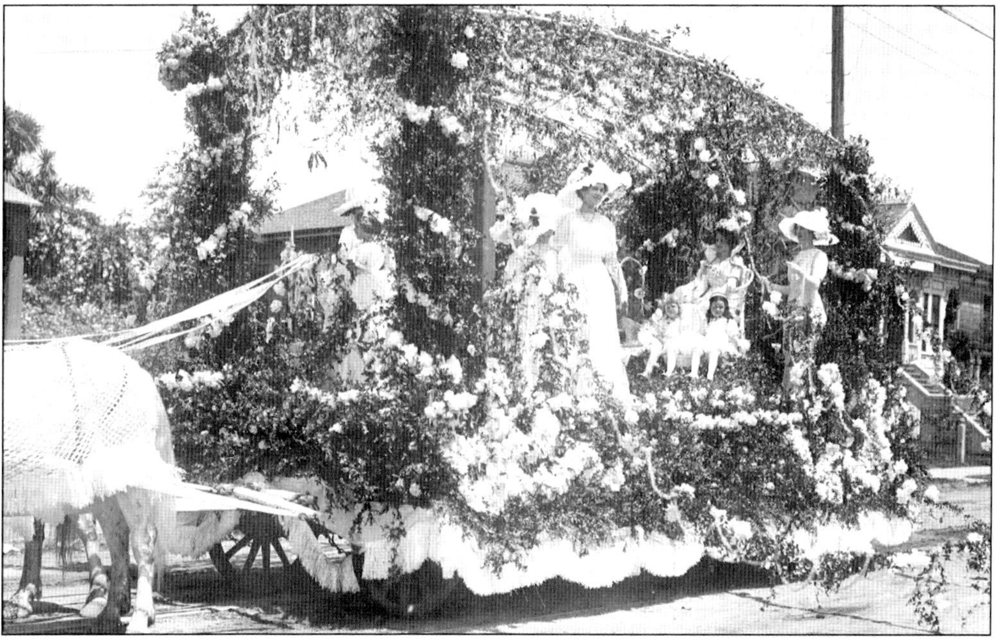

QUEEN'S FLOAT, 1911. This elaborate flower-covered entry carried the 1911 Rose Queen.

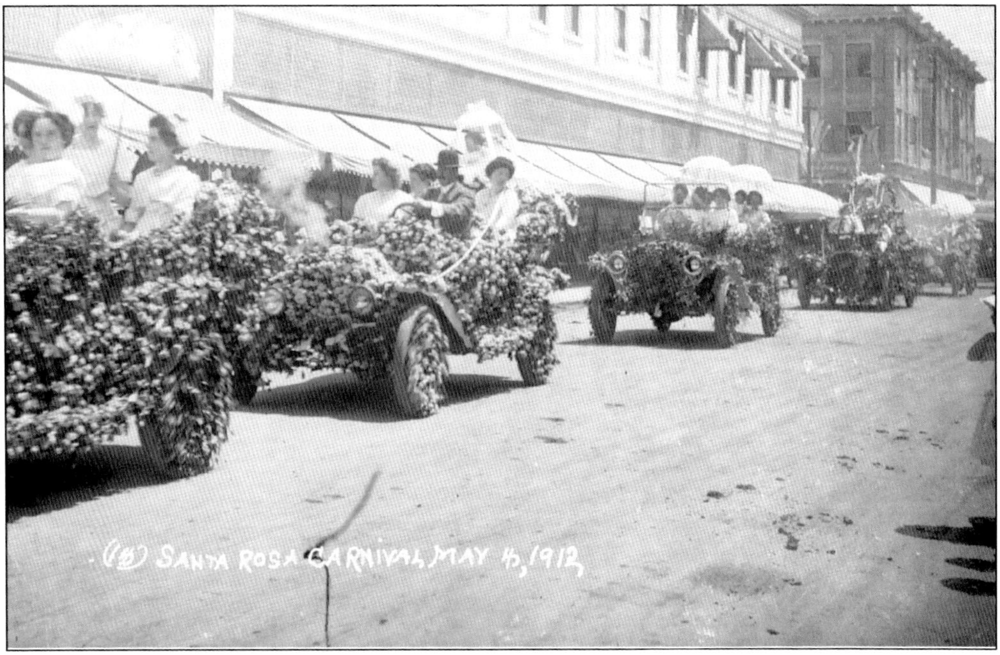

ROSE CARNIVAL, 1912. By 1912 the automobile had replaced many of the horse-drawn entries.

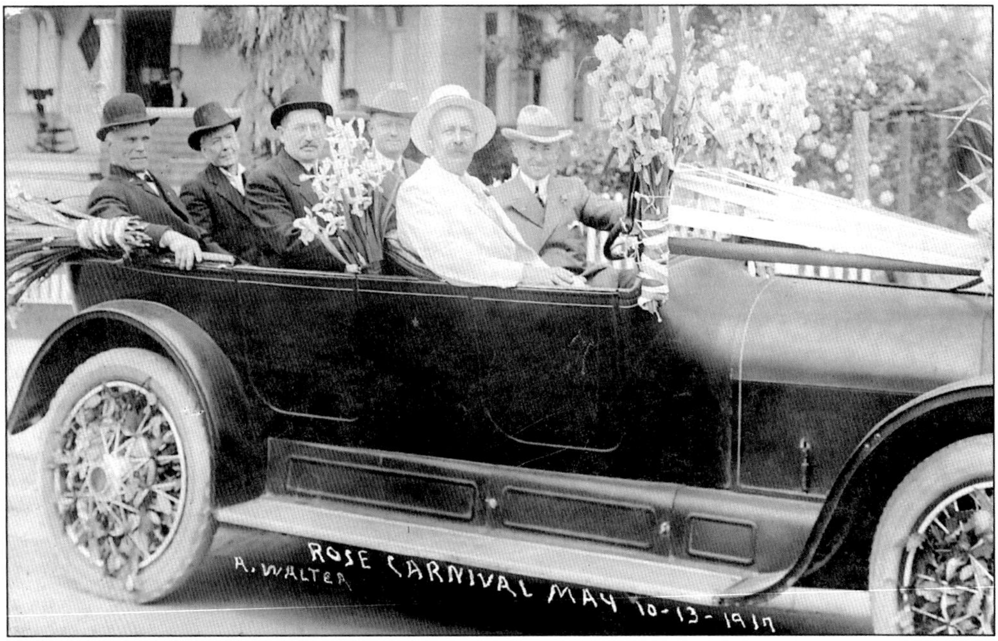

ROSE CARNIVAL, 1917. This year marked the last official Rose Carnival until 1932. Dignitaries pictured in the back seat, from left to right, are Jim Mailer, Luther Burbank, and Max Rosenberg.

Two

STREET SCENES

Street scene postcards provide a fascinating snapshot of daily life in any city. These photographs or lithographic views freeze a moment in time. They show people involved in their daily activity and vehicles moving about the town. Look at these cards with a magnifying glass and little details appear. You can read signs advertising businesses or events long past, each a clue in identifying a location or determining a date.

The Santa Rosa shown in the postcards from 1915 through the 1940s is a busy place, the commercial center for a large geographic area. In many ways it appears to be a larger city than it does today. All of the retail businesses, professional services, and many residences were packed into the downtown area. People lived, worked, and played in much closer confines than today.

Take your time when you look at these postcards—some buildings and businesses will be familiar, others only memories.

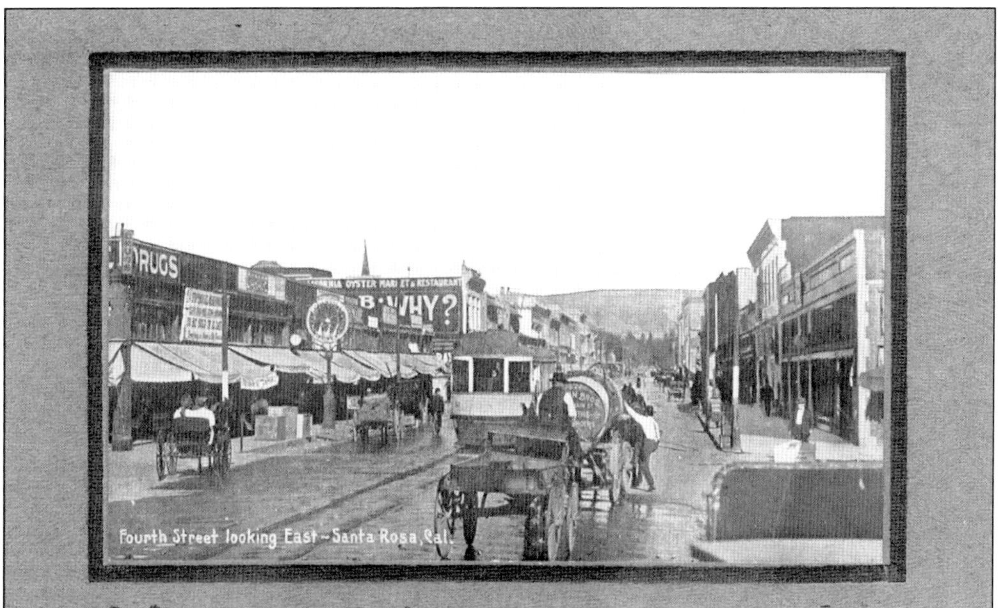

EARLY VIEW OF FOURTH STREET, C. 1900. This photocard shows the 400 block of Fourth Street looking east. Note the water wagon in the foreground washing the streets, and the streetcar and its track down the middle.

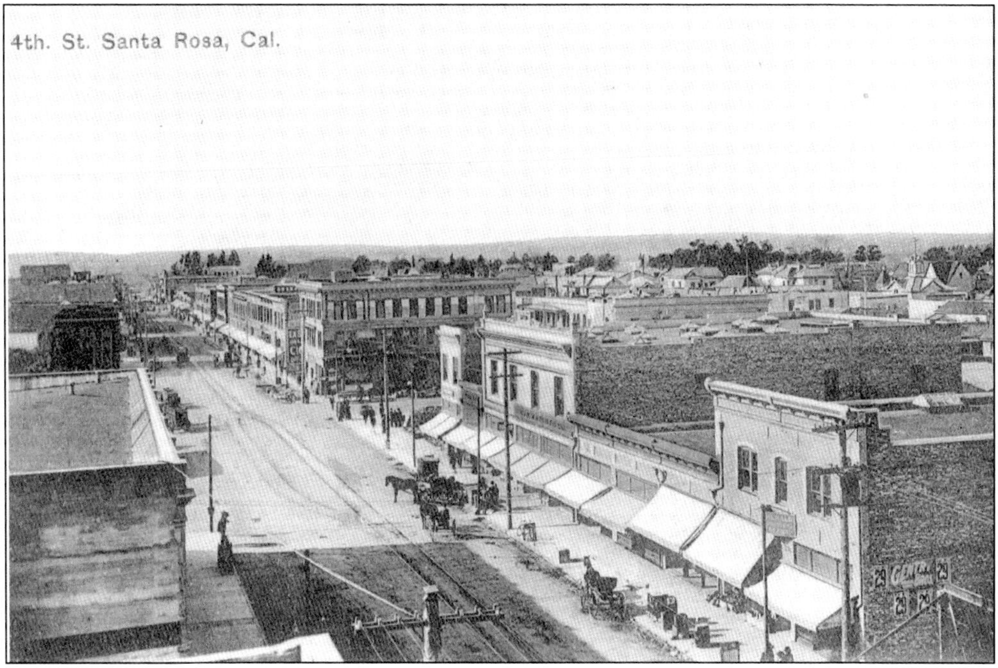

FOURTH STREET, C. 1905. This view looks west at the corner of Mendocino Avenue and Fourth Street. The double tracks enabled busy streetcars to pass each other on Fourth Street.

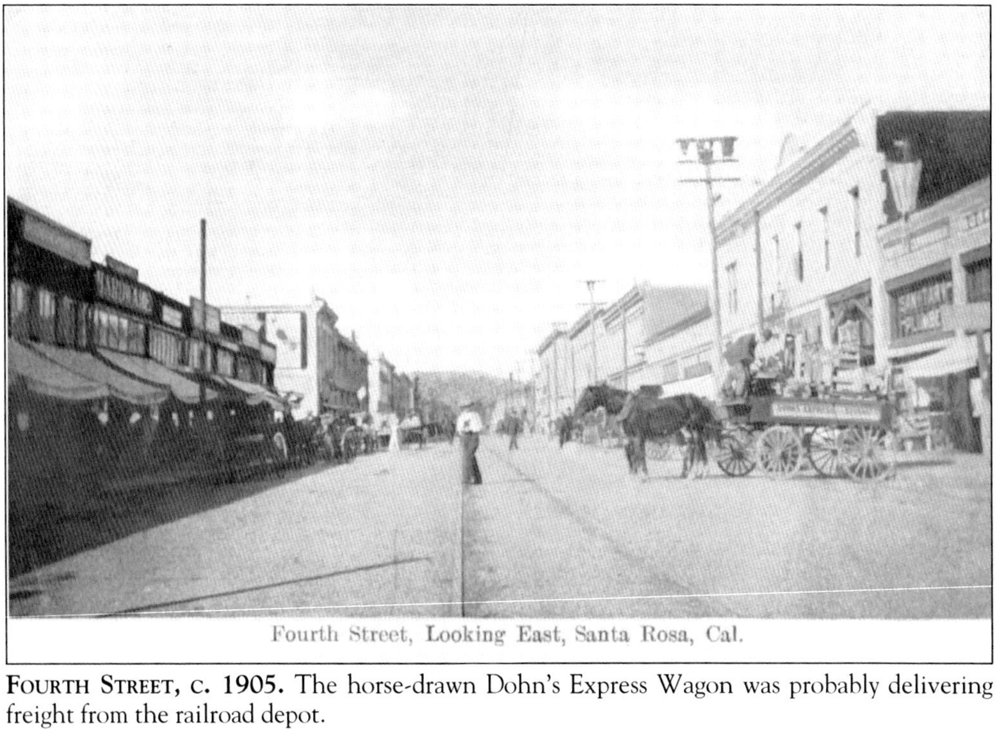

FOURTH STREET, C. 1905. The horse-drawn Dohn's Express Wagon was probably delivering freight from the railroad depot.

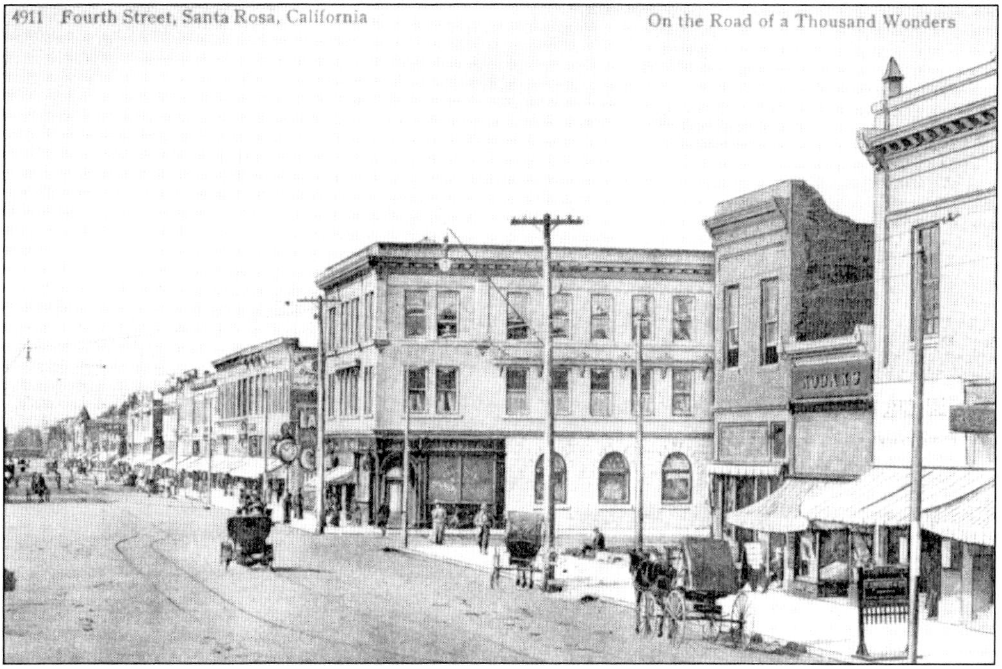

FOURTH STREET, C. 1912. A good view of the Exchange Bank building at the corner of Fourth Street and Mendocino Avenue is visible in this card.

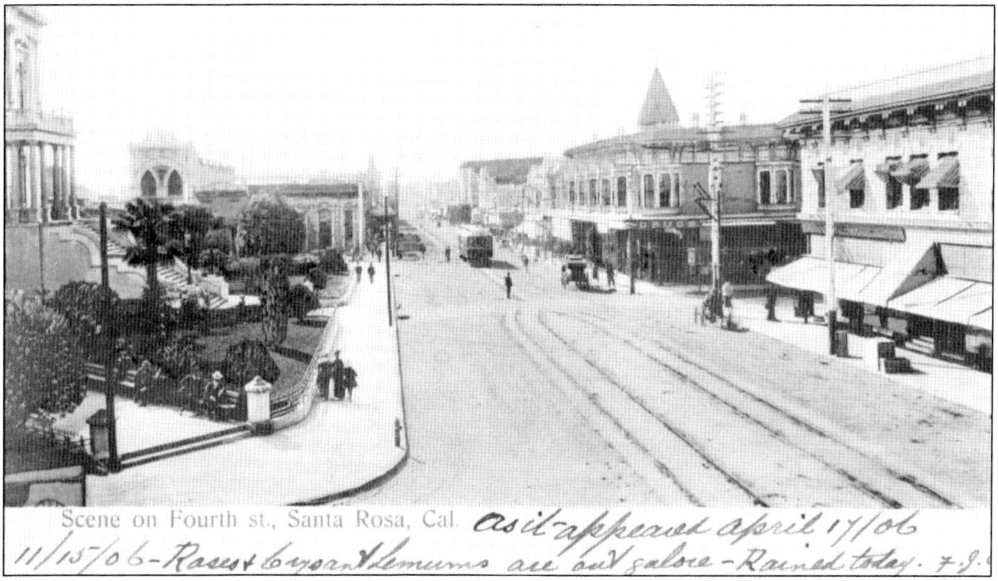

FOURTH STREET, C. 1906. This postcard says, "As it appeared April 17, 1906," one day prior to the earthquake.

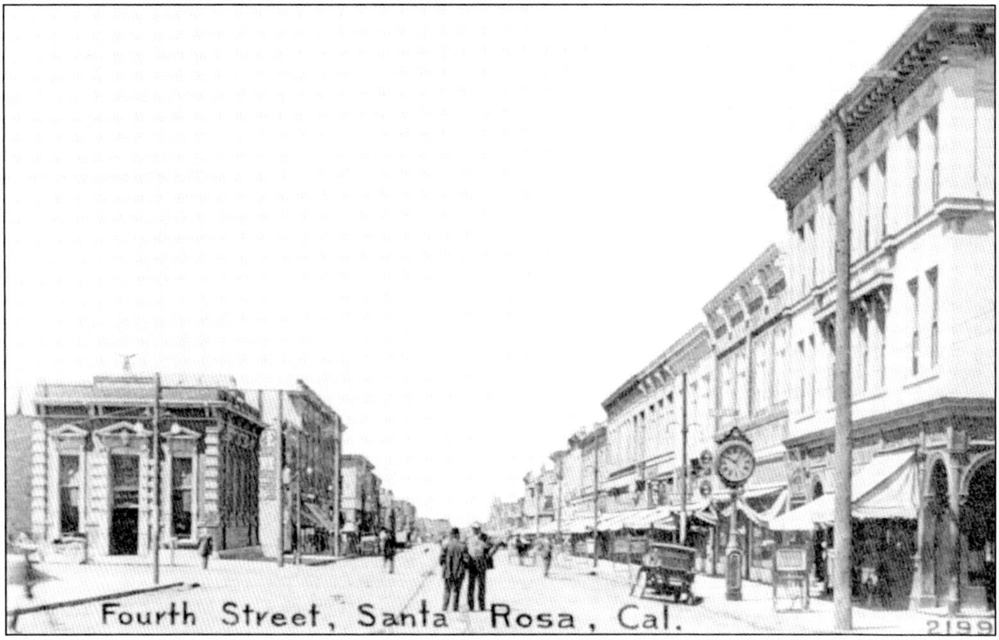

Fourth Street, c. 1915. This printed postcard's view looks west from the intersection of Fourth and Mendocino. The fine cast-iron street clock appears in numerous views of Fourth Street.

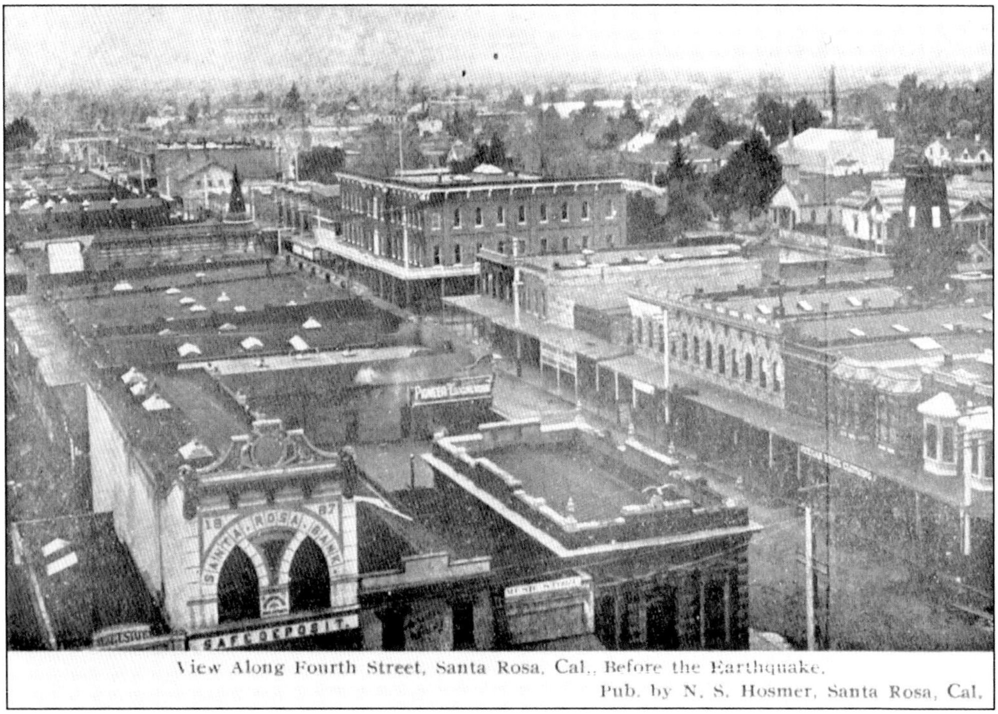

Aerial View of Fourth Street, c. 1905. A photographer climbed to the top of the courthouse tower to get this shot of the intersection of Fourth and B Streets in the center of the postcard.

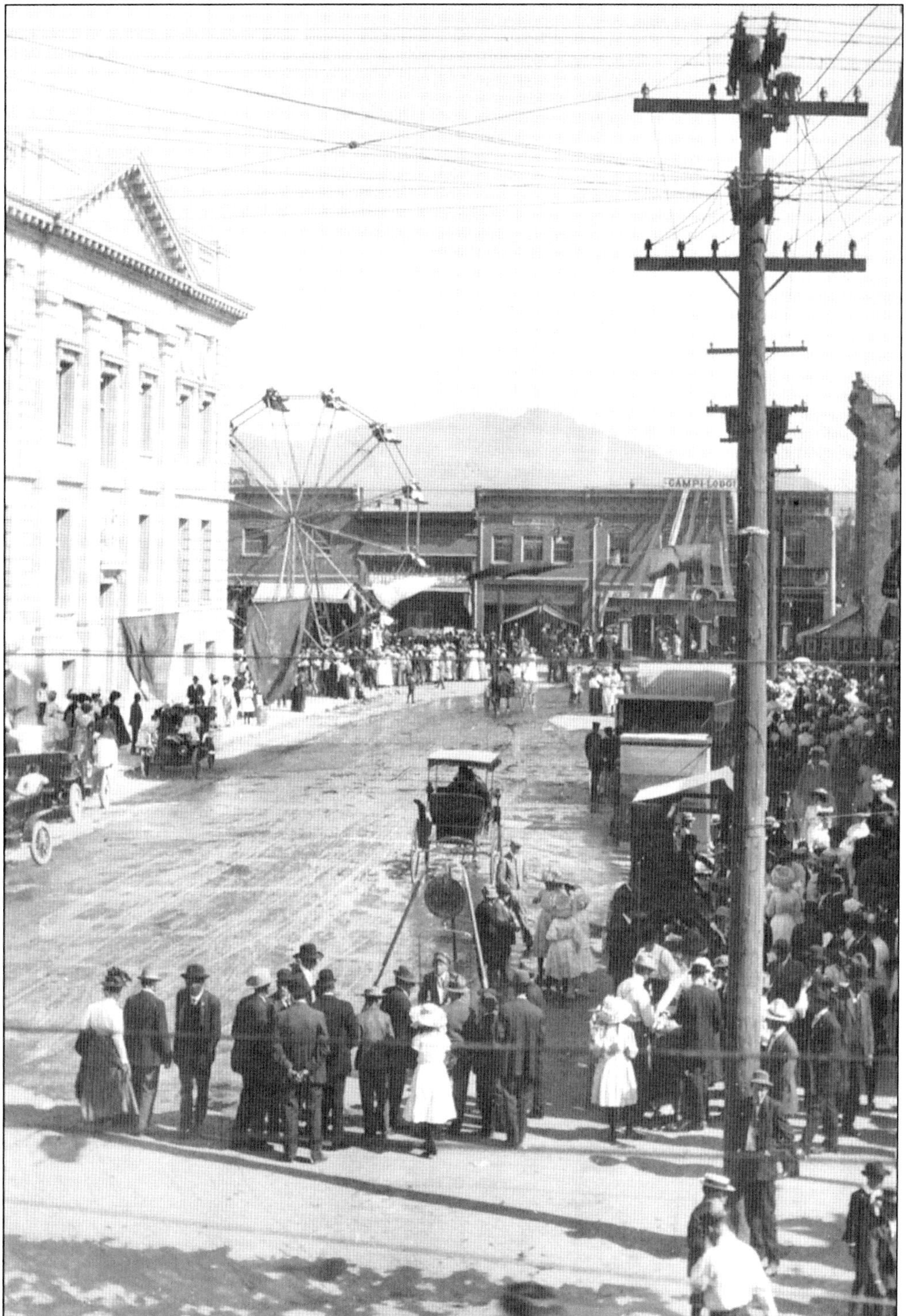

Fourth Street, 1910. A street fair is in progress in this view down Exchange Avenue to Third Street.

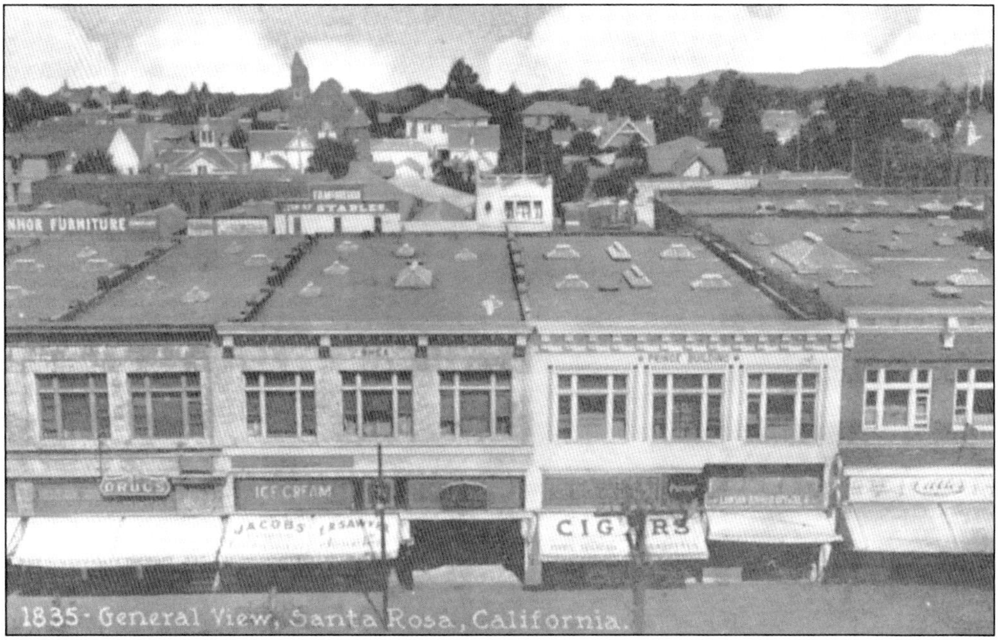

AERIAL VIEW OF FOURTH STREET, C. 1910. This postcard shows several retail establishments in the 500 block of Fourth Street. Note the awning advertising E.R. Sawyer Jewelers.

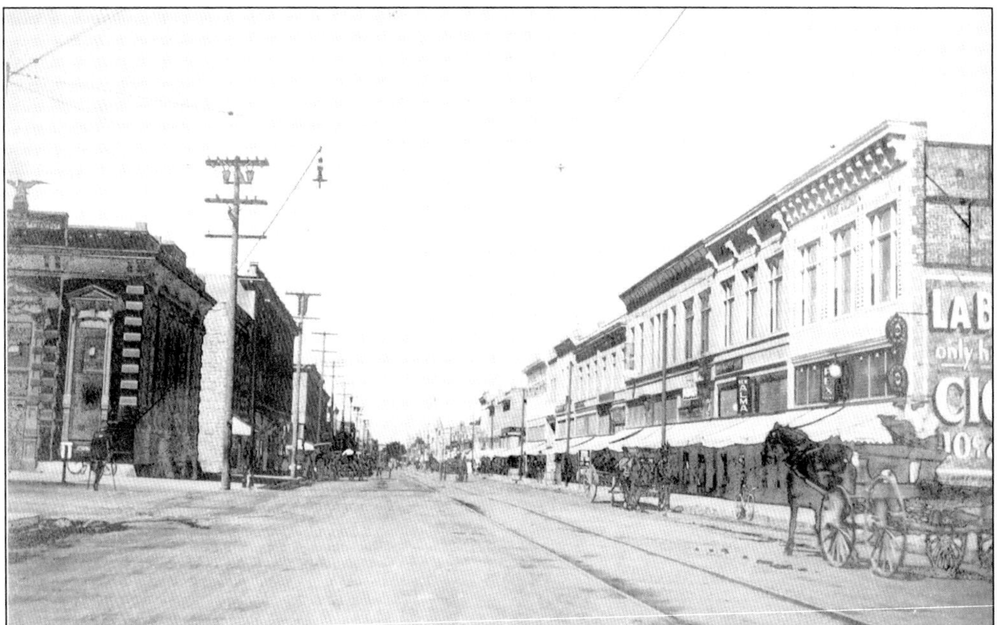

FOURTH STREET, C. 1910. In this view looking west on Fourth Street at the intersection of Exchange Avenue, one can see the LaBria Cigar ad painted on the side of the building. This sign appears in many Fourth Street views.

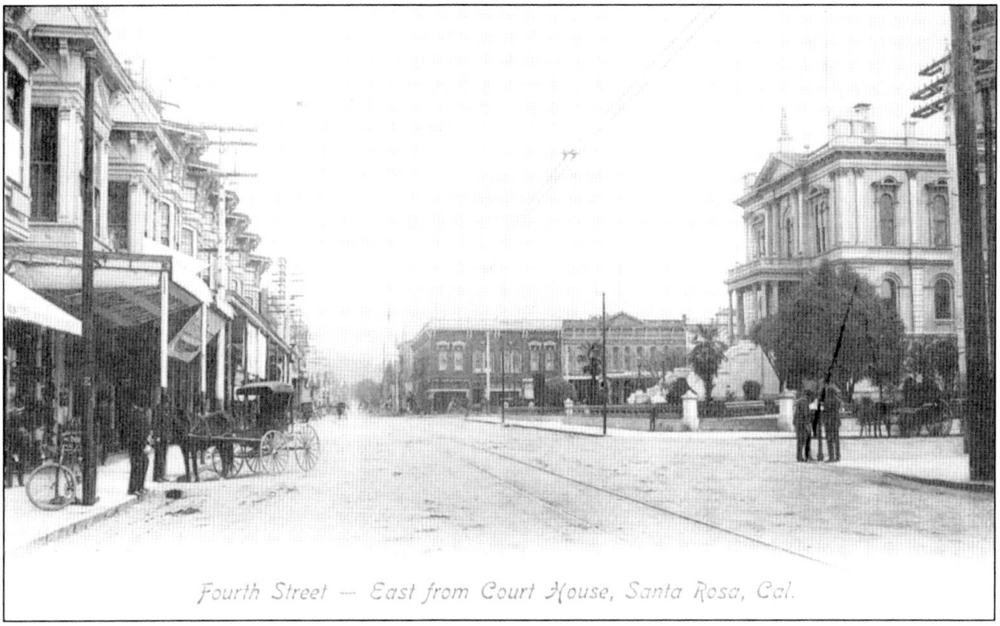

FOURTH STREET, C. 1905. This is Fourth Street looking east from the corner of Exchange Avenue.

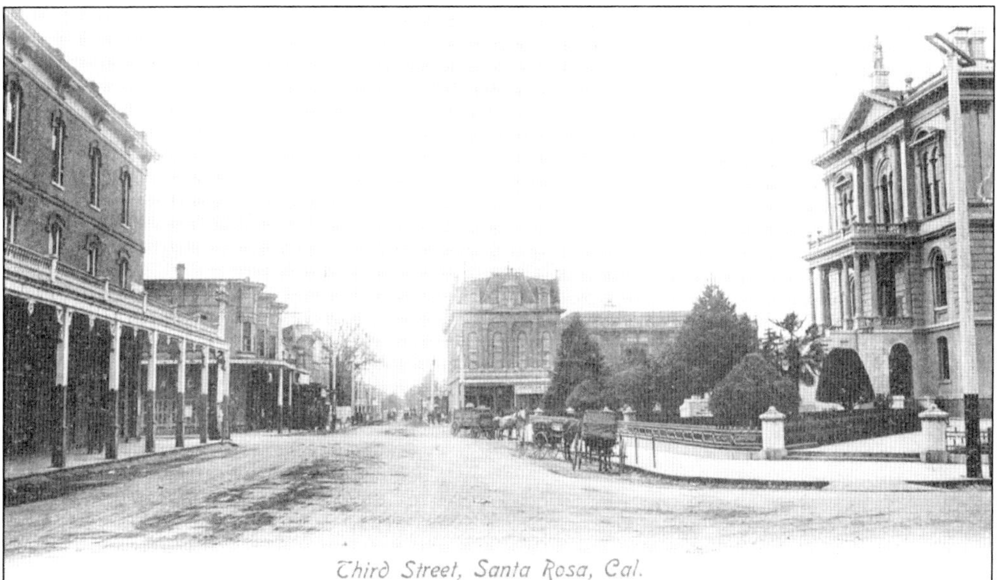

THIRD STREET, C. 1905. In this view looking west on Third Street, the courthouse is visible on the right, bounded by Exchange Avenue on the west and Hinton Avenue on the east. Main Street, now Santa Rosa Avenue, is the intersection on the left.

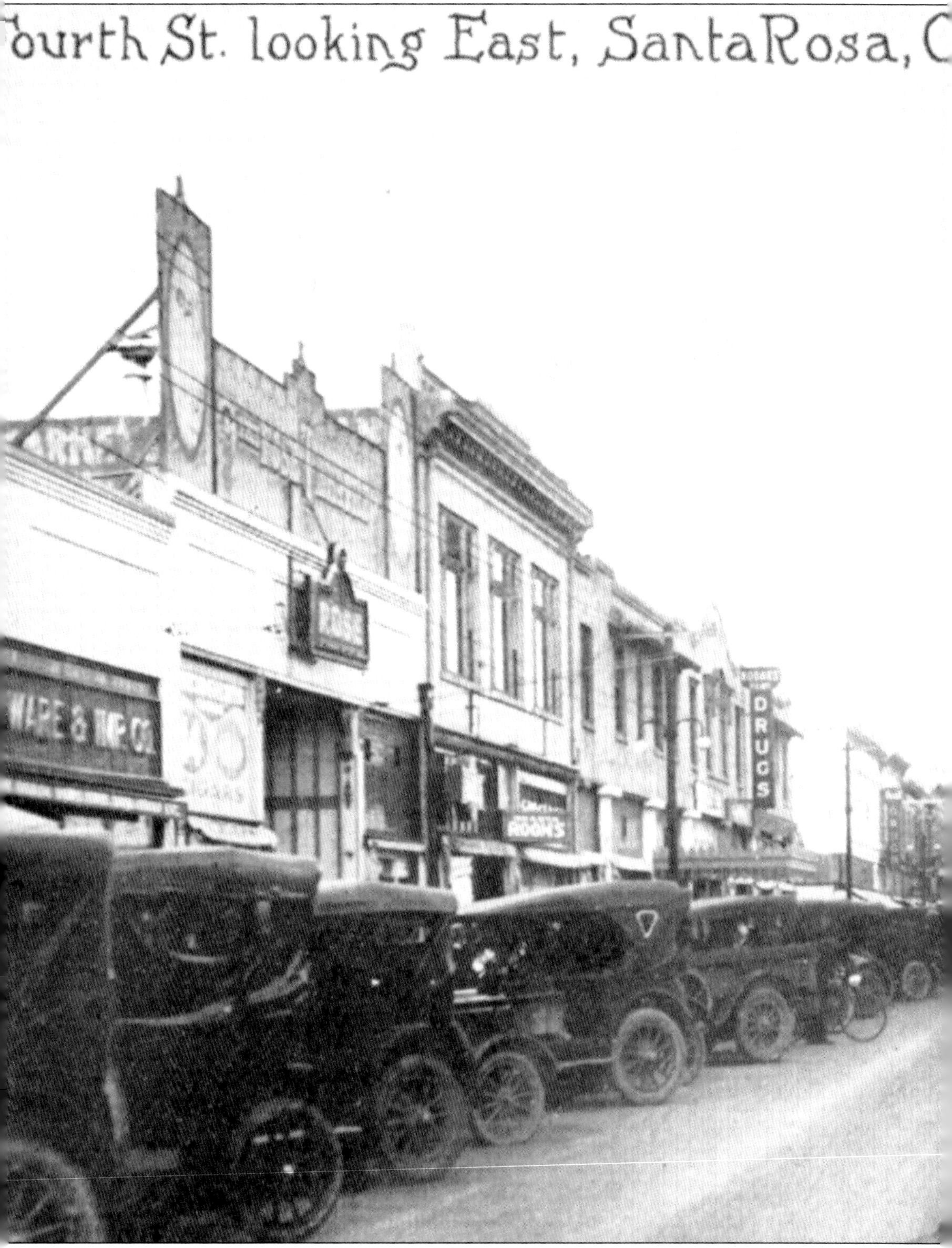

Downtown, 1915. A parking space in downtown Santa Rosa on Fourth Street must have

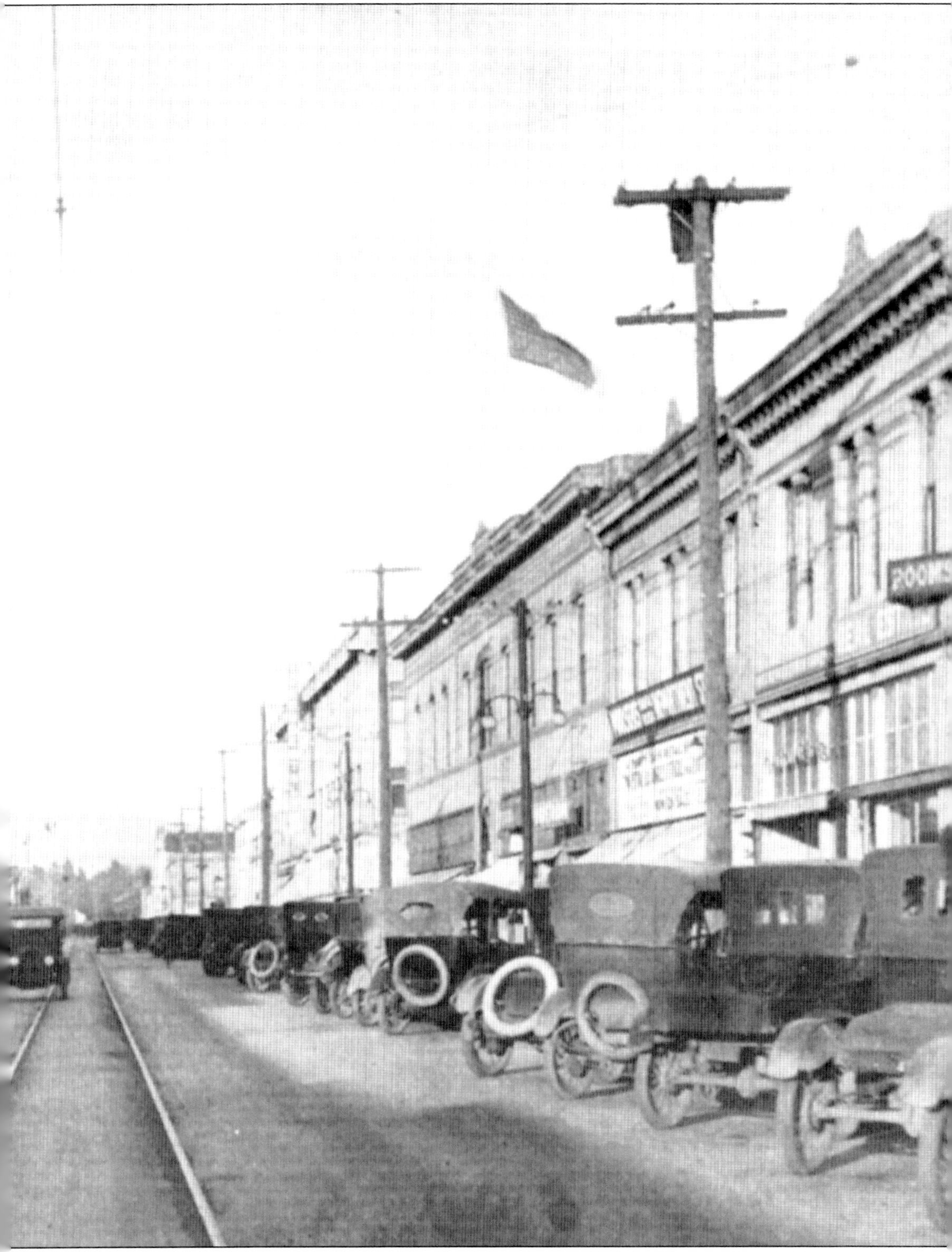

been at a premium in 1915. The same thing can be said for today's parking on Fourth Street!

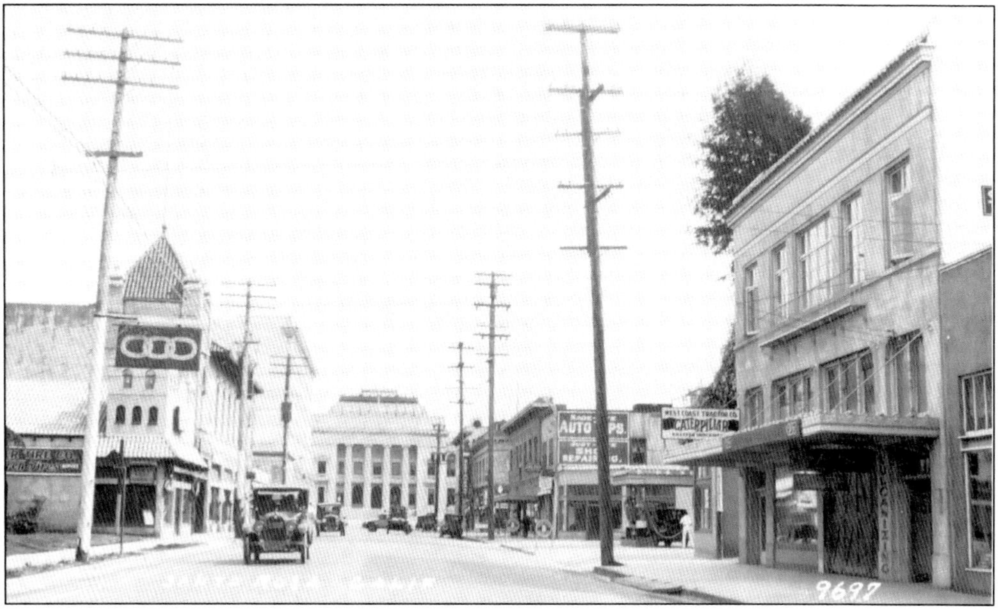

MENDOCINO AVENUE, C. 1925. This view is looking south from Sixth Street toward the courthouse. The Native Sons Building appears on the left.

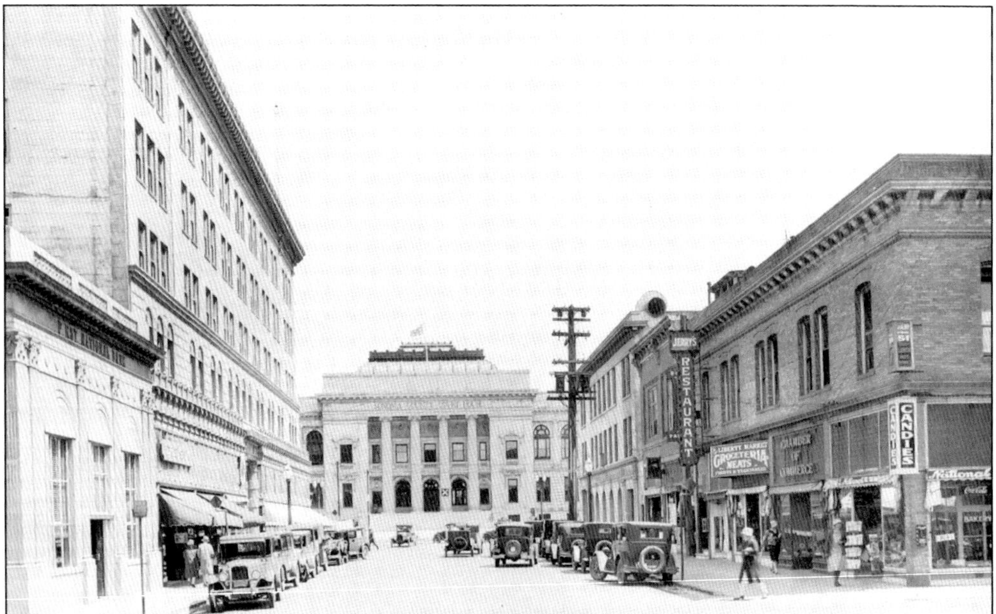

MENDOCINO AVENUE, C. 1925. Looking south from Fifth Street, the Rosenberg Building is visible on the left and the Chamber of Commerce occupies an office on the right.

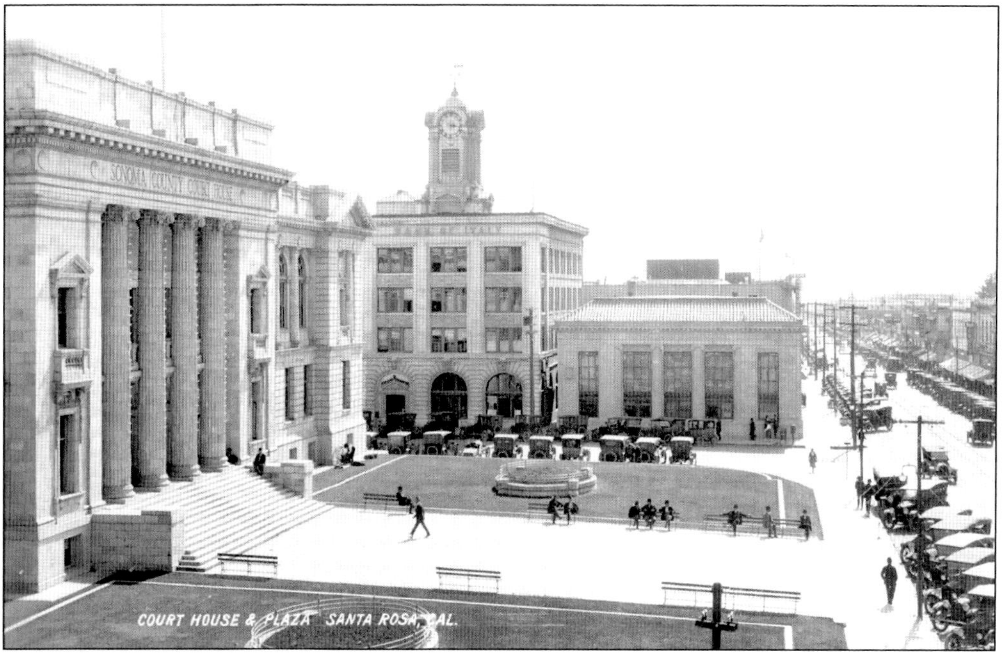

COURTHOUSE AND PLAZA, C. 1917. A photocard view of the plaza with Fourth Street and Exchange Avenue shows the former Santa Rosa Bank Building, which became the Bank of Italy.

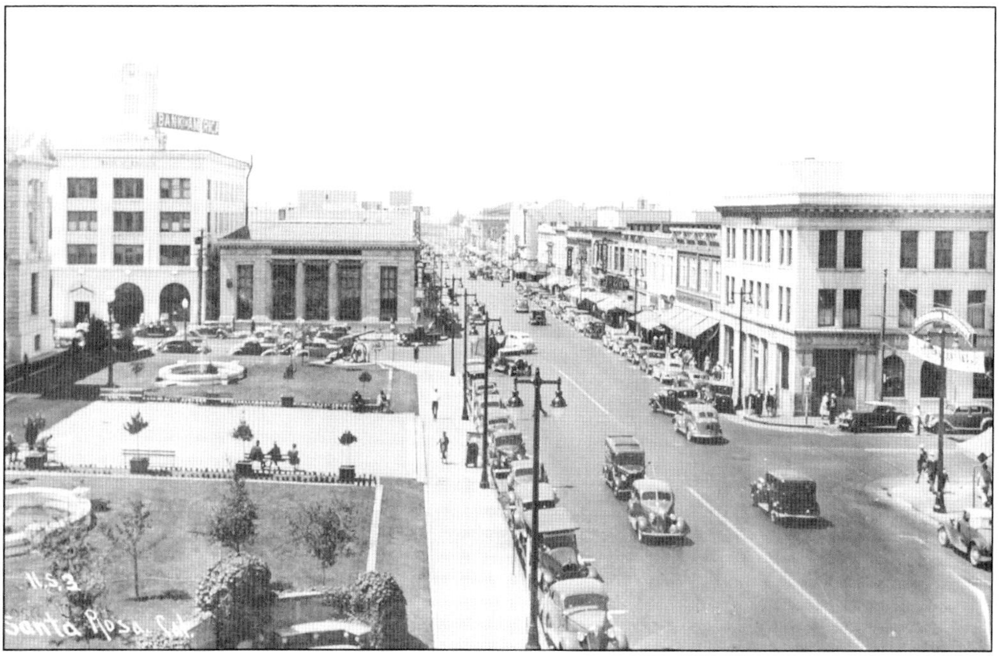

COURTHOUSE AND PLAZA, C. 1930. The Bank of Italy by this time had changed to Bank of America. Note the large cannon on the corner of the plaza.

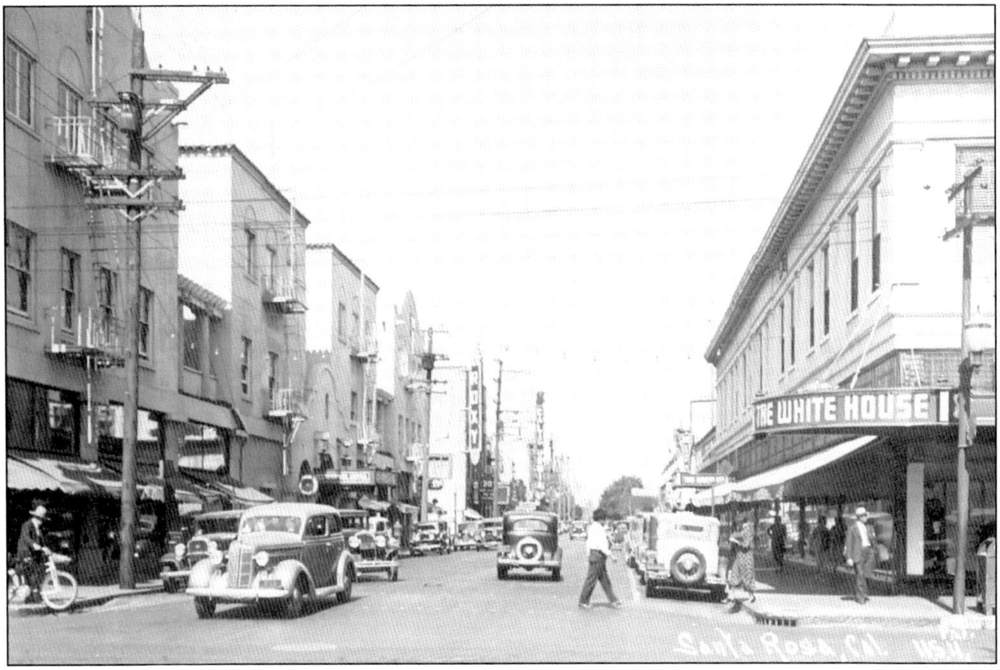

FOURTH STREET, C. 1930. This view looking north on B Street from the intersection of Fourth Street shows several landmarks, all of them now gone. They are The White House, the Roxy and California Theaters, and the Occidental Hotel.

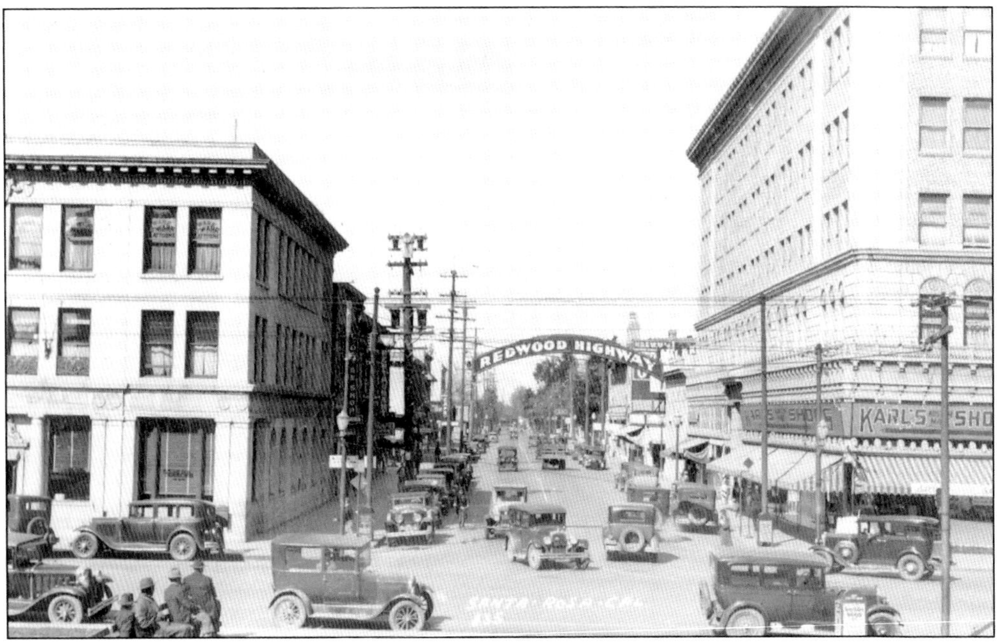

MENDOCINO AVENUE, C. 1935. The intersection of Mendocino Avenue and Fourth Street was the focal point of downtown. This view taken from the courthouse shows the Redwood Highway sign that arched over Mendocino Avenue until the new Highway 101 was constructed in 1948.

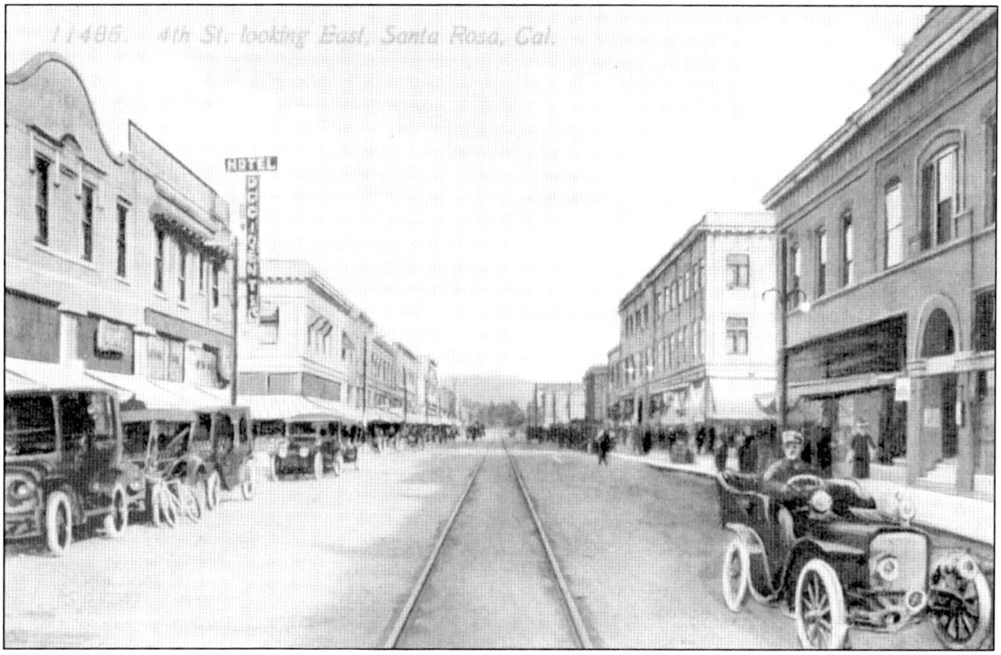

Fourth Street, c. 1917. This postcard shows Fourth Street looking east past the Occidental Hotel. The unusual feature of this card is the "tipped-in" or painted-in automobile in the foreground. Many publishers used this device to make a scene more interesting.

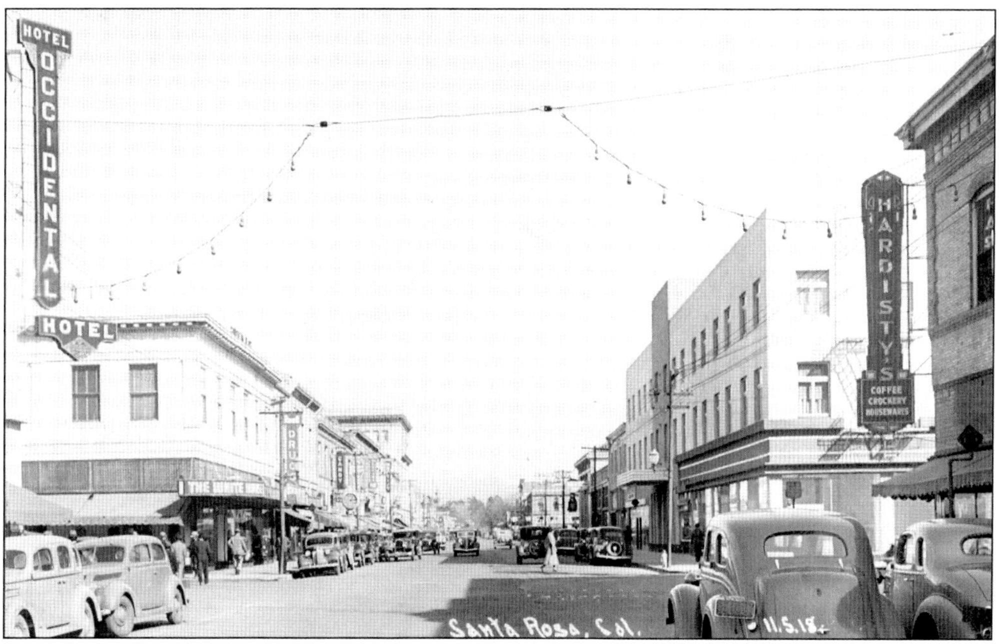

Fourth Street, c. 1935. This is the same scene as above, but years later. Hardisty's Homewares was located on the corner of Fourth and B Streets.

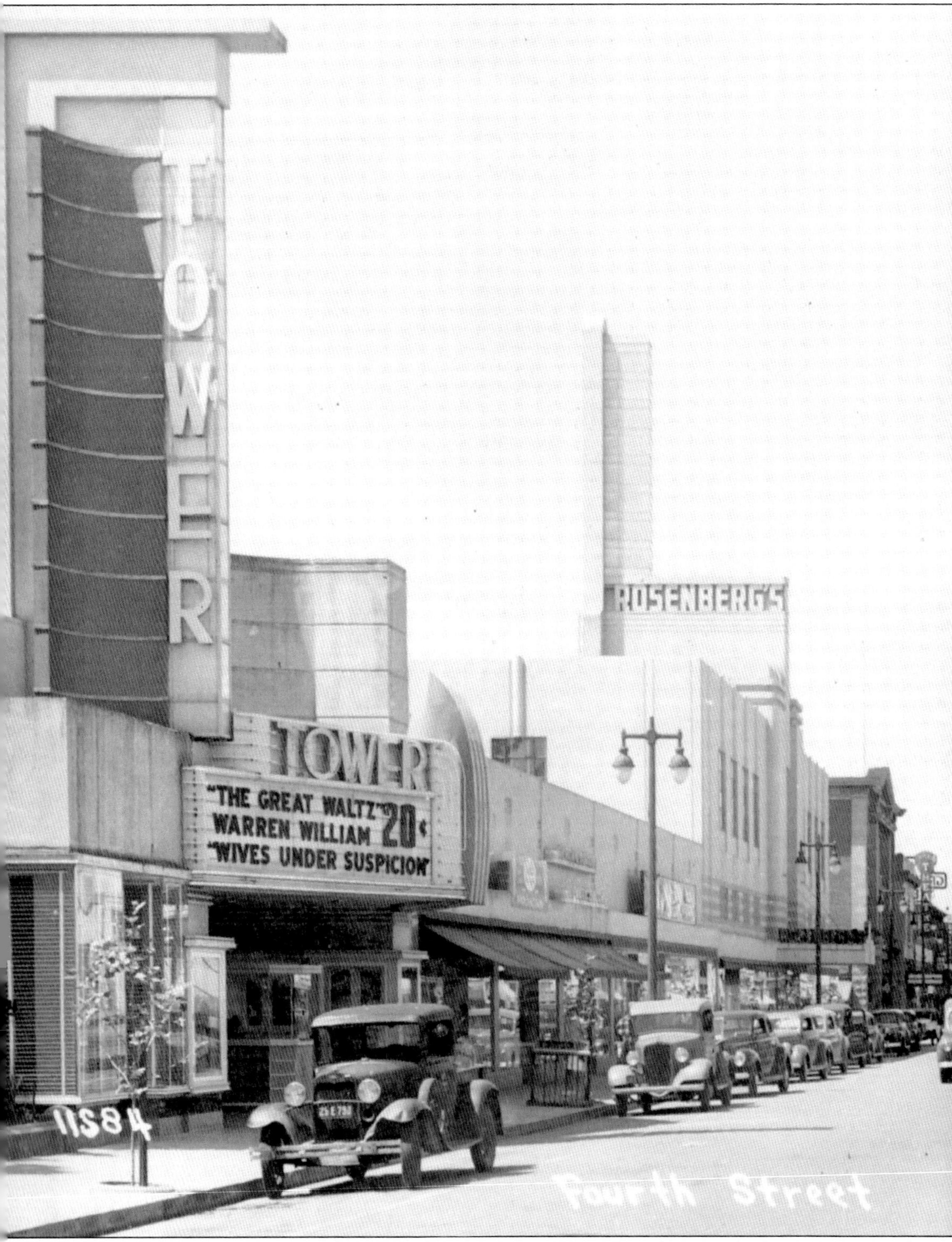

FOURTH STREET, c. 1937. This great photocard view shows Fourth Street looking west toward Railroad Square. The Tower Theater, located at 730 Fourth Street, and Rosenberg's Department

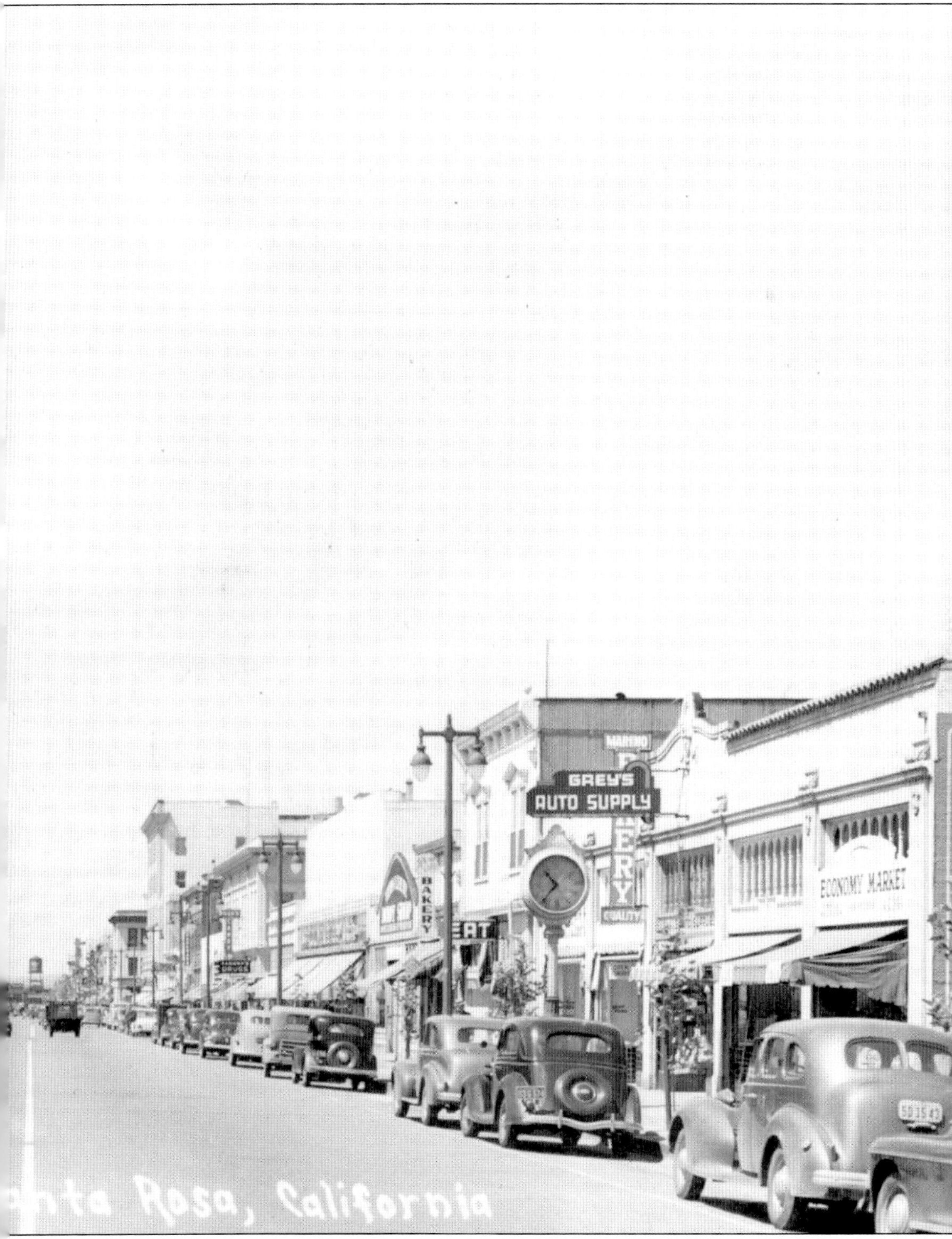

Store are pictured on the left. One could catch a double feature at the movies for 20¢. The water tower west of the NWP railroad depot is visible in the background.

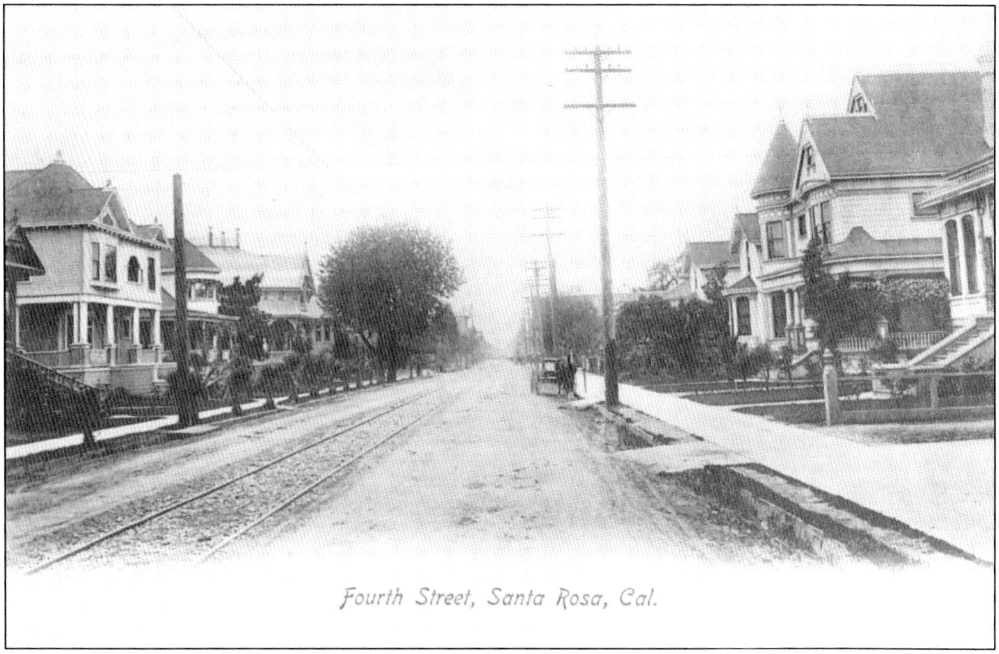

UPPER FOURTH STREET, C. 1905. This postcard view shows upper Fourth Street looking west toward downtown. Notice the beautiful Victorian homes on both sides of the dirt street.

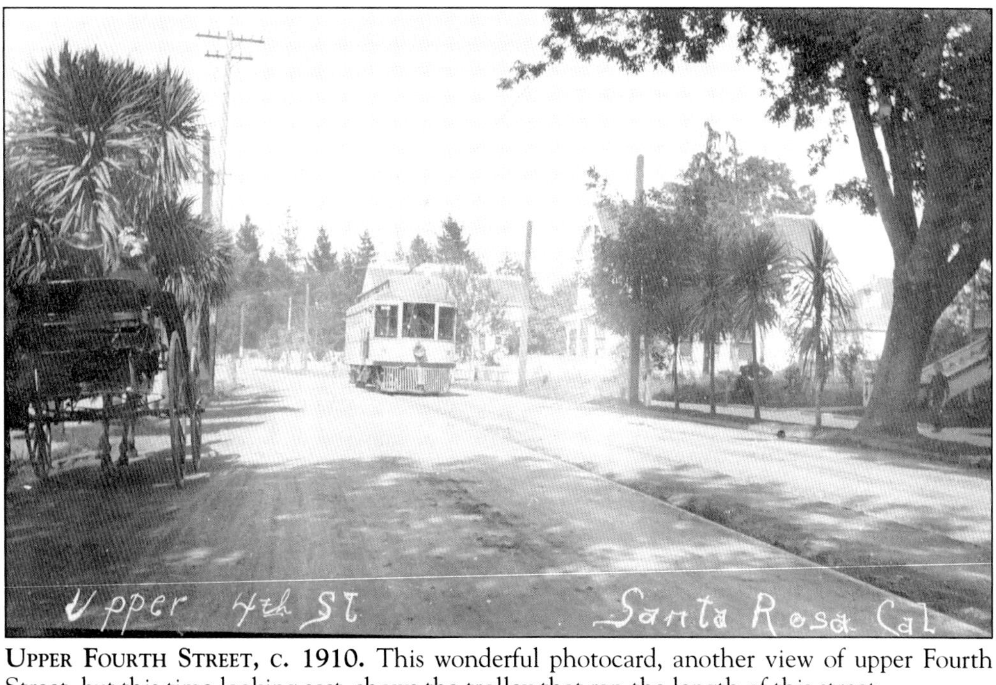

UPPER FOURTH STREET, C. 1910. This wonderful photocard, another view of upper Fourth Street, but this time looking east, shows the trolley that ran the length of this street.

Three

Luther Burbank Favorite Son

No other single person brought more national attention to Santa Rosa, California, than Luther Burbank (1849–1926). The Chamber of Commerce and the local media were quick, ready, and able to capitalize on this fact.

A world-renowned horticulturist, Burbank came to Santa Rosa in 1875. In his working career of over 50 years he developed over 800 new varieties of fruits, flowers, nuts, grains, and vegetables. Thousands of visitors flocked to his home properties just to see and talk to him. A few famous notables included Thomas Edison, Henry Ford, Harvey Firestone, Helen Keller, and his friend and neighbor, Jack London.

To this end, the postcard industry flourished with our hometown celebrity from 1900 through 1930. The following selections are only a sampling.

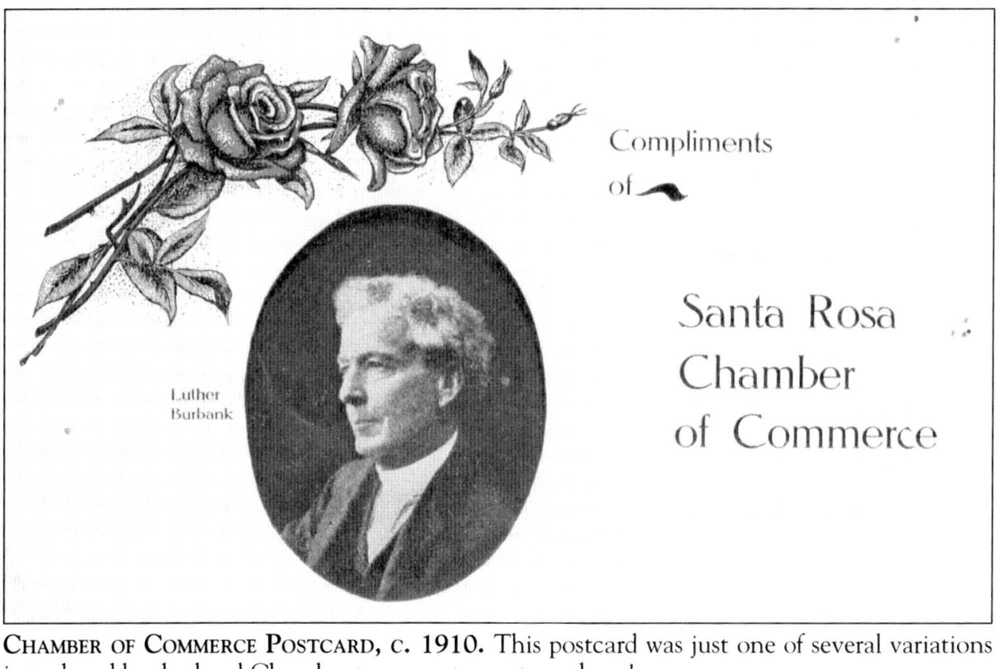

Chamber of Commerce Postcard, c. 1910. This postcard was just one of several variations introduced by the local Chamber to promote our town hero!

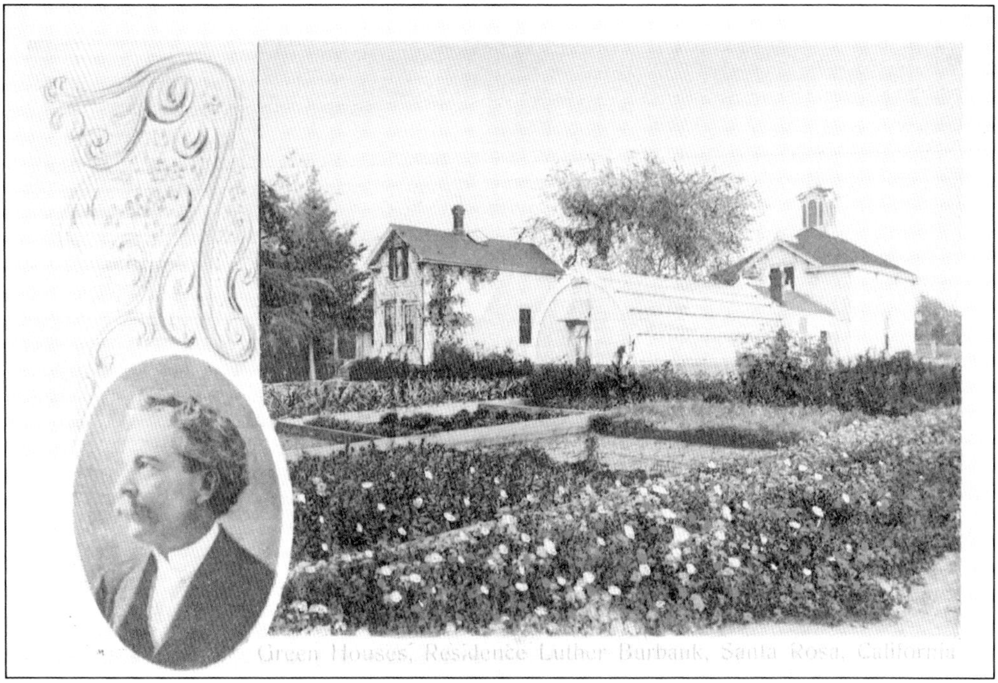

OLD HOME PLACE, c. 1905. Luther Burbank's home, greenhouse, and carriage house, located at the corner of Santa Rosa Avenue and Tupper Streets, is the subject of this postcard. Burbank purchased the house and 4 acres in 1884.

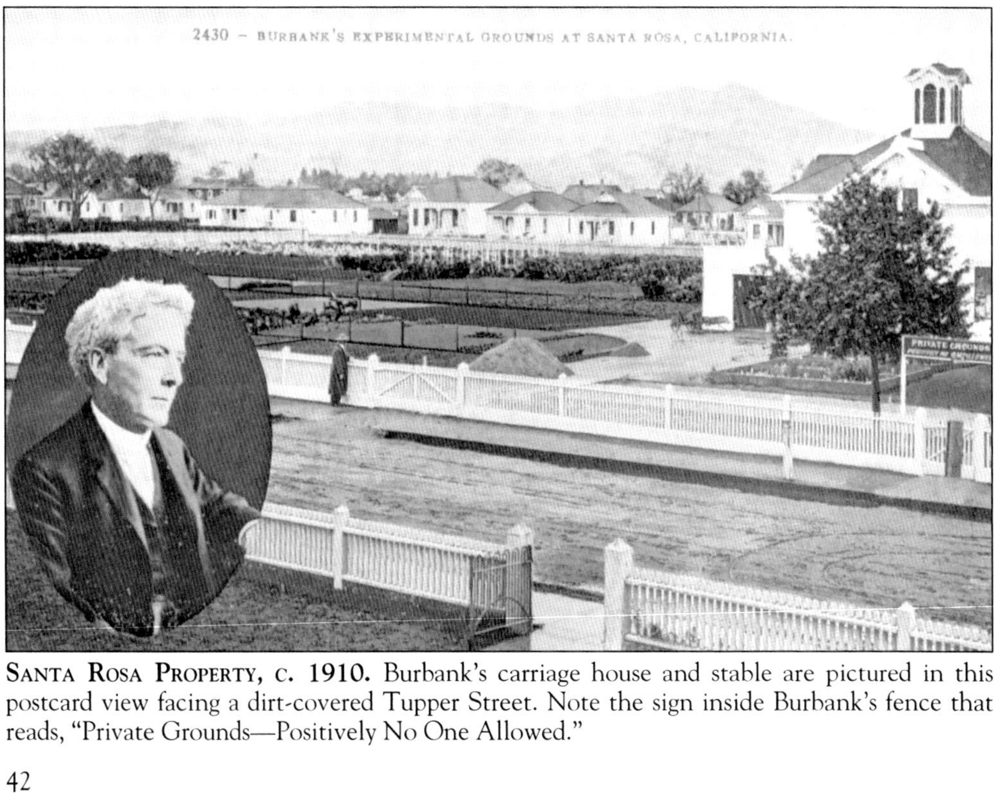

SANTA ROSA PROPERTY, c. 1910. Burbank's carriage house and stable are pictured in this postcard view facing a dirt-covered Tupper Street. Note the sign inside Burbank's fence that reads, "Private Grounds—Positively No One Allowed."

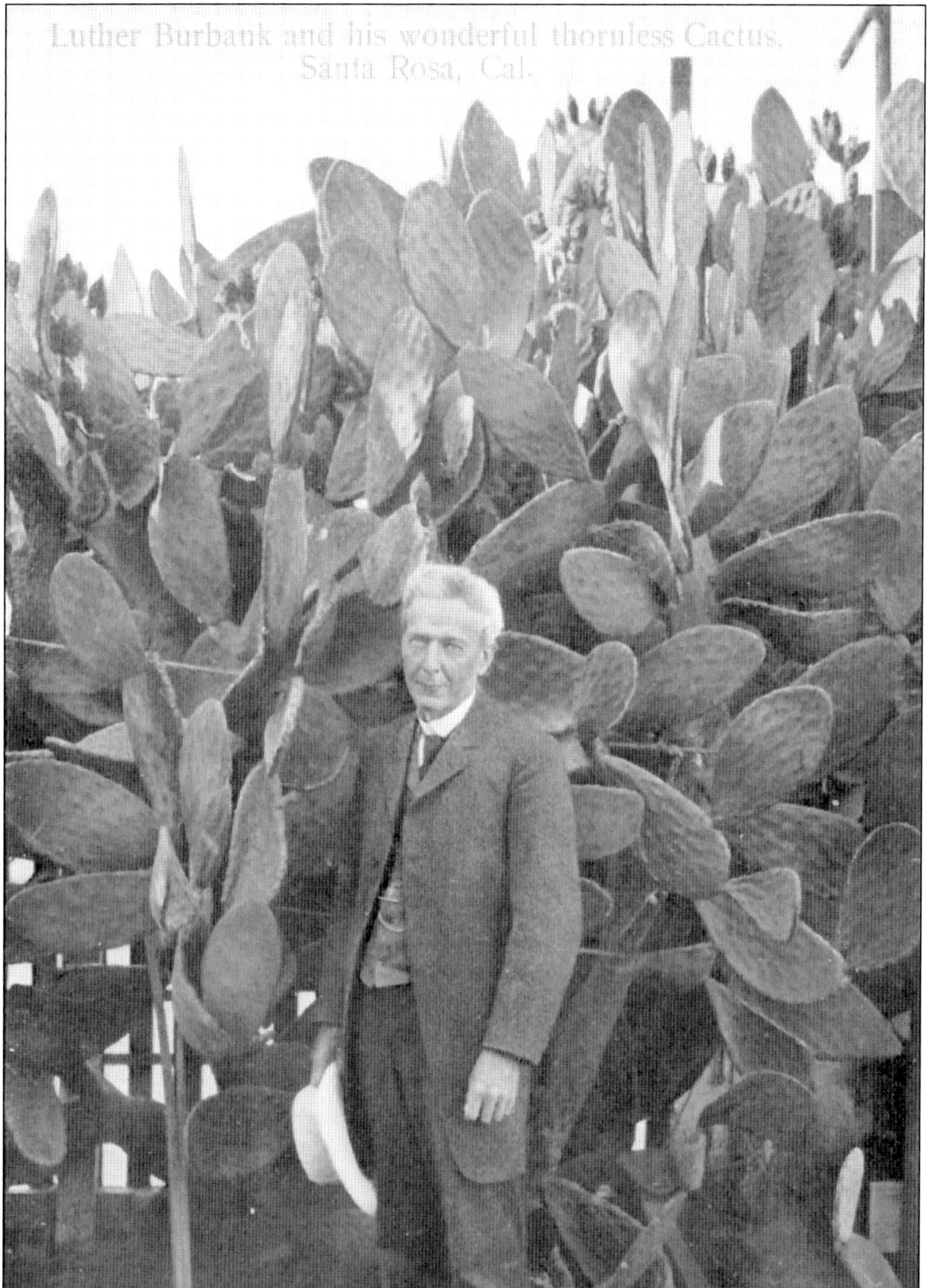

Burbank and Spineless Cactus, c. 1909. Burbank poses in front of his spineless cactus, the most popular backdrop on postcards of his plant introductions. On the back, Maude writes to her friend in Germany, "This picture does not do Mr. Burbank justice as the sun shone too strongly in his face. We will send you a better one soon."

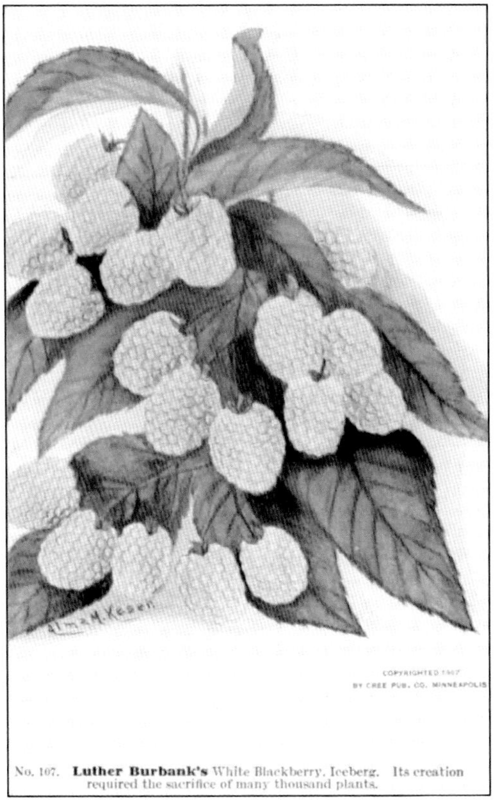

BURBANK'S NOVELTY FRUIT, C. 1907. Luther Burbank developed this White Blackberry in 1894, but it seemed to be accepted by the public as a novelty item. Perhaps homemakers preferred to bake their pies with *black*berries!

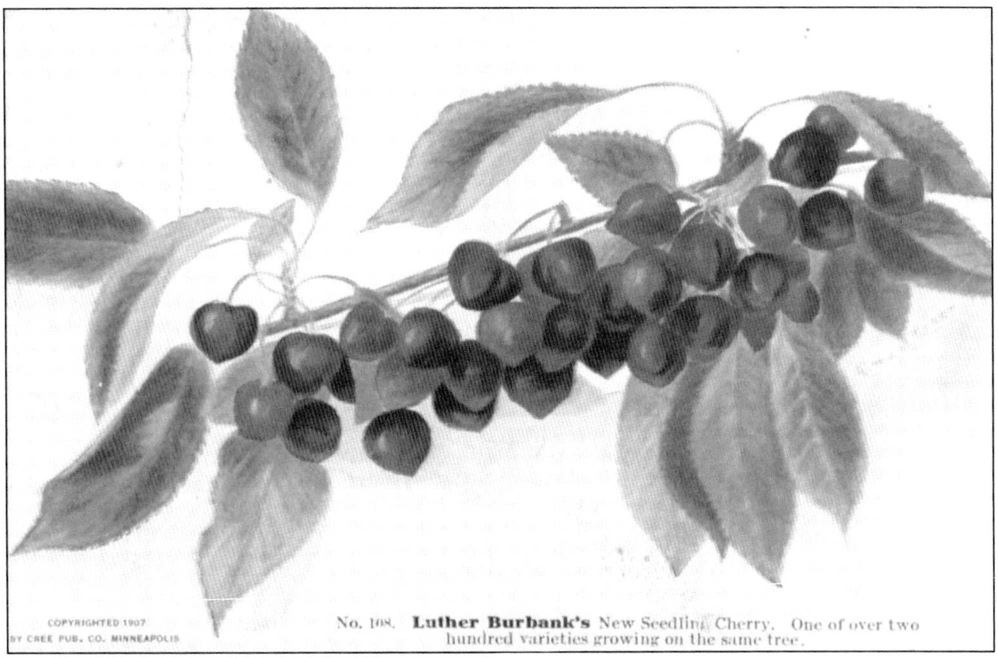

BURBANK NEW SEEDLING CHERRY, C. 1907. Burbank's New Seedling Cherry was introduced in 1903, championing his methods of grafting as many as two hundred varieties on a single tree.

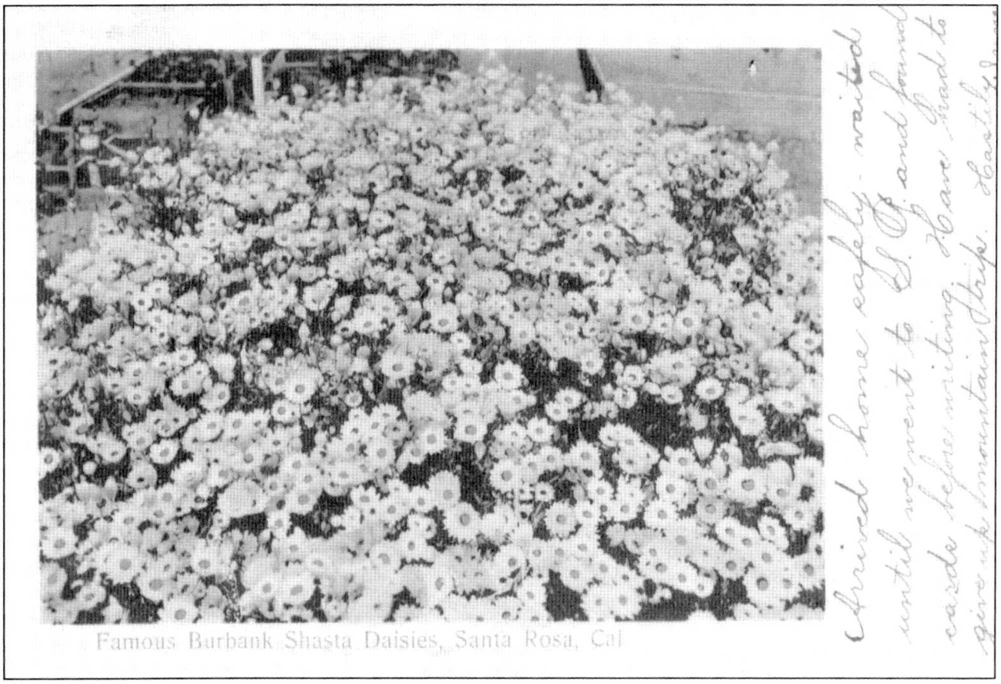

LUTHER BURBANK'S SHASTA DAISY, C. 1906. This postcard shows the results of 17 years of Burbank's work. In 1901, he introduced his famous Shasta daisy, named for the beautiful snow-covered peak of Mount Shasta in Northern California.

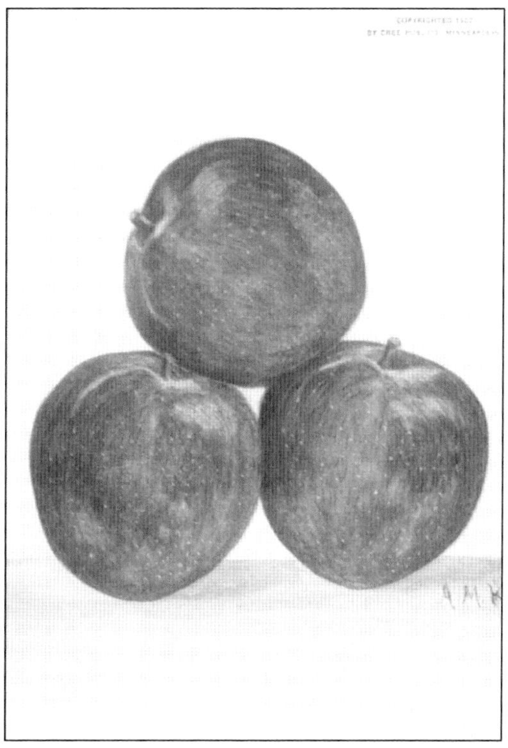

BURBANK PLUM, A GOLD MEDAL WINNER, C. 1907. Burbank's delicious Santa Rosa Plum, introduced in 1906, continues to be popular and available in produce markets today.

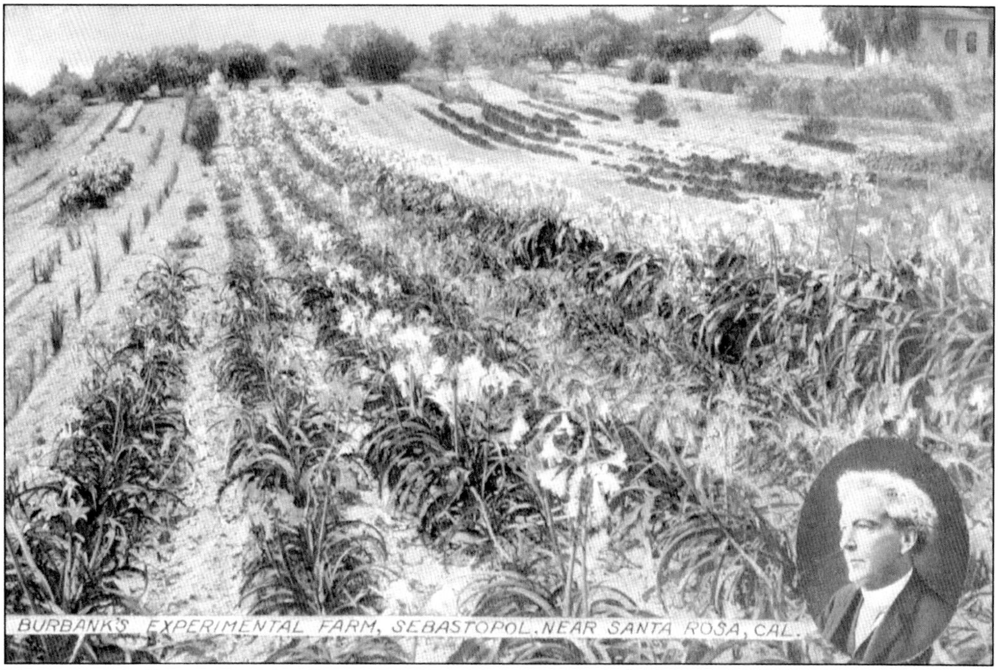

FIELDS OF FLOWERS IN SEBASTOPOL, C. 1910. This postcard highlights Luther Burbank's Experimental Farm in nearby Sebastopol, which made good use of 18 acres for plant propagation.

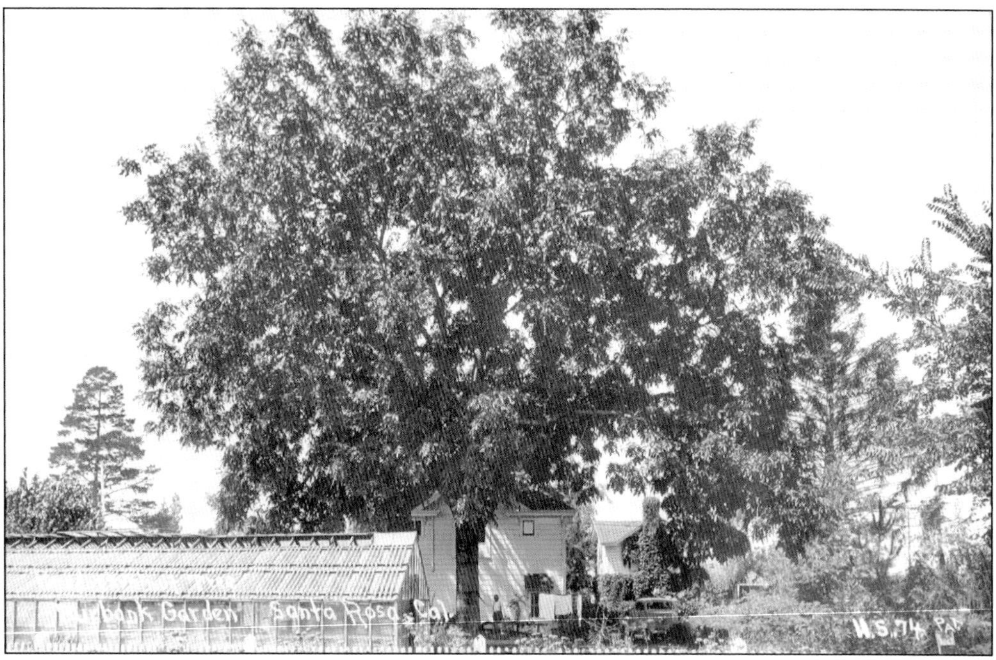

BURBANK'S PARADOX WALNUT TREE, C. 1940. Burbank's home property, featuring his Paradox Walnut tree, is the focus of this photocard. This walnut is a fast-growing hardwood that he introduced in 1893.

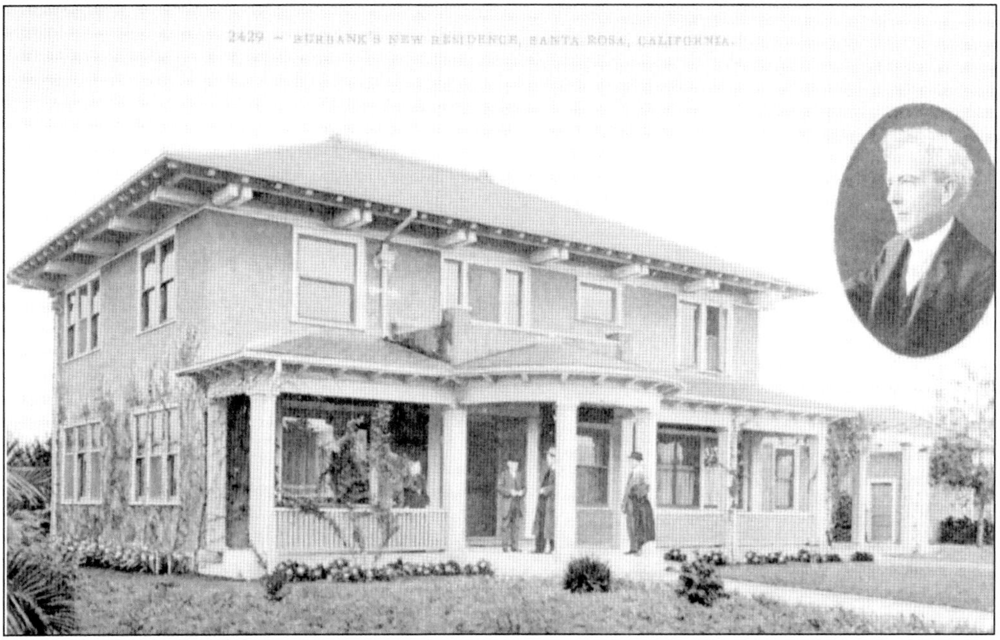

BURBANK'S "NEW RESIDENCE," C. 1907. Burbank and some gentlemen callers pose on the front porch of his new home on Tupper Street, built in 1906.

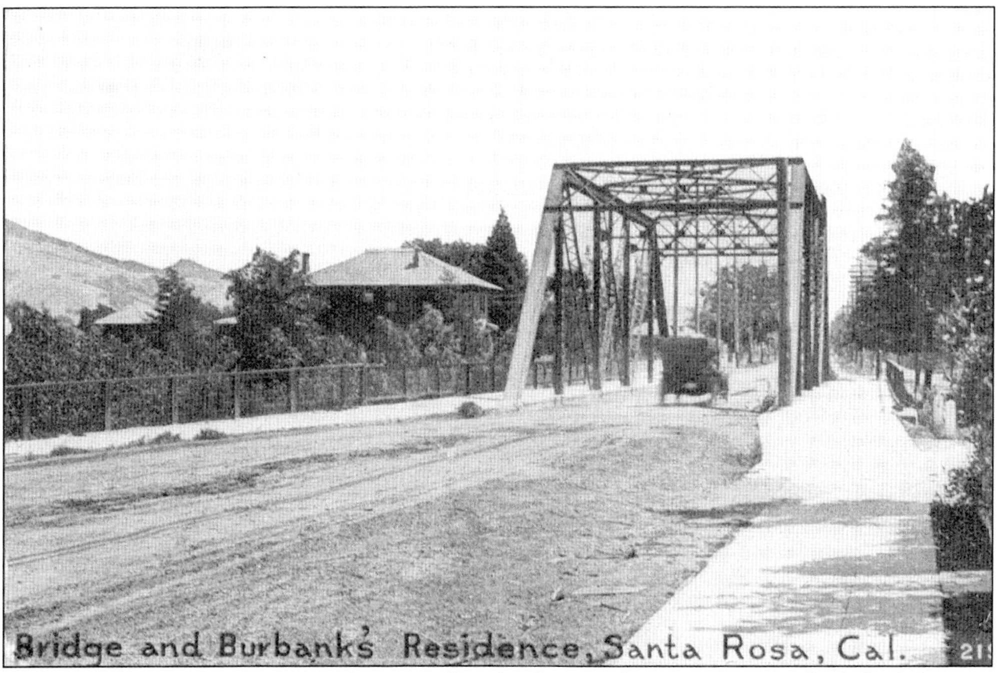

"THE IRON BRIDGE," C. 1910. The rear of Burbank's new home appears to the left of the iron bridge located on Santa Rosa Avenue.

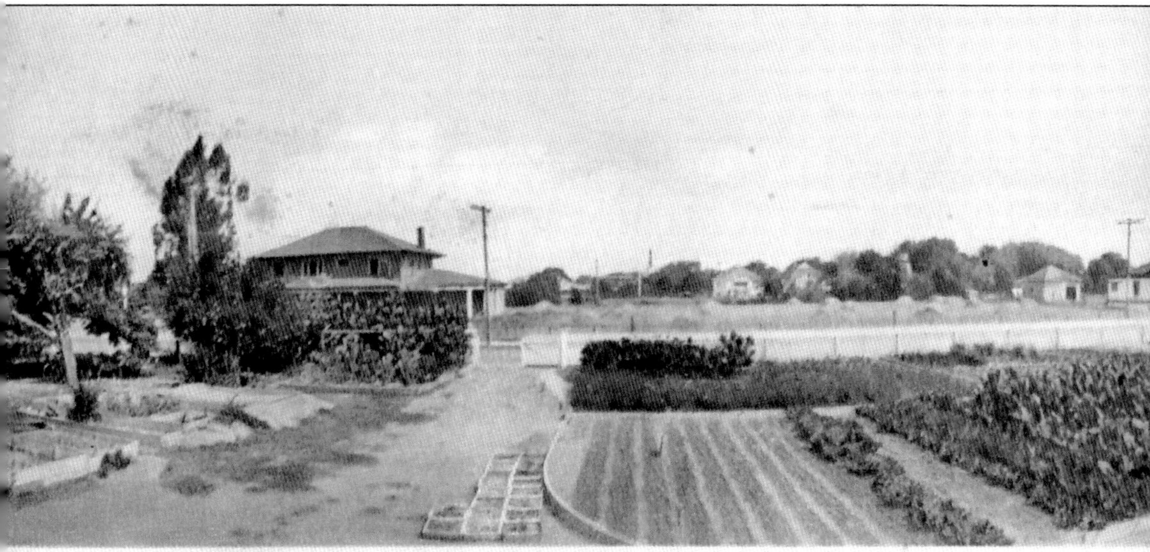

102. Bird's-eye View of **Luther Burbank's** Experiment Grounds at Santa Rosa, looking North and East.

BIRD'S-EYE VIEW, C. 1907. This panoramic view of Luther Burbank's original 4-acre property in Santa Rosa looks north and east. Luther Burbank Home & Gardens, a National, State, and

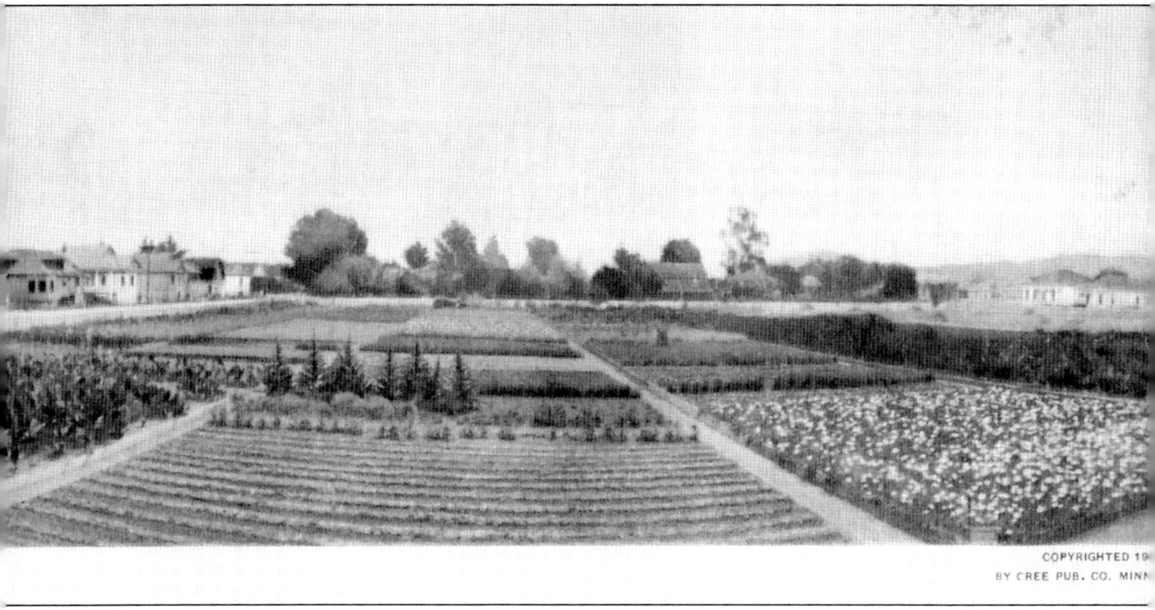

City Registered Historic Landmark, today occupies a little more than 1 acre.

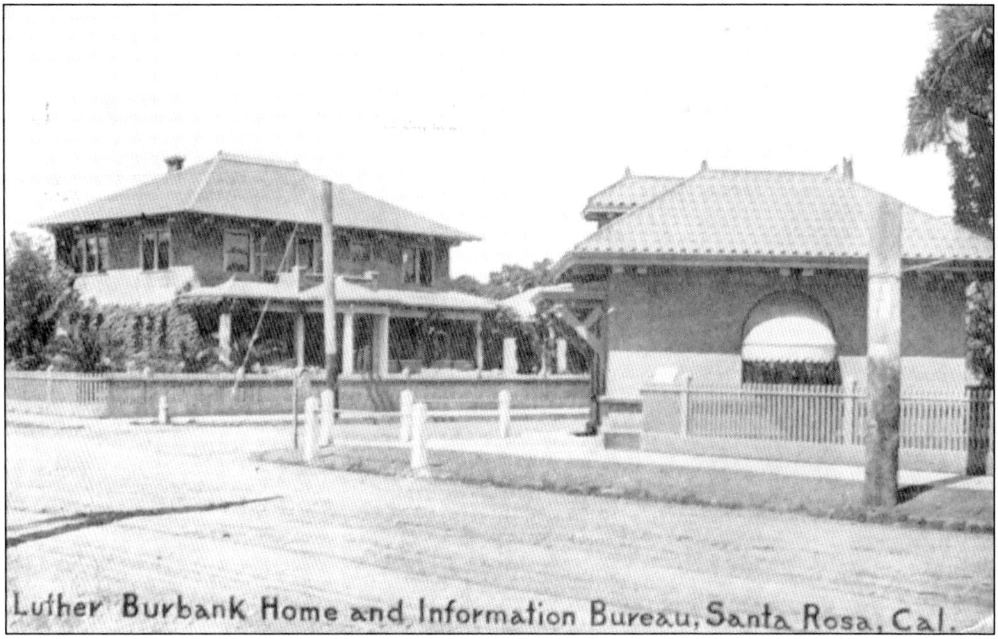

Burbank House and Sales Structure, c. 1914. After Burbank's death in 1926, his widow sold this house to move into the "old homestead" across the street. Following several commercial occupants, the house was demolished in the early 1960s as part of a major redevelopment project.

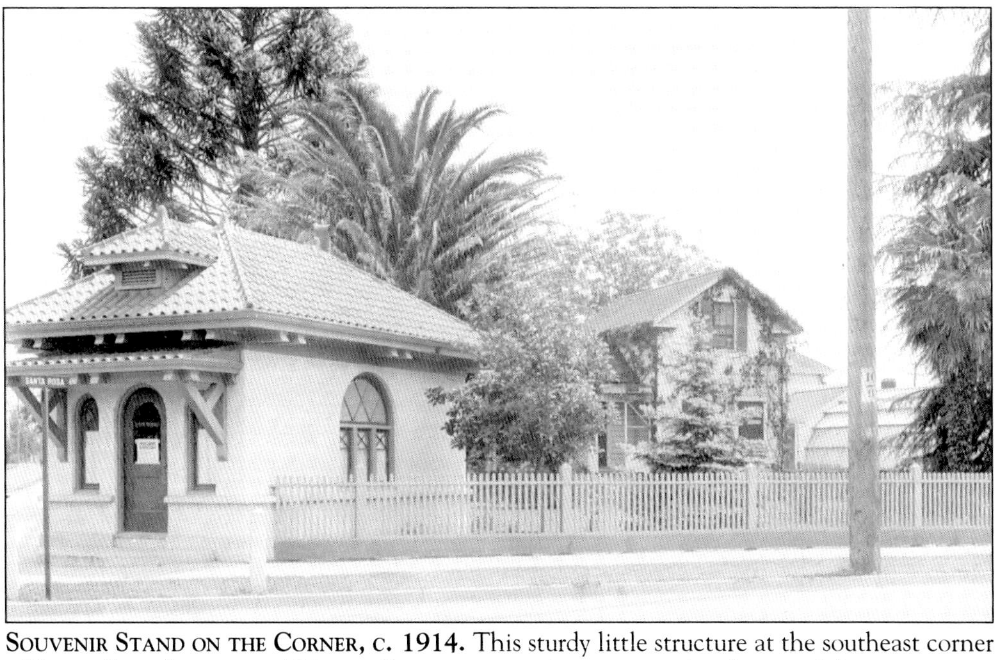

Souvenir Stand on the Corner, c. 1914. This sturdy little structure at the southeast corner of Santa Rosa Avenue and Tupper Streets was used as a souvenir sales stand for many years. Burbank's old residence is visible to the right. After Burbank's death, Mrs. Burbank sent the little building to Henry Ford's Greenfield Village Museum in Dearborn, Michigan, at Ford's request. It remains there today.

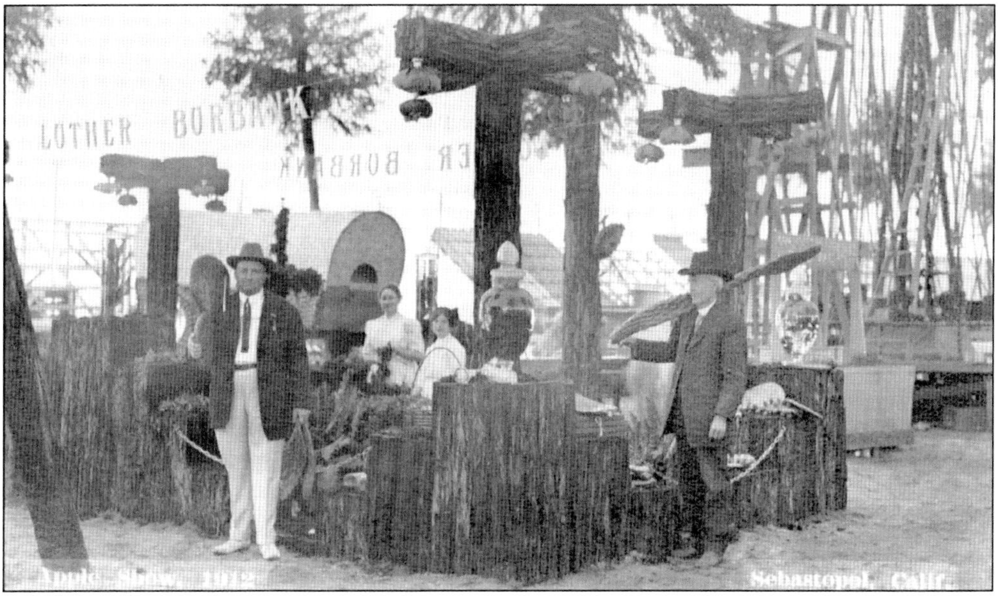

SEBASTOPOL APPLE SHOW, 1912. Luther Burbank was famous all over the world, and he enjoyed his celebrity status right here in Sonoma County. Burbank appears in this photocard on the right, participating in an apple show in Sebastopol, California.

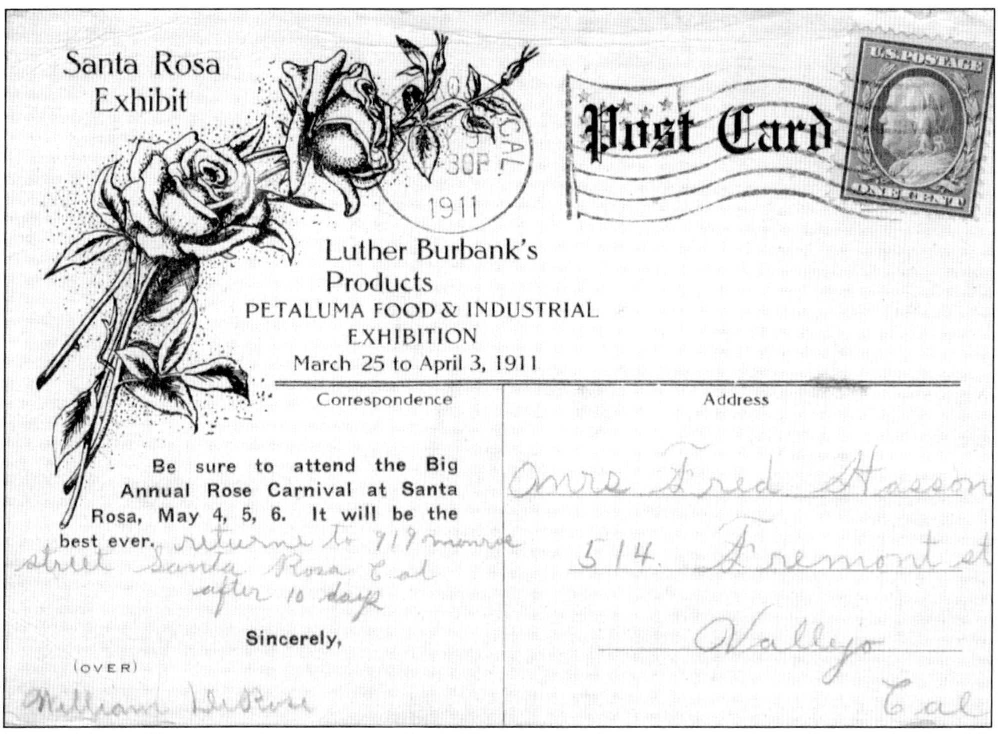

SANTA ROSA EXHIBIT IN PETALUMA, 1911. This postcard was imprinted to advertise Burbank's plant products at an exhibition in Petaluma, California.

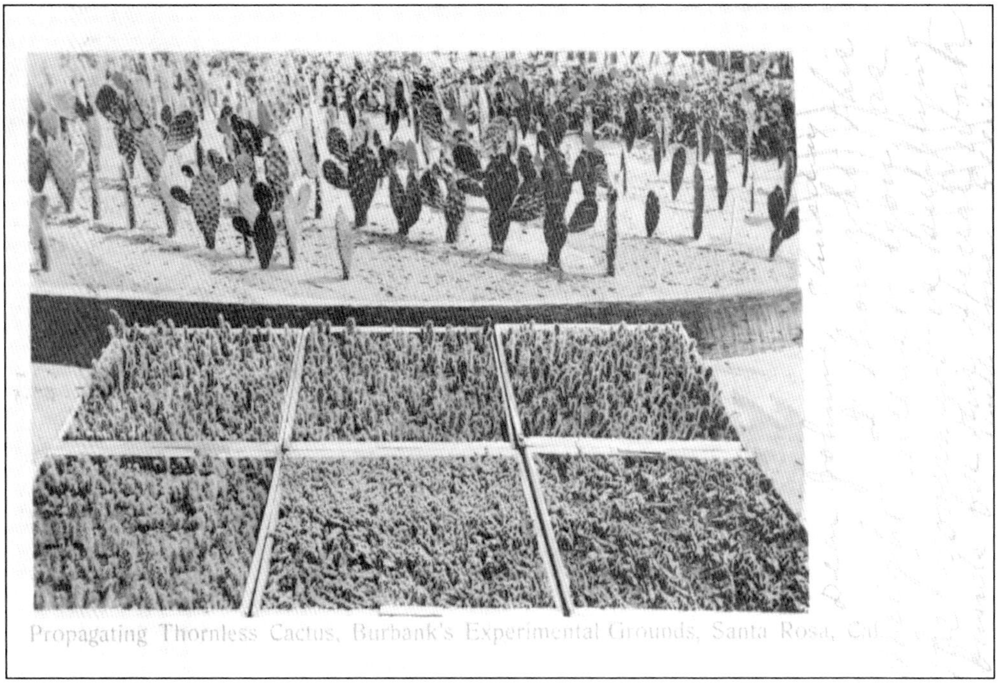

Burbank's Spineless Cactus, c. 1907. Burbank's "thornless" or "spineless" cactus, which he spent nearly 20 years developing and improving, is the subject of this card.

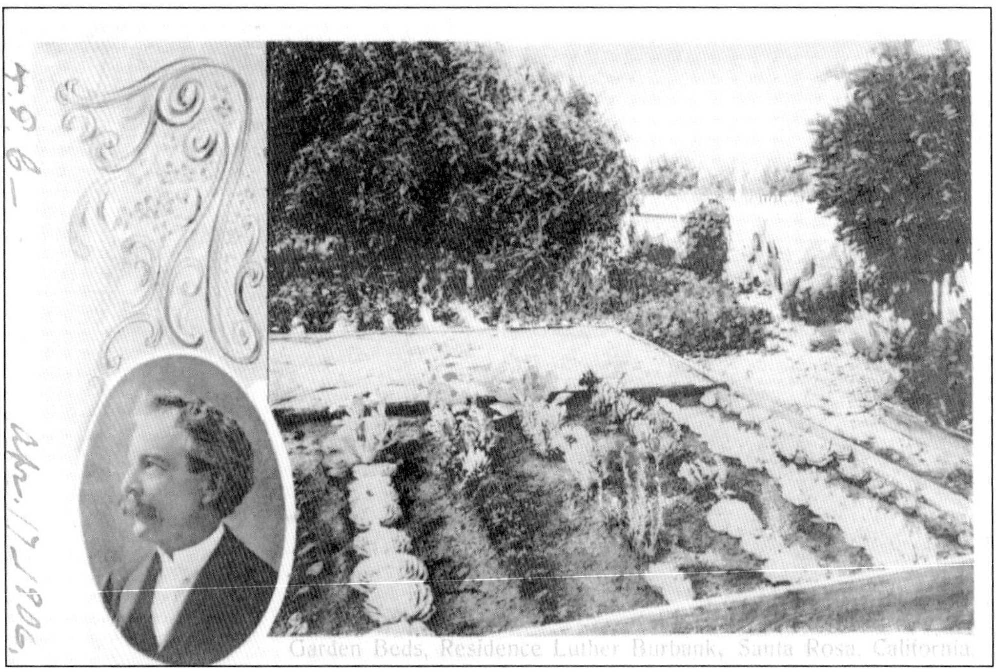

Garden Beds, c. 1906. Burbank's gardening methods included using raised beds for planting.

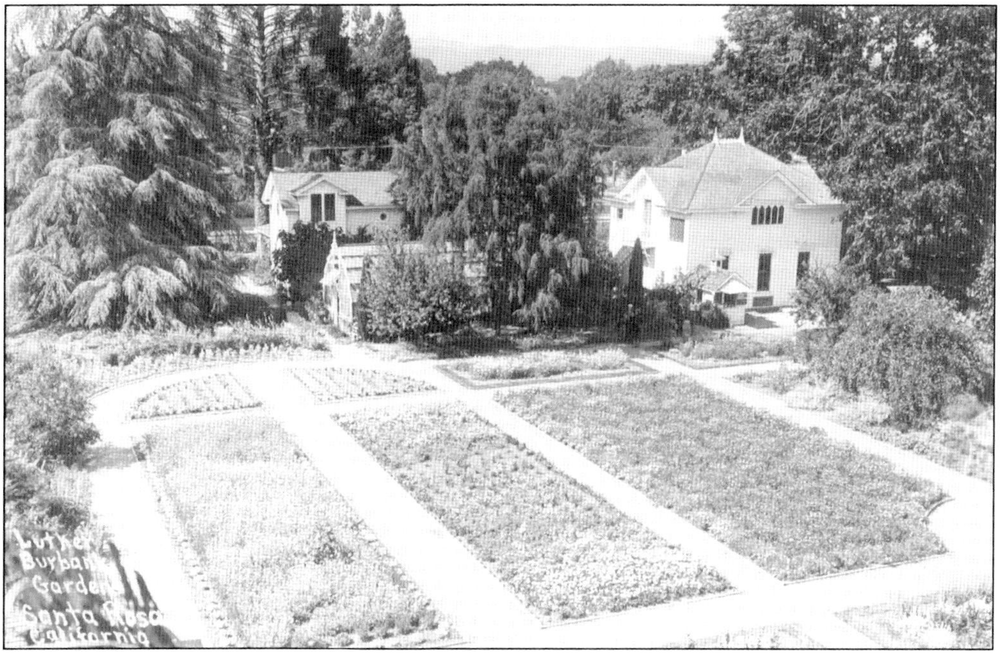

AERIAL VIEW OF THE PROPERTY, C. 1945. After Luther Burbank's death in 1926, the Santa Rosa garden property went through numerous changes in design and use.

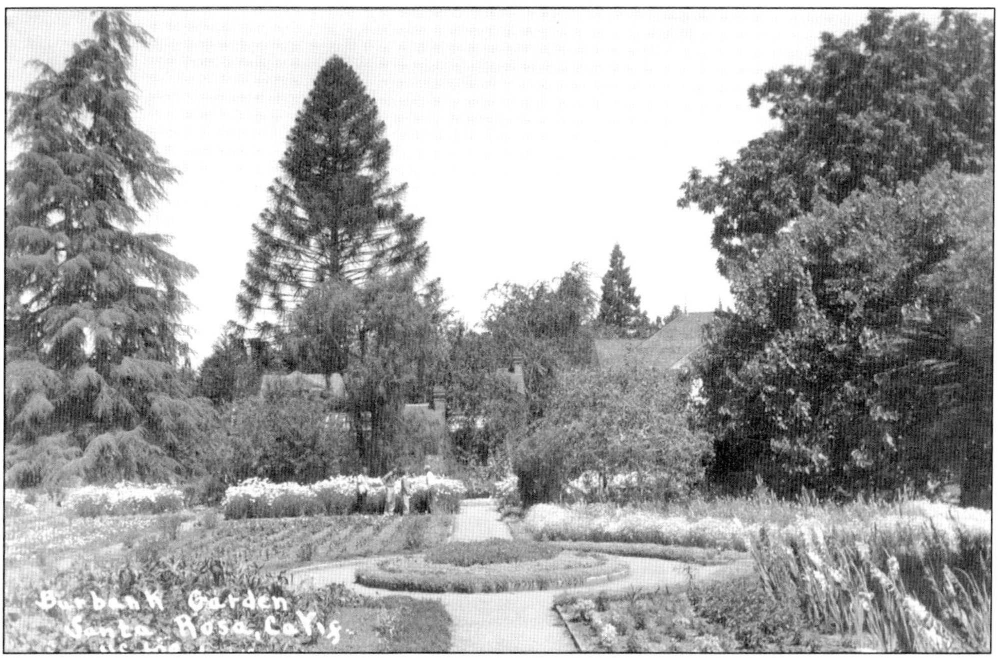

GARDEN CENTER POINT, C. 1945. This view was taken standing at the center of the gardens looking north toward Tupper Street. The giant Cedar of Lebanon tree appears at the far left, and a Monkey Puzzle tree is visible on its right.

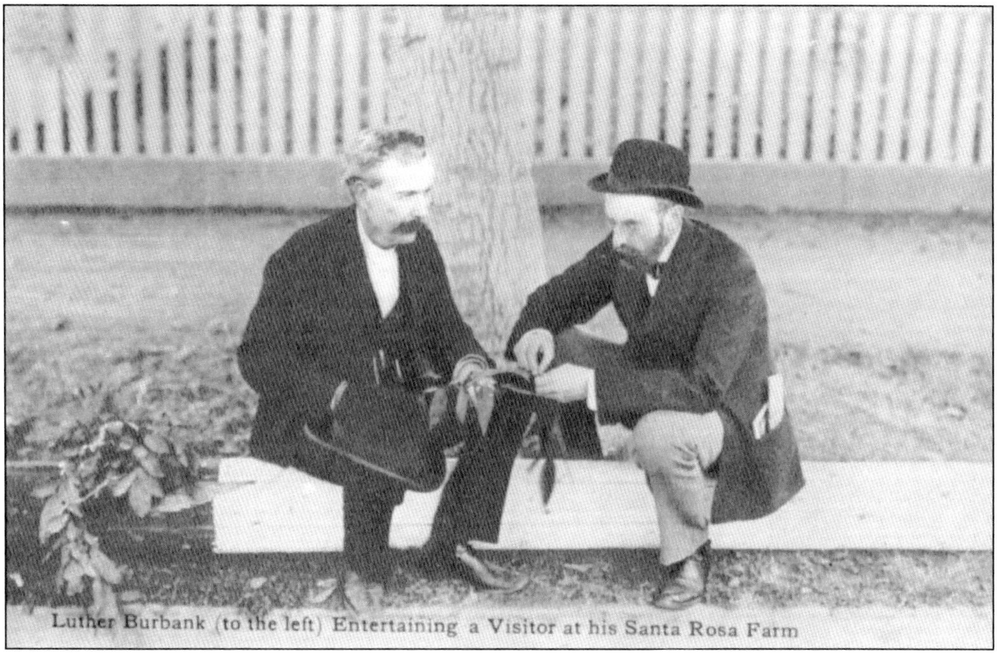

CHAT WITH A VISITOR, c. 1900. This very early photocard shows Luther Burbank on the left with a visitor at his Santa Rosa property.

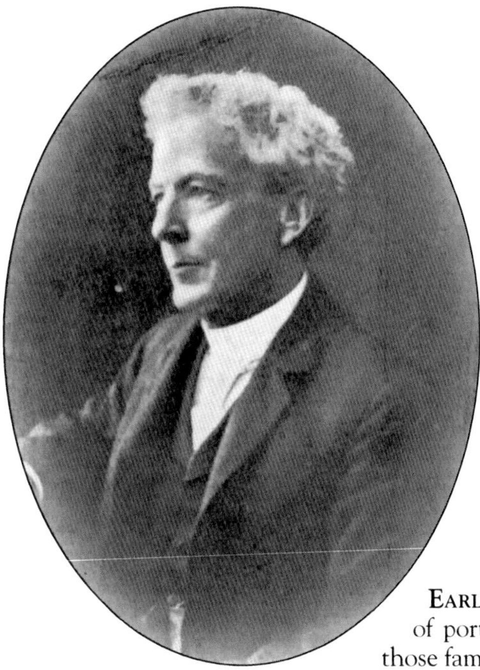

EARLY PORTRAIT, c. 1910. Burbank posed for a series of portraits during his career. This postcard is one of those familiar photographs.

EARLY ADVERTISING, C. 1914. The front of this postcard says that everyone could have "a Burbank Flower Garden" for $1! This image was also used on the front of a small seed box.

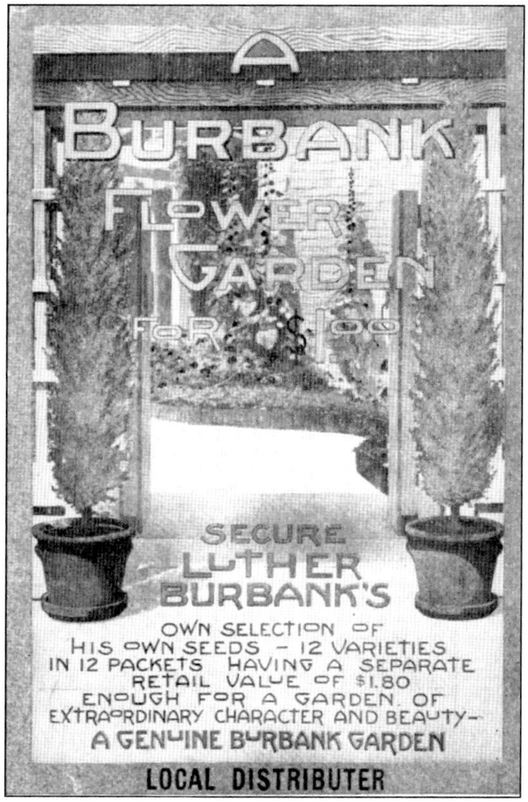

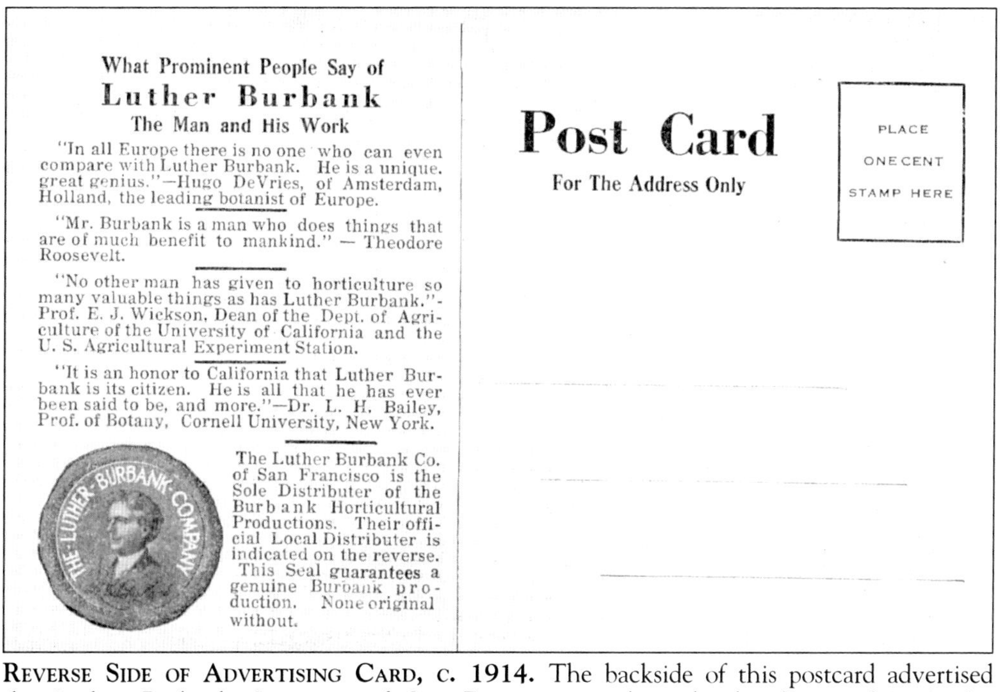

REVERSE SIDE OF ADVERTISING CARD, C. 1914. The backside of this postcard advertised the Luther Burbank Company of San Francisco as the sole distributor of Burbank's plant productions.

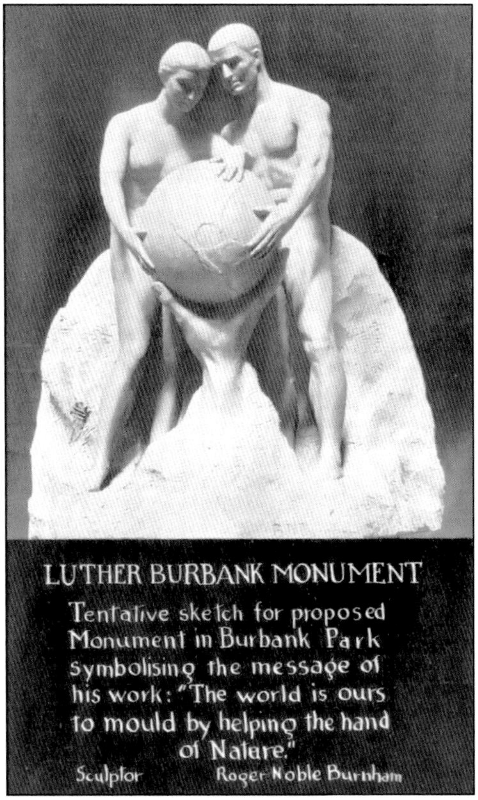

TESTIMONIALS, c. 1930. After Burbank's death, many ideas surfaced in an effort to pay lasting tribute to this plant genius. This postcard was one of those ideas.

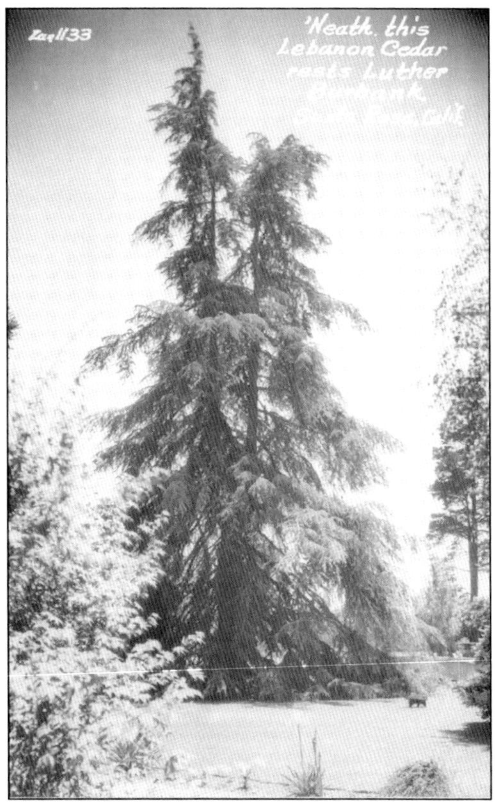

FINAL RESTING PLACE, c. 1930. A photocard shows the Cedar of Lebanon tree that Burbank himself planted in the front lawn of his home facing Santa Rosa Avenue. When he died, his wish to be buried near this tree in an unmarked grave was granted. Unfortunately, the cedar needed to be removed in 1989 due to root disease.

Four

Churches, Schools, and Residences

This chapter covers the non-commercial structures in Santa Rosa, which proved to be the most challenging to research. The churches were easy to locate from old directories, though names did change, but most are no longer standing. Remodeling and rebuilding have made many changes to most Santa Rosa residential neighborhoods, making some of the private residences nearly impossible to locate. The schools portrayed in this chapter seemed to have best withstood the changes of time. The photocards of the private residences really show a more genteel era in Santa Rosa. From the large residences of McDonald Avenue to the smaller homes on Cherry Street, the photographs show families very proud of their well-kept houses and streets.

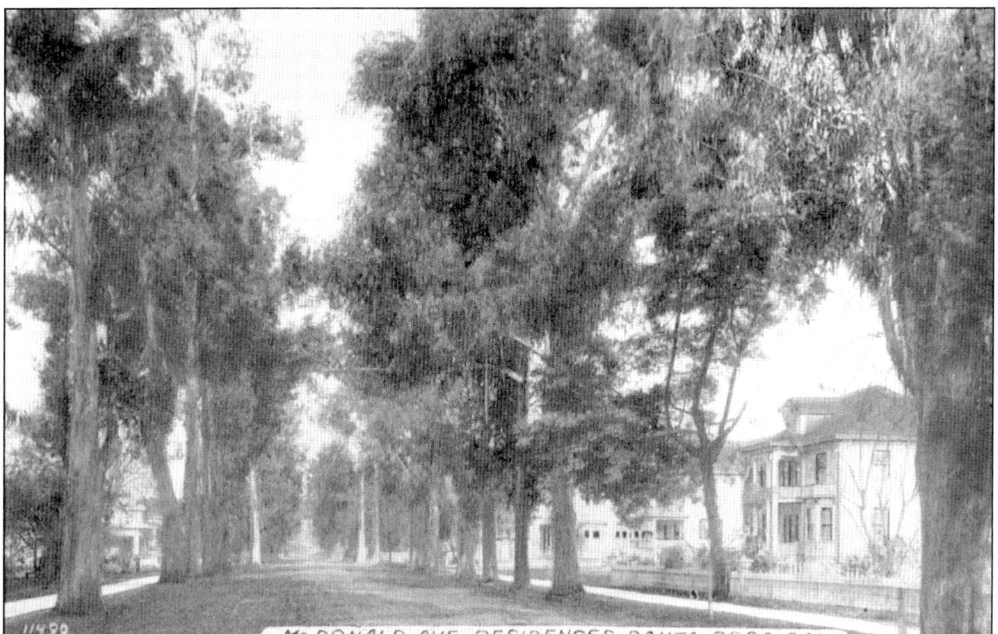

McDonald Avenue, c. 1915. McDonald Avenue has always been one of Santa Rosa's most prominent residential streets. Many of these stately homes, built in the late 1870s, stand today.

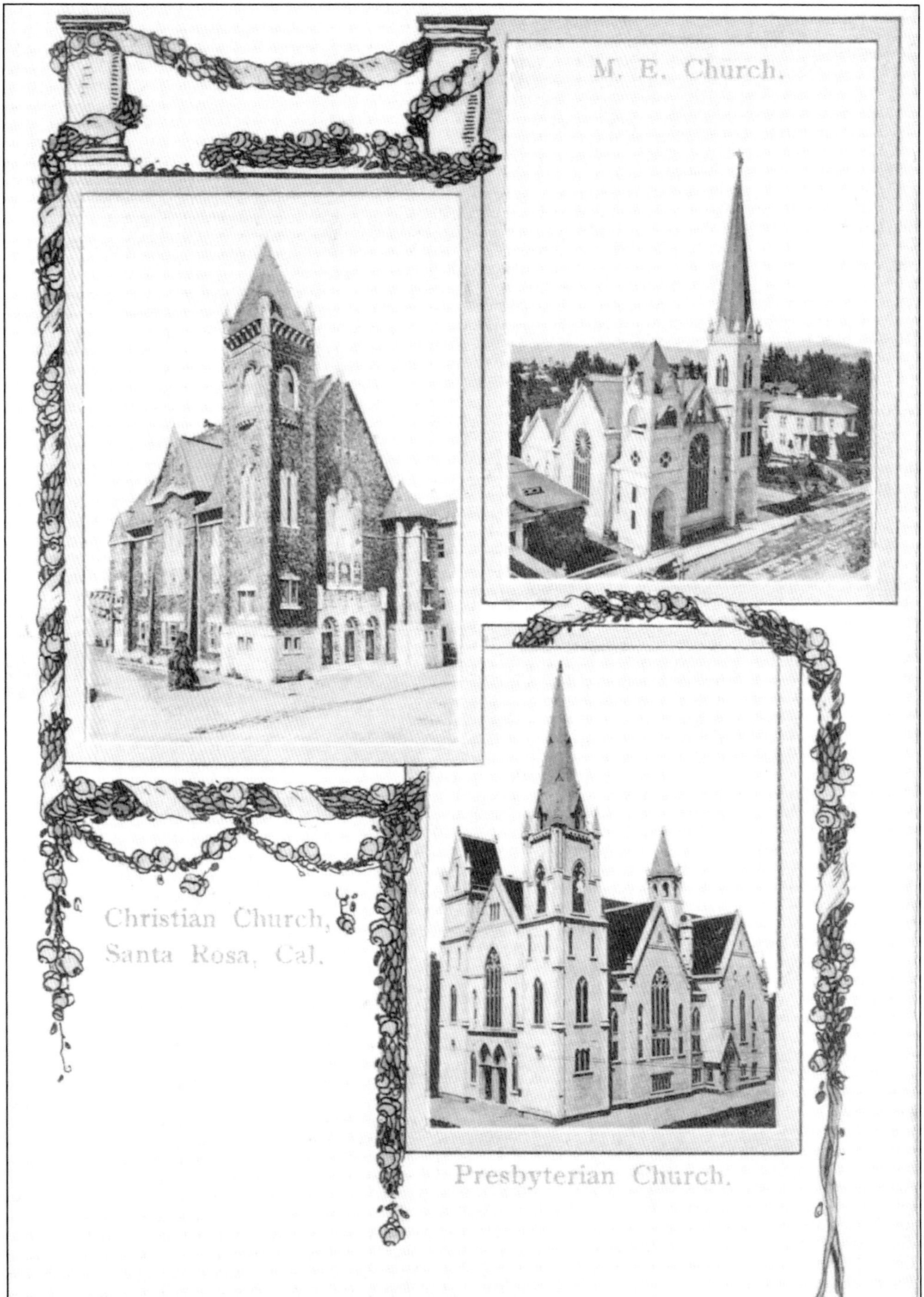

THREE EARLY SANTA ROSA CHURCHES, C. 1905. The Christian Church was located on Ross Street near B Street. The Methodist Episcopal Church, built in 1894, was located at 905 Mendocino Avenue; its remodeled building is now St. Luke Evangelical Lutheran. The Presbyterian Church was on the corner of Johnson and Humboldt Streets.

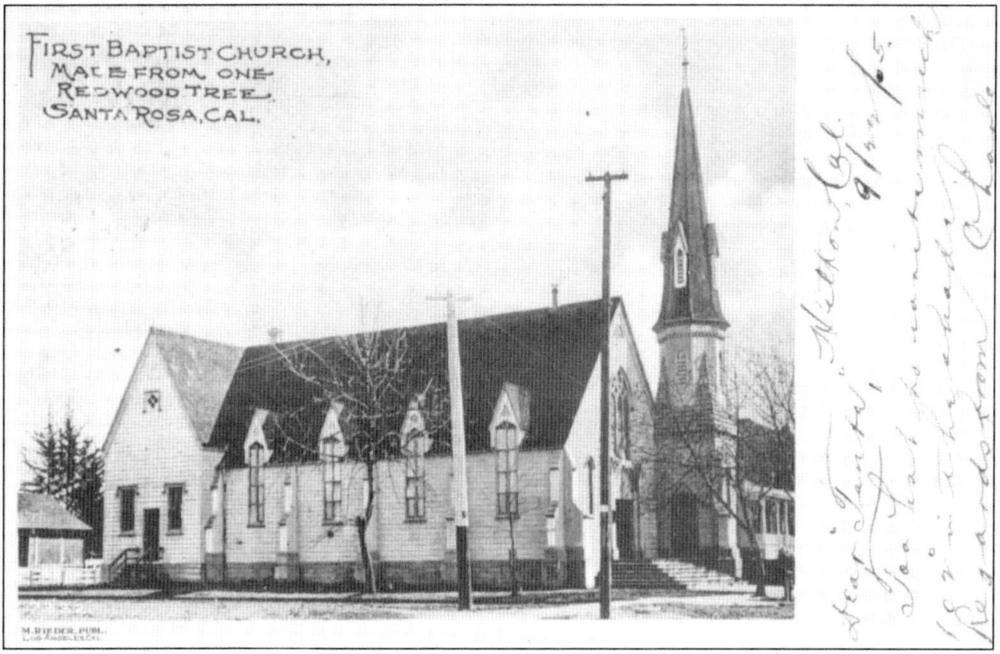

First Baptist Church, c. 1905. The First Baptist Church was built in 1874 of lumber taken from one redwood tree, giving it the nickname, "The Church of One Tree." It was originally located at Ross and B Streets.

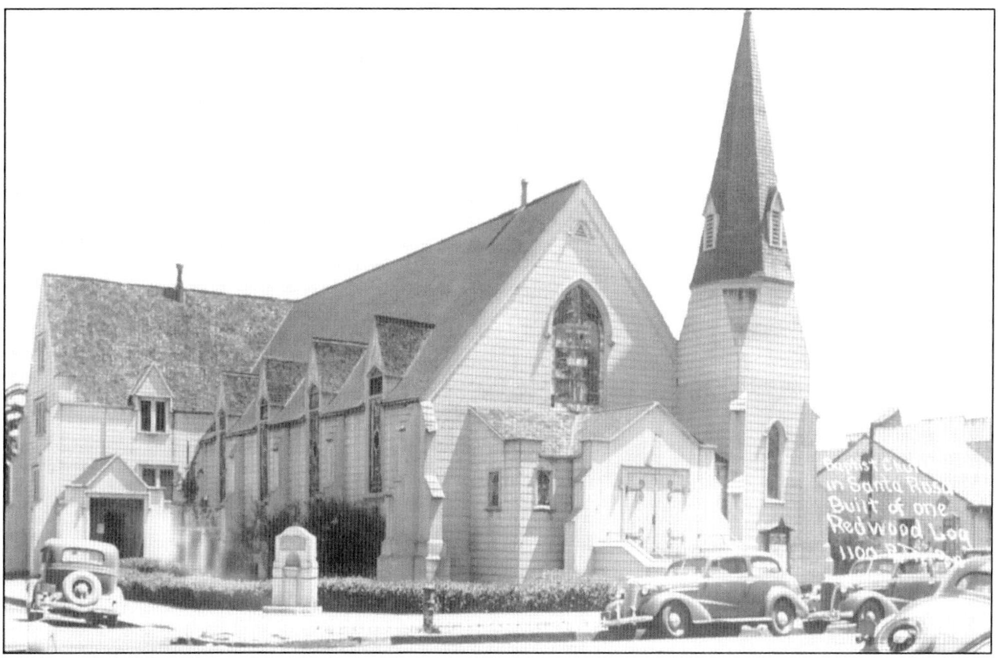

First Baptist Church, c. 1940. "The Church of One Tree" was moved to its present location at 488 Sonoma Avenue in 1959. Local cartoonist Robert Ripley made this church famous in his syndicated column, "Ripley's Believe It or Not."

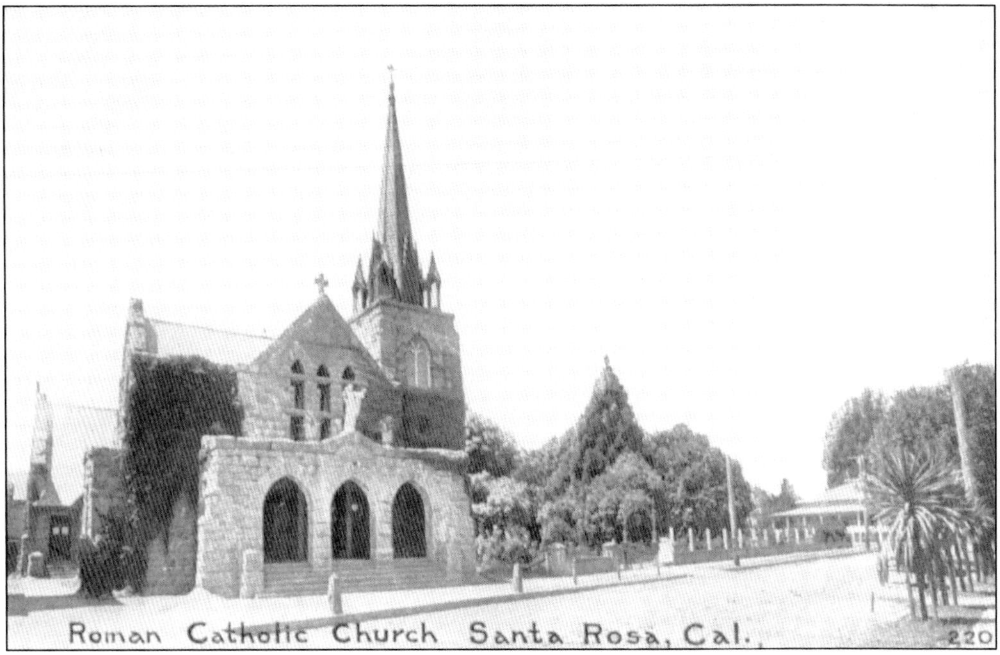

St. Rose Roman Catholic Church, c. 1915. St. Rose Church, dedicated in 1900, was the first stone structure in Santa Rosa. The steeple shown in this postcard withstood the 1906 earthquake, but is gone today.

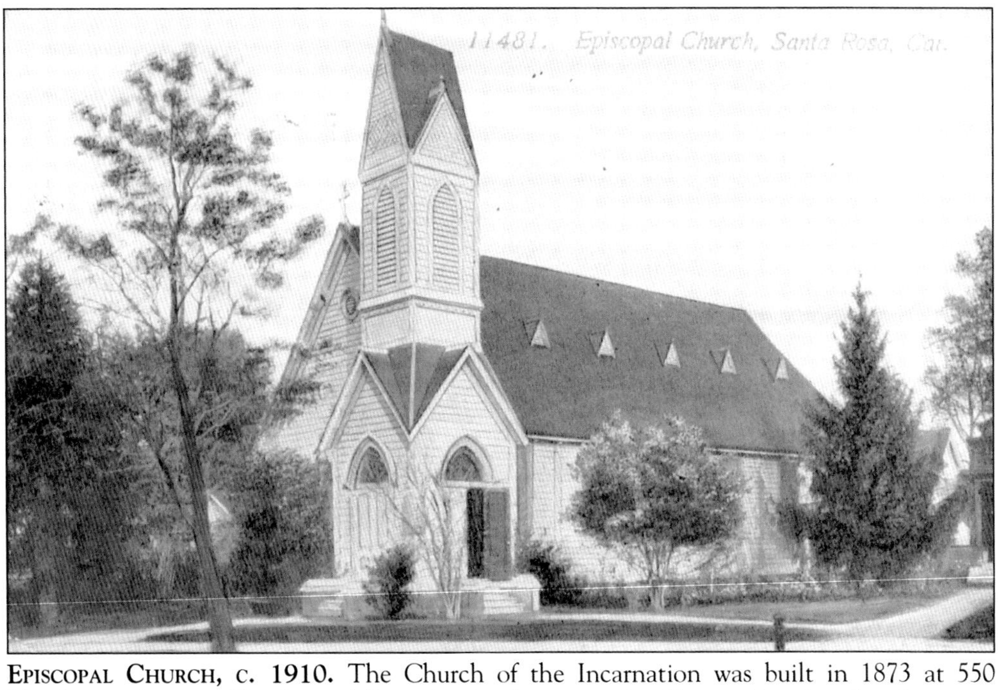

Episcopal Church, c. 1910. The Church of the Incarnation was built in 1873 at 550 Mendocino Avenue. This beautifully maintained structure is still an active church today.

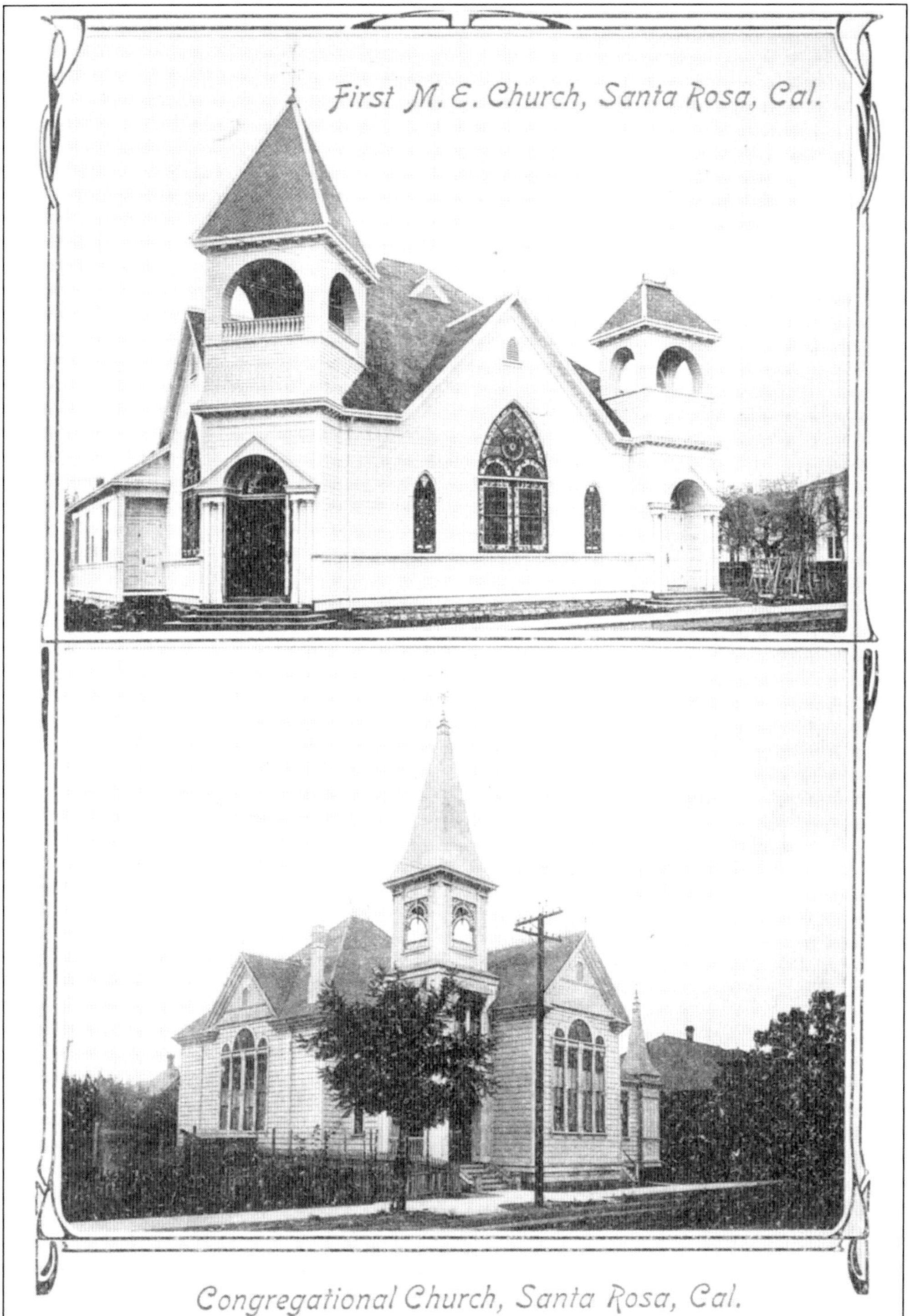

Two Early Santa Rosa Churches, c. 1905. The First Methodist Episcopal Church was located on the corner of Fifth and Orchard Streets, and the Congregational Church was on E Street between Third and Fourth Streets.

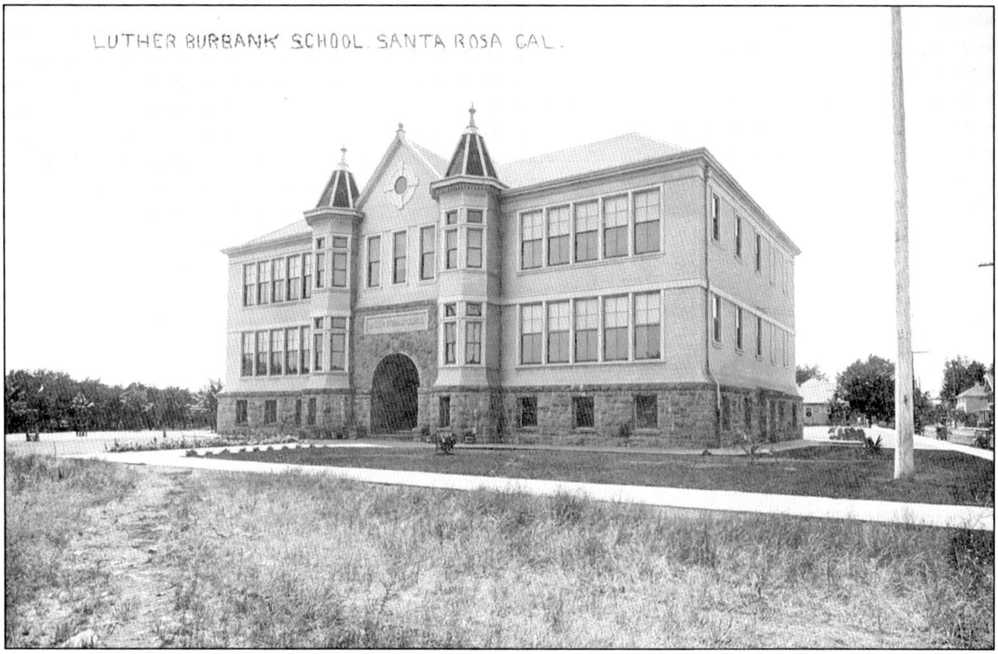

LUTHER BURBANK SCHOOL, C. 1910. This postcard photo shows Burbank School as it was when built in 1907 at South A and Ellis Streets. The school still operates today on the same site but in a building constructed in the 1940s.

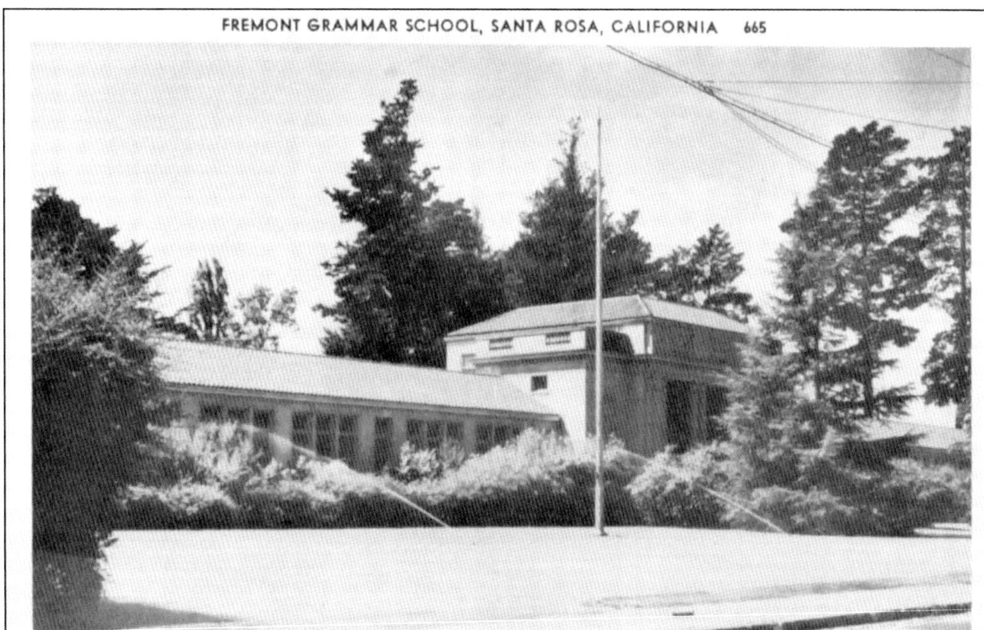

FREMONT SCHOOL, C. 1940. The original Fremont School was built at Fourth and North Streets. This grammar school at College Avenue and E Street is now home to the Santa Rosa Middle School.

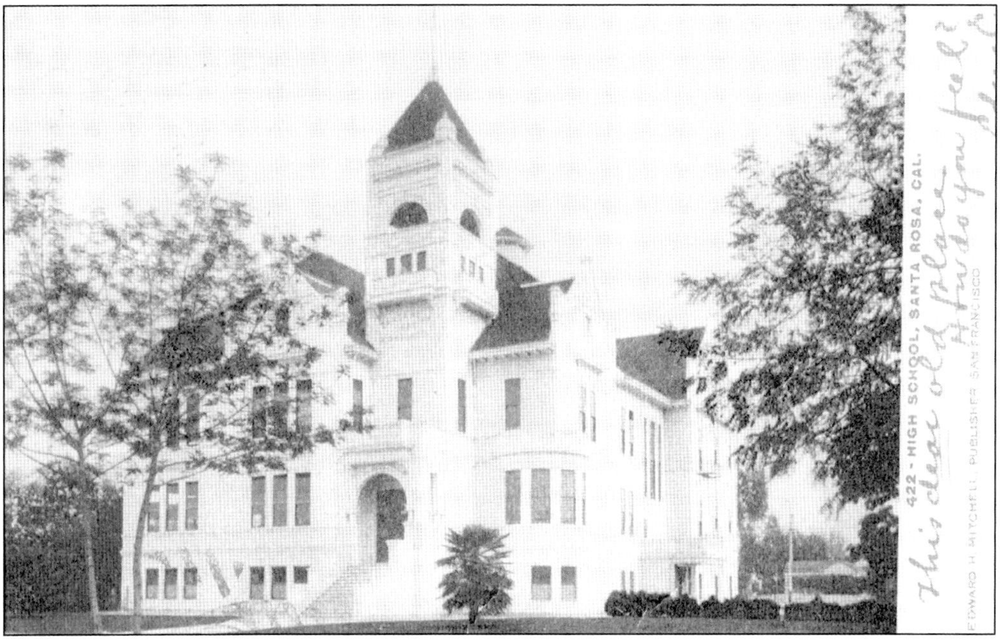

SANTA ROSA HIGH SCHOOL, C. 1905. The first Santa Rosa High School was completed in 1895 and was located on Humboldt Street between College Avenue and Benton Street. On this postcard, Edna writes, "This dear old place."

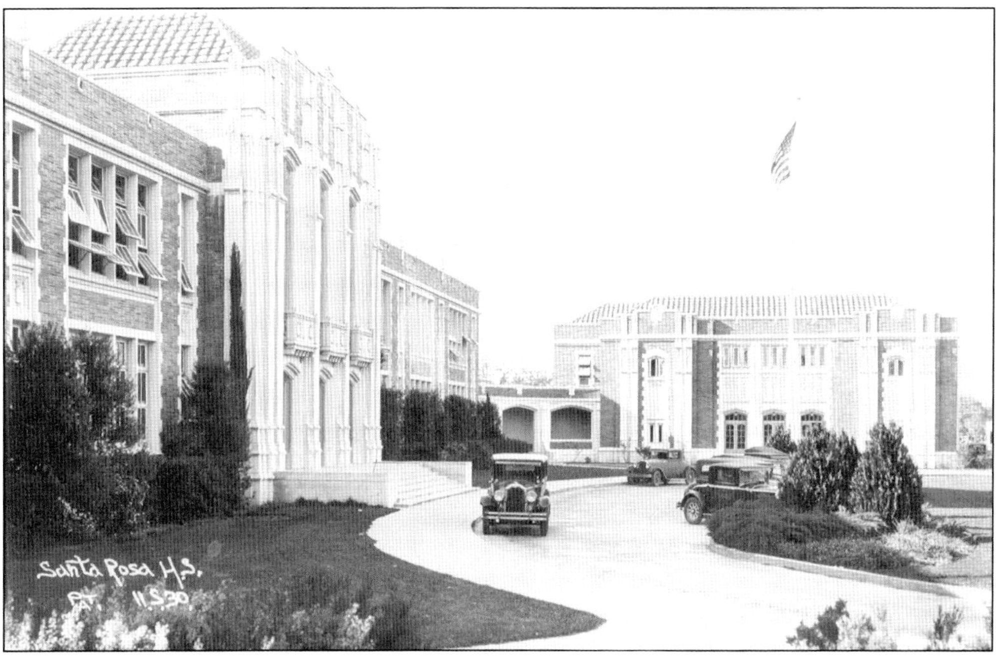

SANTA ROSA HIGH SCHOOL, C. 1925. This stately structure at 1141 Mendocino Avenue was built in 1924, after a fire destroyed the original high school in 1921.

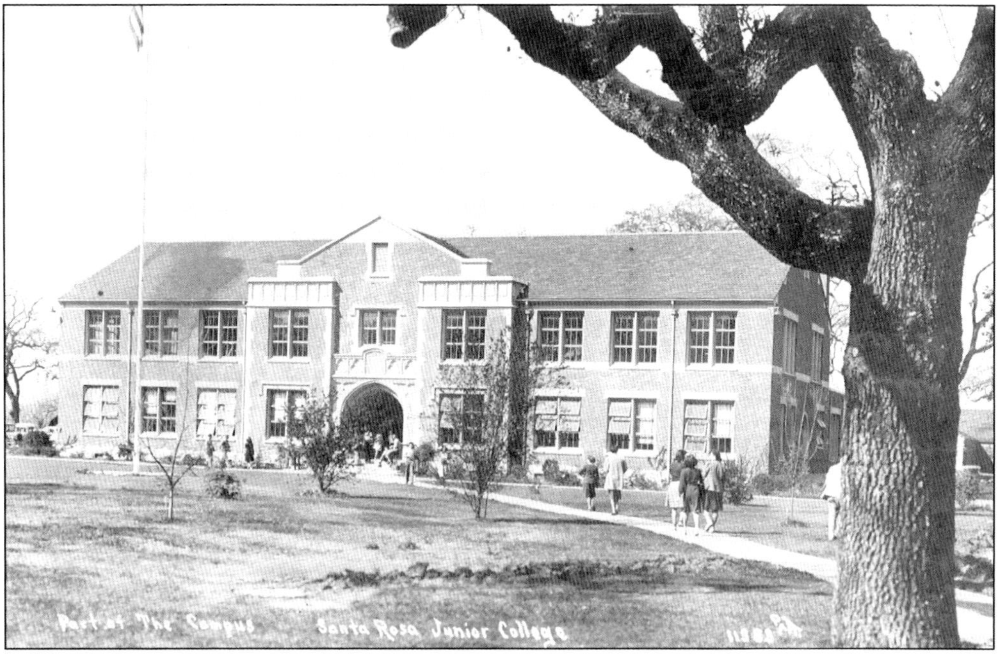

SANTA ROSA JUNIOR COLLEGE, C. 1940. Analy Hall, shown in this photocard, was completed on the Santa Rosa Junior College campus in 1940. This college is located at 1501 Mendocino Avenue.

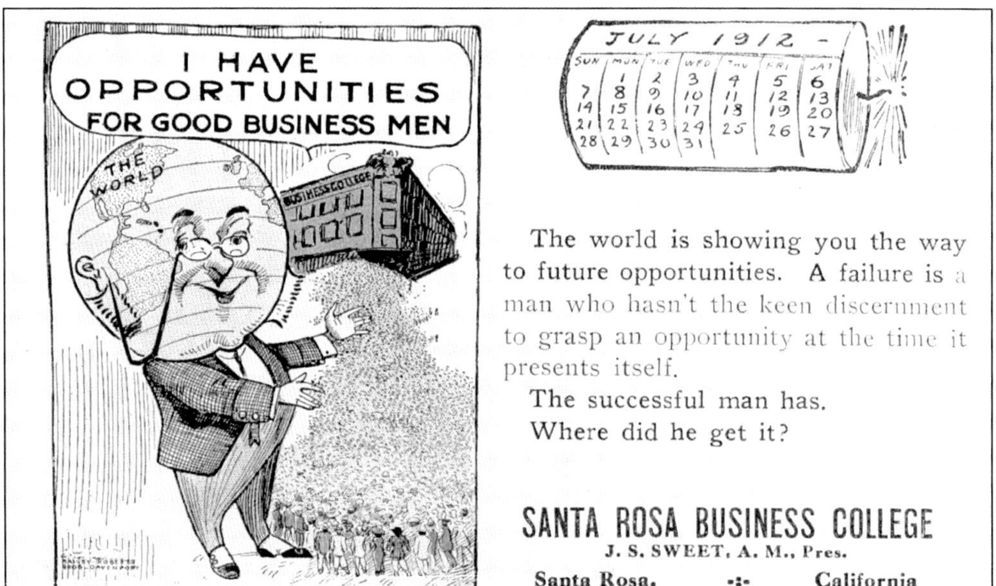

SANTA ROSA BUSINESS COLLEGE, 1912. This local college was located on Ross near Mendocino Avenue. On his postcard, President J.S. Sweet assures us that the books, the courses of study, and the teachers at his facility are the best that can be found.

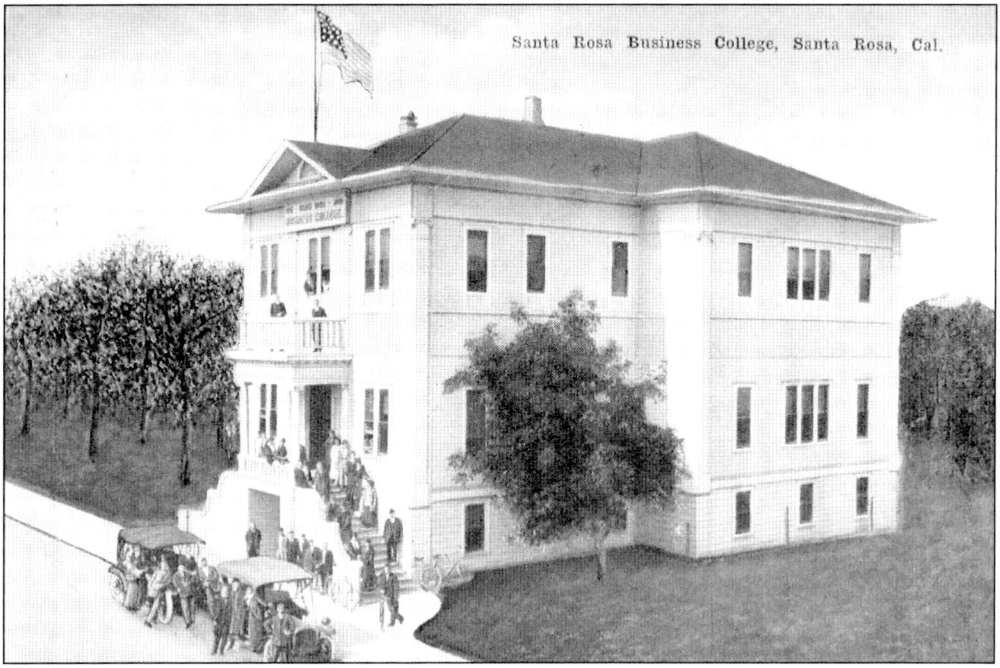

SANTA ROSA BUSINESS COLLEGE, 1910. President Sweet, consistent in his quest for new students, writes to Eugene Carrillo in Sebastopol, "Do not fail to be with us at the opening of the fall term, September 4. We want 200 graduates qualified to fill good positions the coming year."

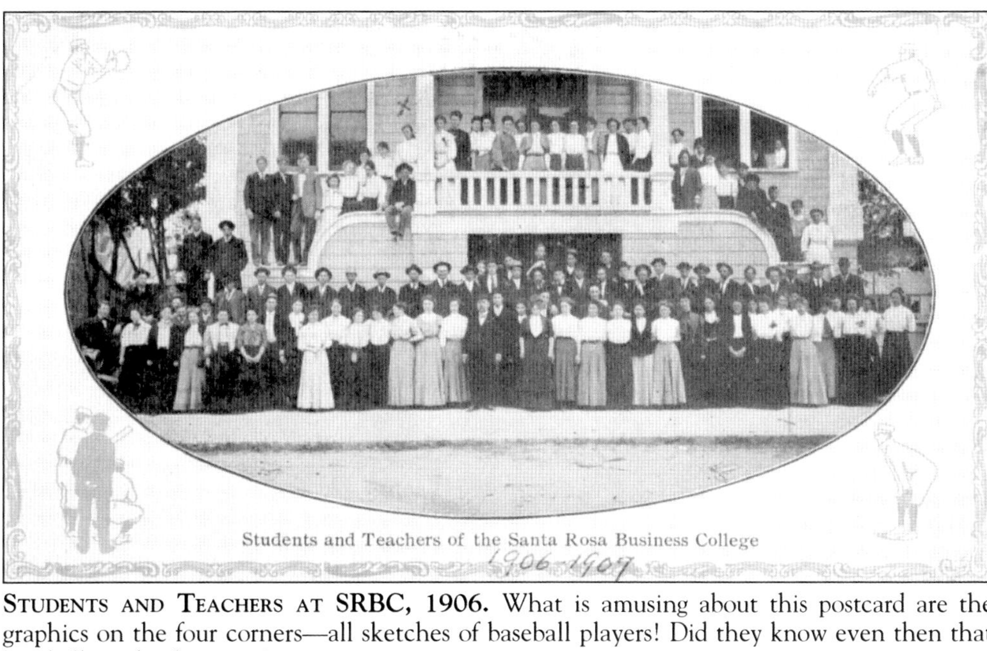

STUDENTS AND TEACHERS AT SRBC, 1906. What is amusing about this postcard are the graphics on the four corners—all sketches of baseball players! Did they know even then that baseball was big business?

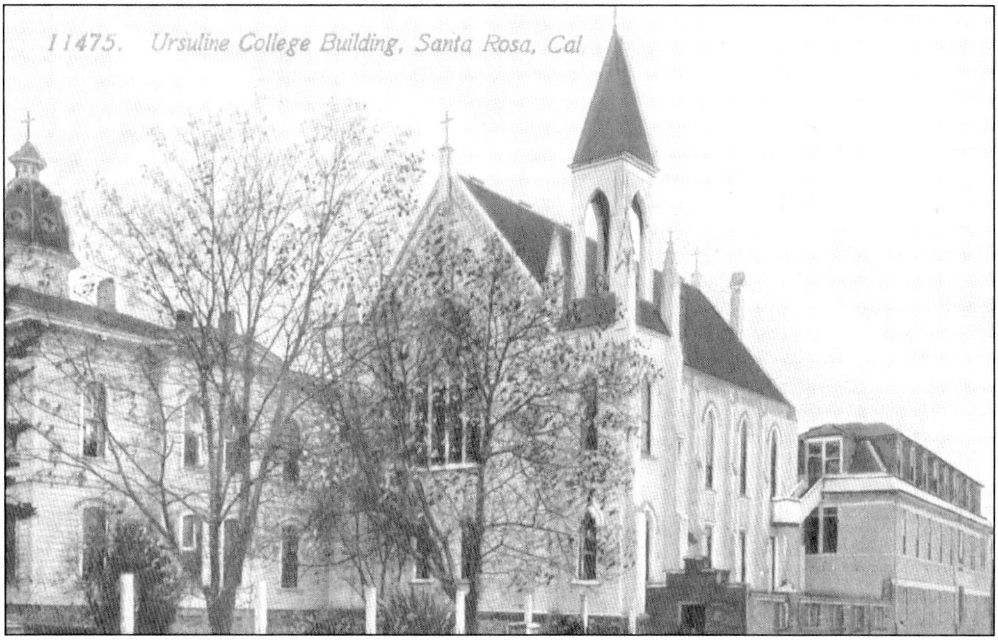

URSULINE COLLEGE BUILDING, C. 1912. A liberal arts college was chartered in 1901 by the Sisters of St. Ursula, and degrees continued to be offered until 1936.

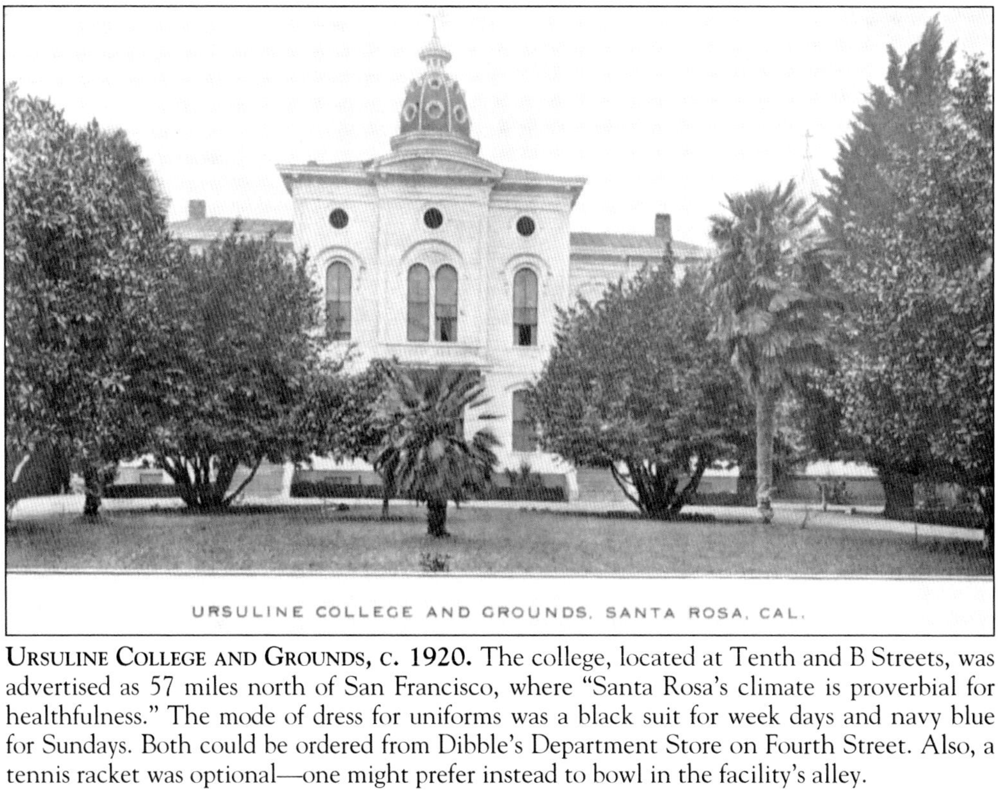

URSULINE COLLEGE AND GROUNDS, C. 1920. The college, located at Tenth and B Streets, was advertised as 57 miles north of San Francisco, where "Santa Rosa's climate is proverbial for healthfulness." The mode of dress for uniforms was a black suit for week days and navy blue for Sundays. Both could be ordered from Dibble's Department Store on Fourth Street. Also, a tennis racket was optional—one might prefer instead to bowl in the facility's alley.

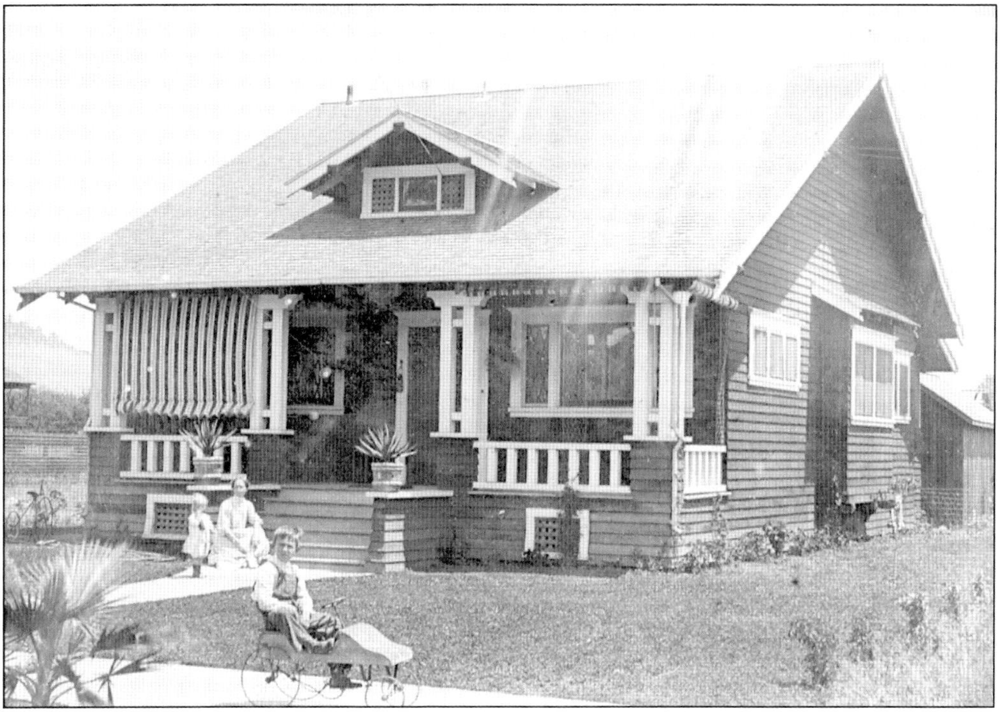

HOMES, C. 1910. There are many photocards of families posed in front of their homes in Santa Rosa. Homes were a great source of pride and joy to their owners. The top card shows an address of 725 Monroe Street, but the house is now remodeled. The house shown in the bottom card may have been located on Hoen Avenue.

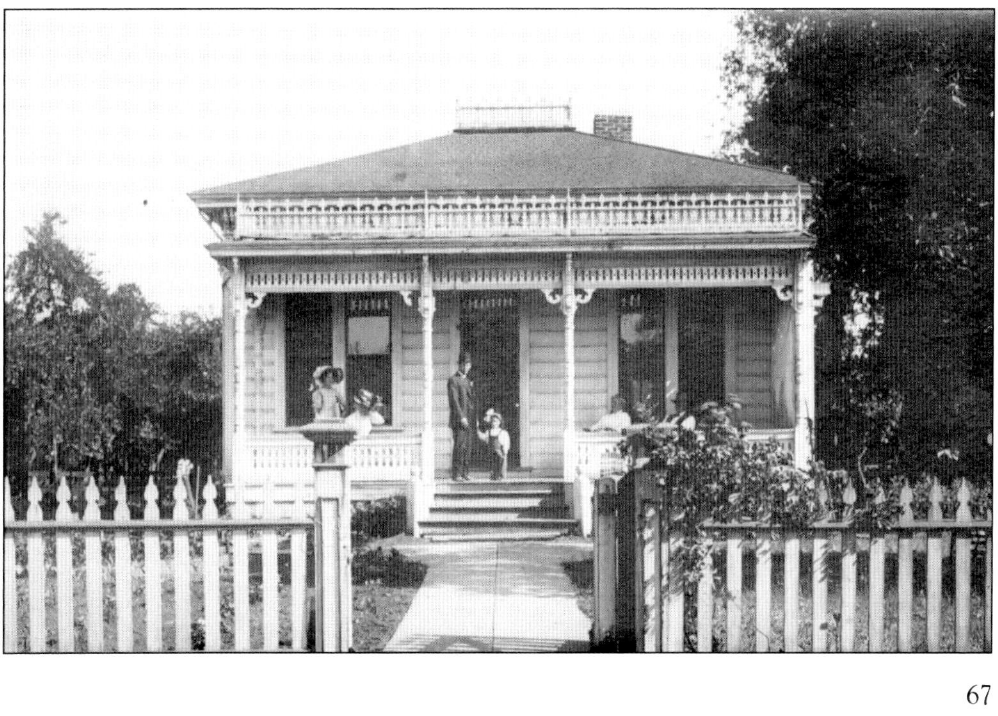

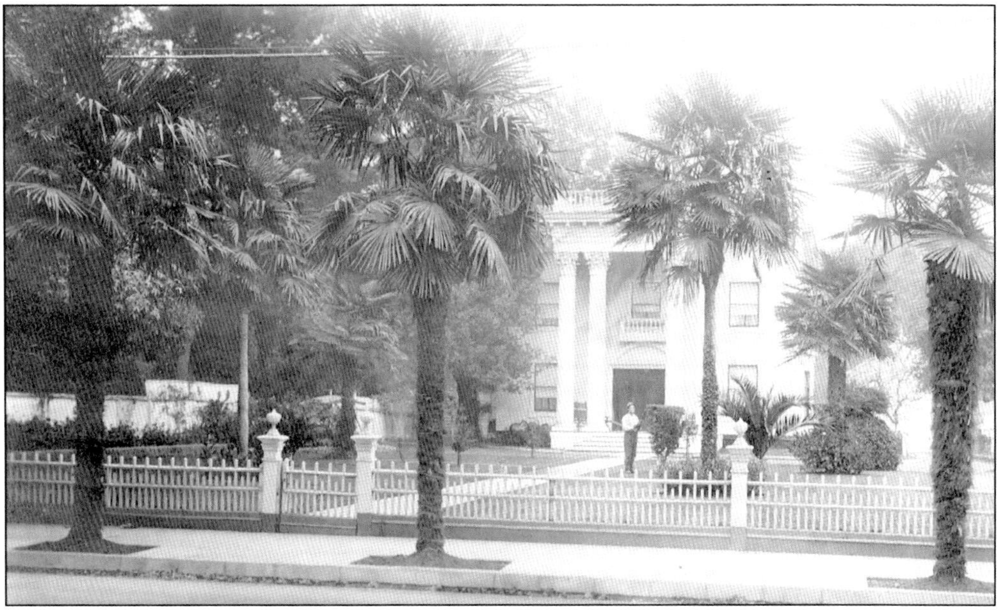

Grace Home, c. 1910. This stately home at 1116 Fourth Street belonged to Joseph Grace. It was built by Henry Kroncke with a public park beside it. Grace's house was located where the Safeway store stands now on Fourth Street.

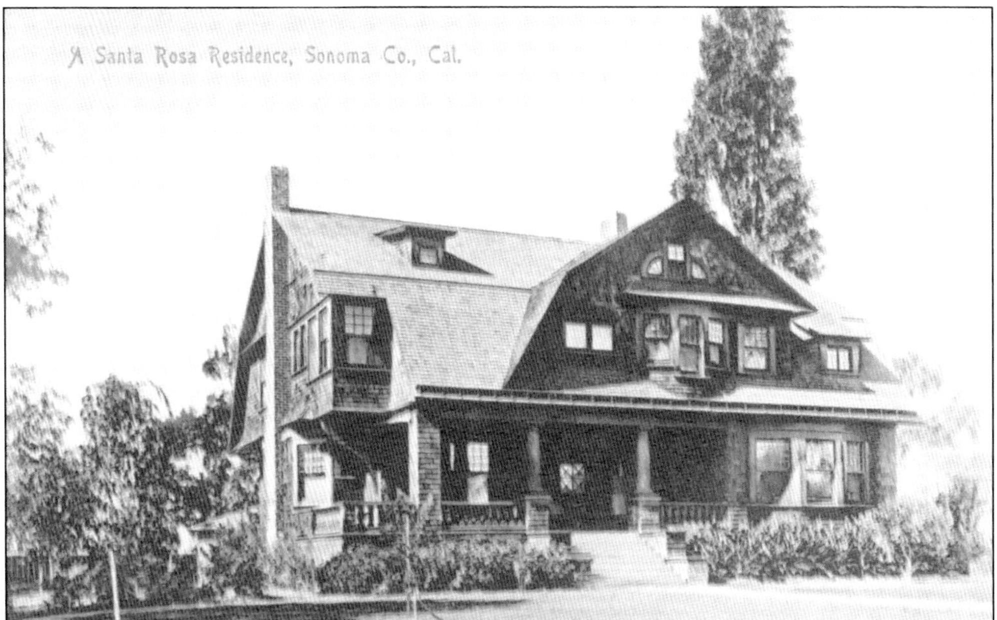

Comstock Home, c. 1910. Brainerd Jones designed this house in 1905 for local lawyer James Oates. Mrs. Nellie Comstock purchased the home in 1916 when Oates died. Her son, Judge Hilliard Comstock, and his family members owned the home at 767 Mendocino Avenue until 1991.

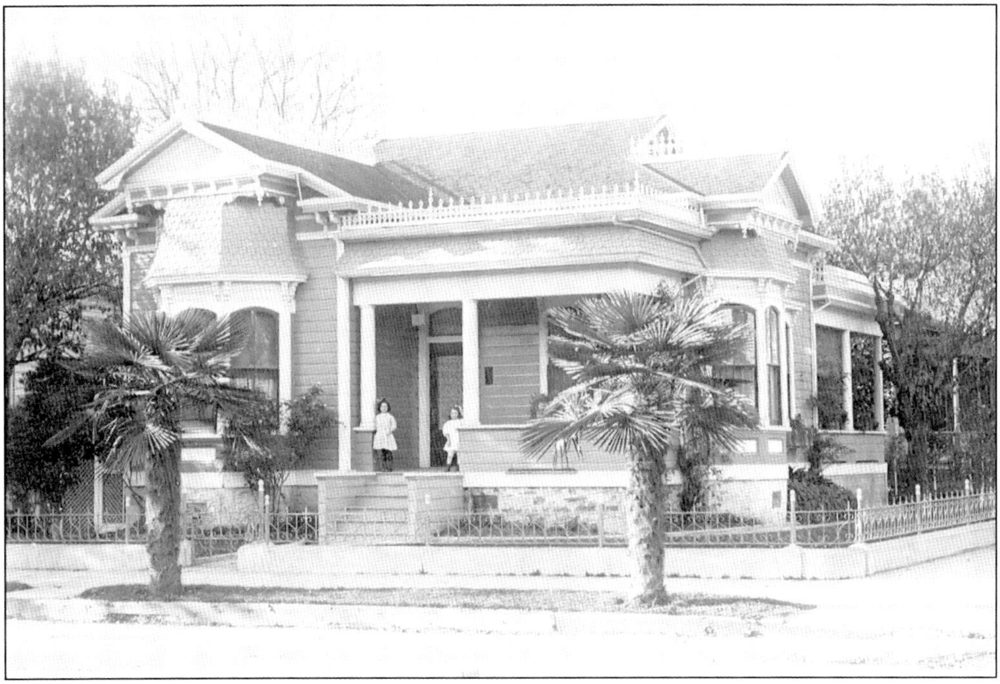

HOME, c. 1910. The home in this photocard, unfortunately unable to be identified, occupied a nice corner somewhere in downtown Santa Rosa.

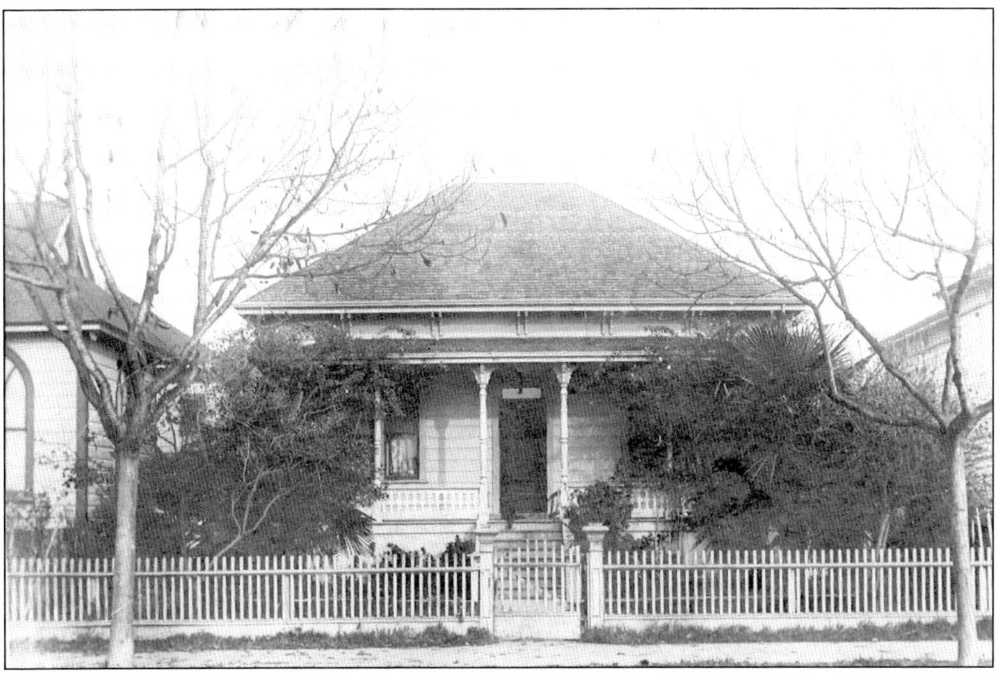

RIPLEY HOME, c. 1910. This charming little house is listed as Robert Ripley's childhood home on Orchard Street—believe it or not!

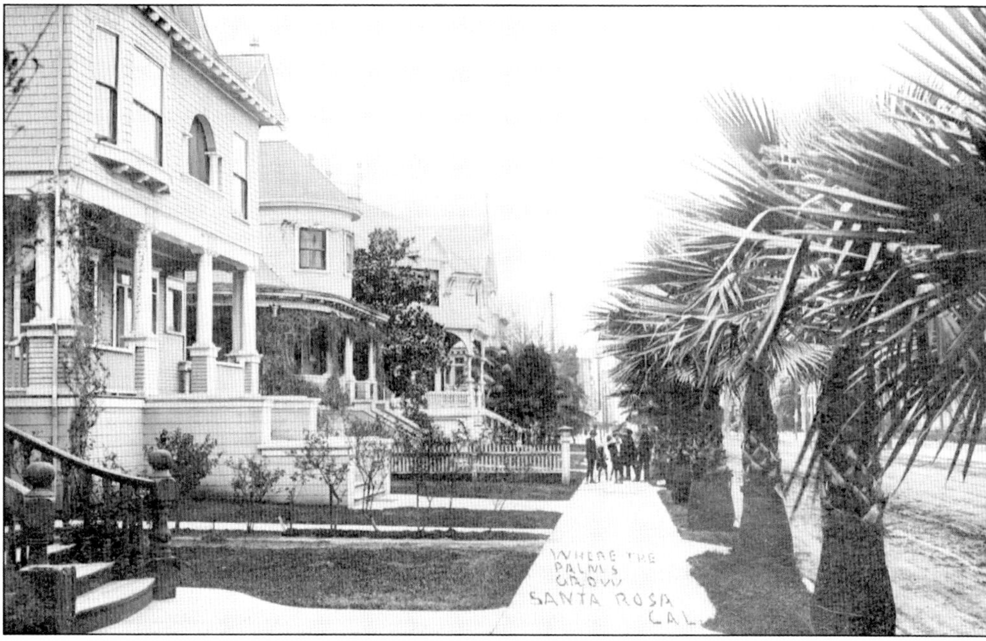

"WHERE THE PALMS GROW," C. 1915. Can you imagine Fourth Street in the early years lined with palm trees? Streetcar tracks are visible in the center of the dirt street.

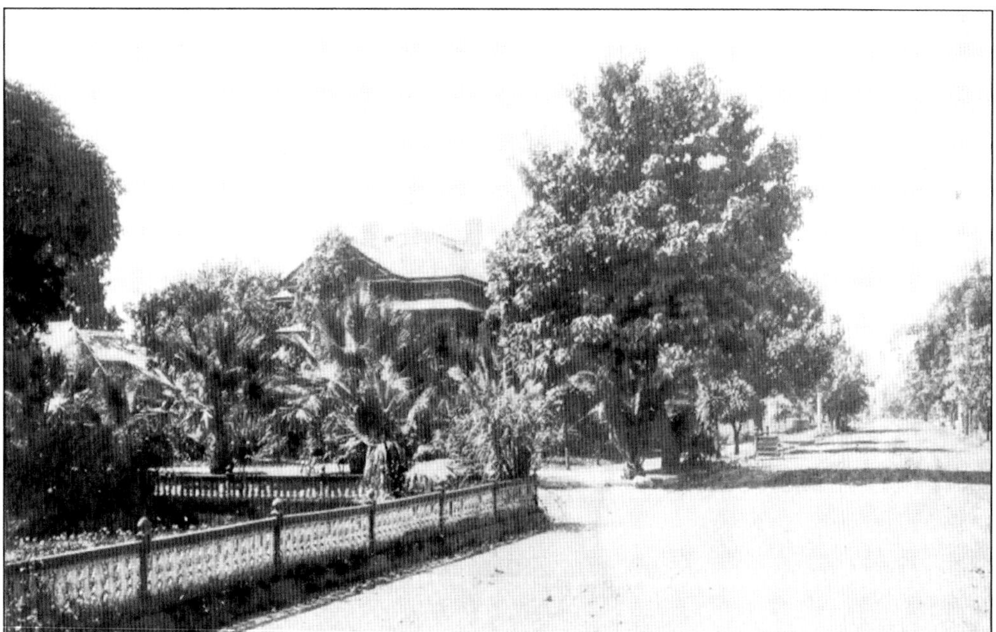

JOHNSTON AND BEAVER STREETS, C. 1915. This postcard publisher's advertising card is unusual in that Johnston Street does not appear on any Santa Rosa map. This view was the corner of Johnson and Beaver Streets. Johnson Street is now Seventh Street.

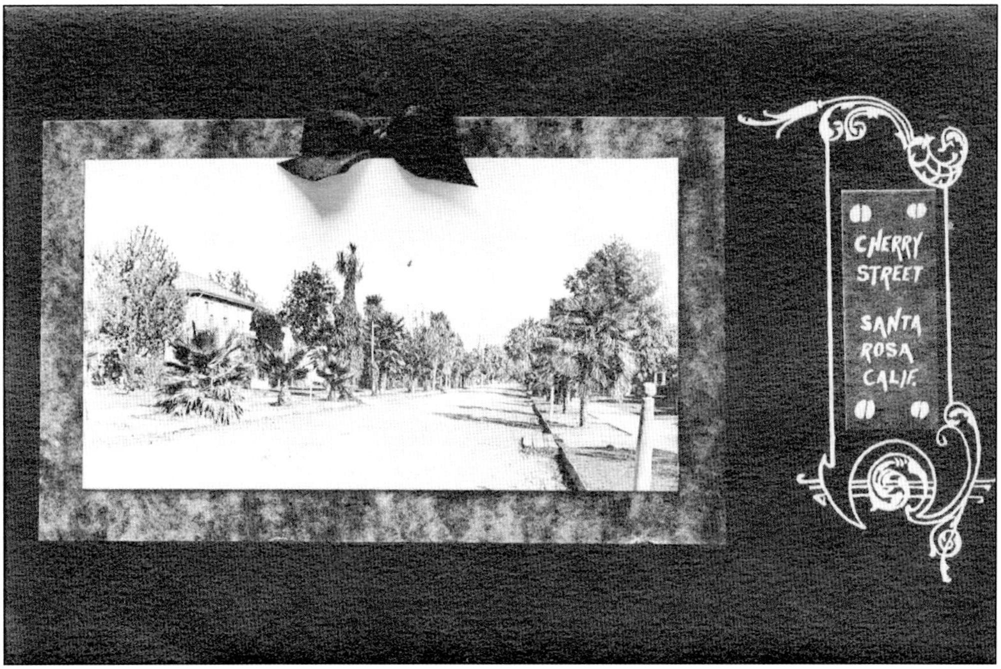

CHERRY STREET, C. 1915. The photograph on this 1930s postcard was taken much earlier than 1930. Cherry Street was and still is a beautiful area in our town.

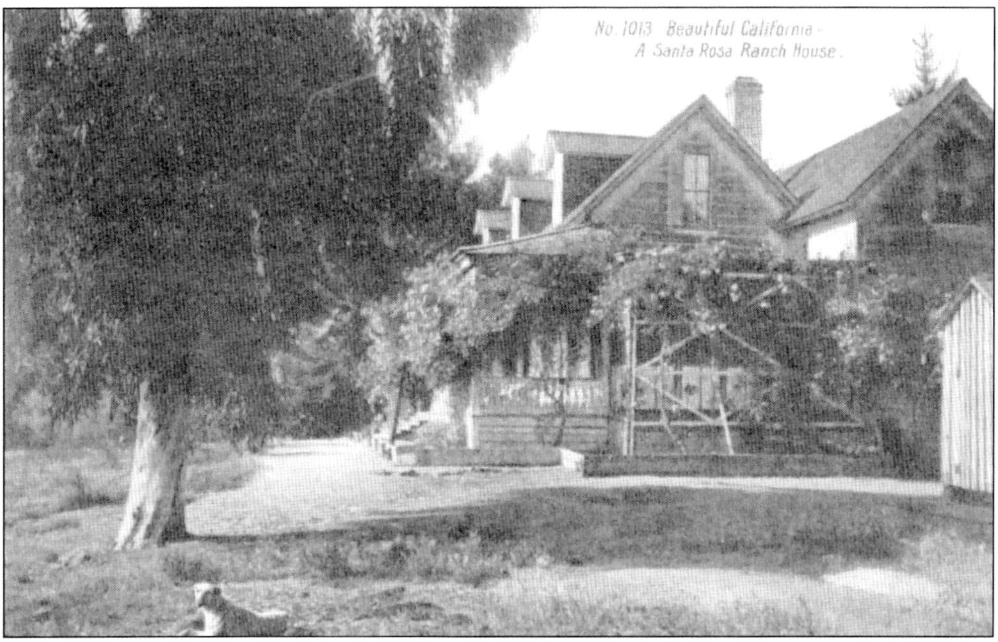

RANCH HOUSE, C. 1925. This rural scene shows flowering trees bordering a Santa Rosa ranch house. Even the dog posed for the photographer.

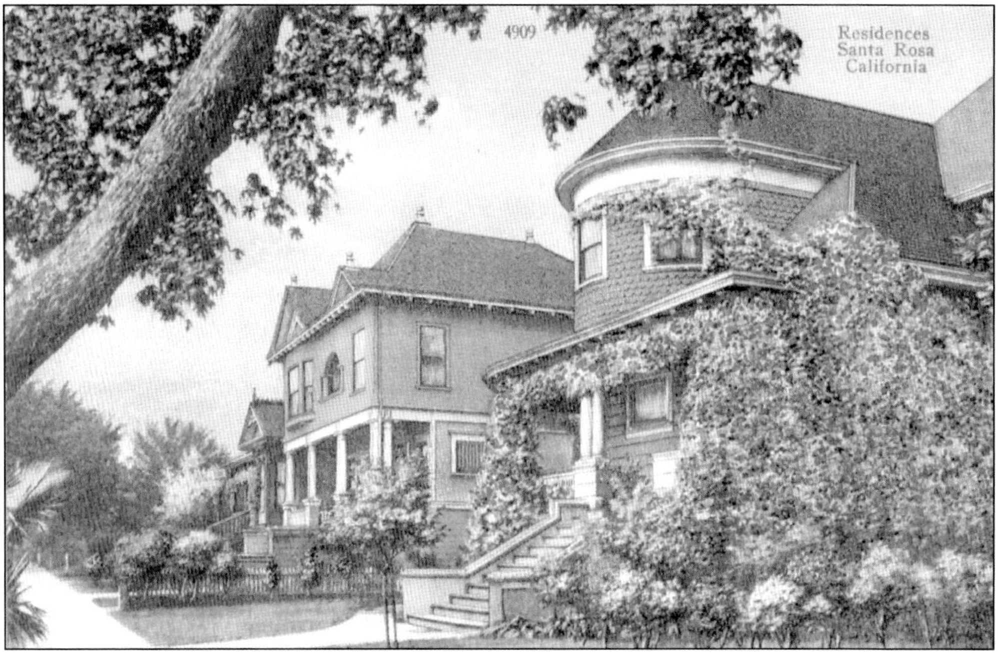

SANTA ROSA RESIDENCES, C. 1920. These stately homes were typical of many residential neighborhoods in Santa Rosa. This was part of a series of postcards entitled, "On the Road of a Thousand Wonders," intended to promote the beauty of California.

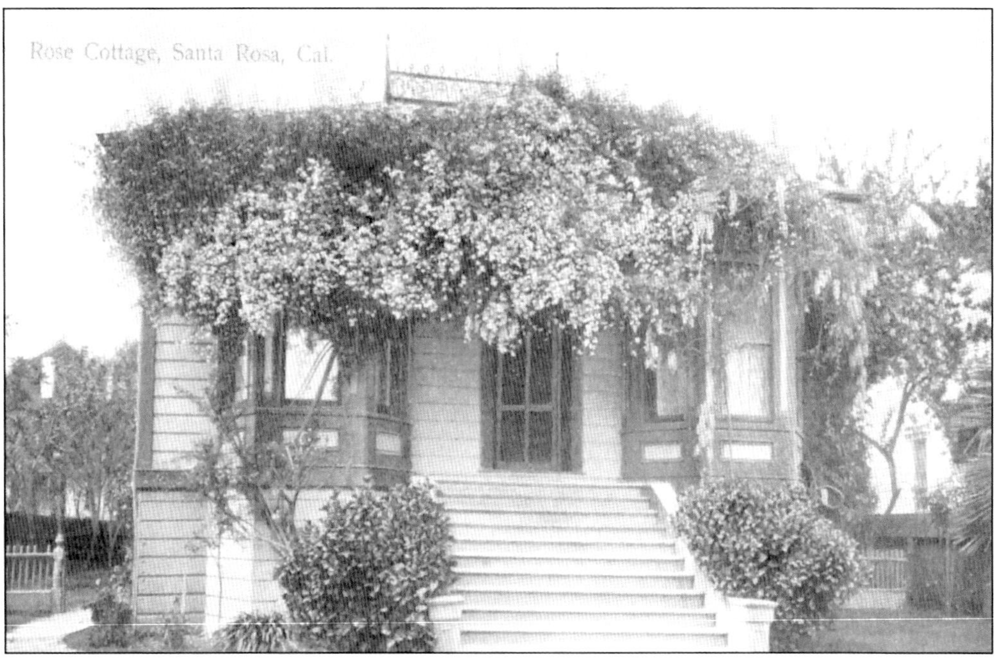

ROSE COTTAGE, C. 1920. The authors were unable to locate this lovely little cottage. While its garden was in bloom, this house presented a beautiful sight in the neighborhood, and must have been a gardener's challenge too!

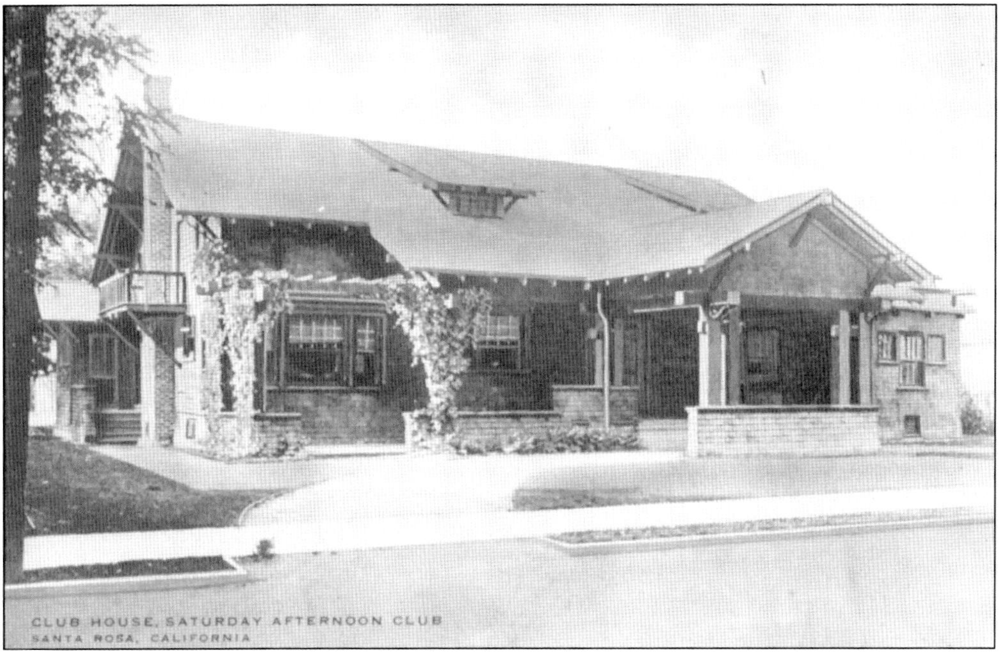

SATURDAY AFTERNOON CLUB, C. 1920. This club, still active today, was founded in 1894. It was built in 1908 at Tenth and B Streets and heavily remodeled in the 1940s.

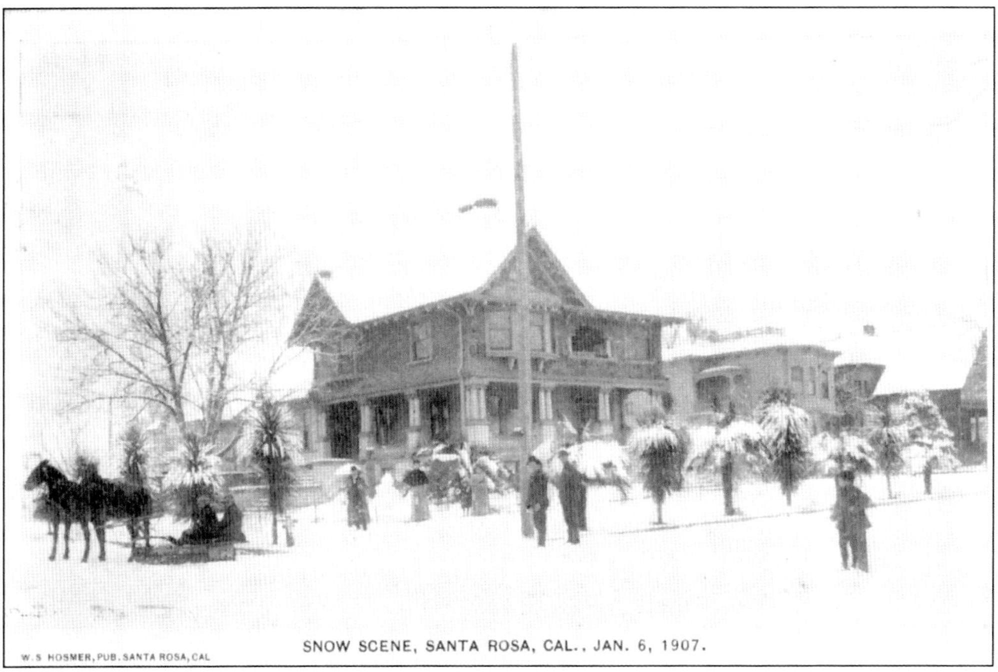

SNOW SCENE, 1907. On January 6, 1907, Santa Rosa experienced a real Midwestern type of snowstorm. In three hours, three to four inches of snow fell on the town. The *Press Republican* newspaper reported on January 8 that there had been numerous snowball fights in the downtown area.

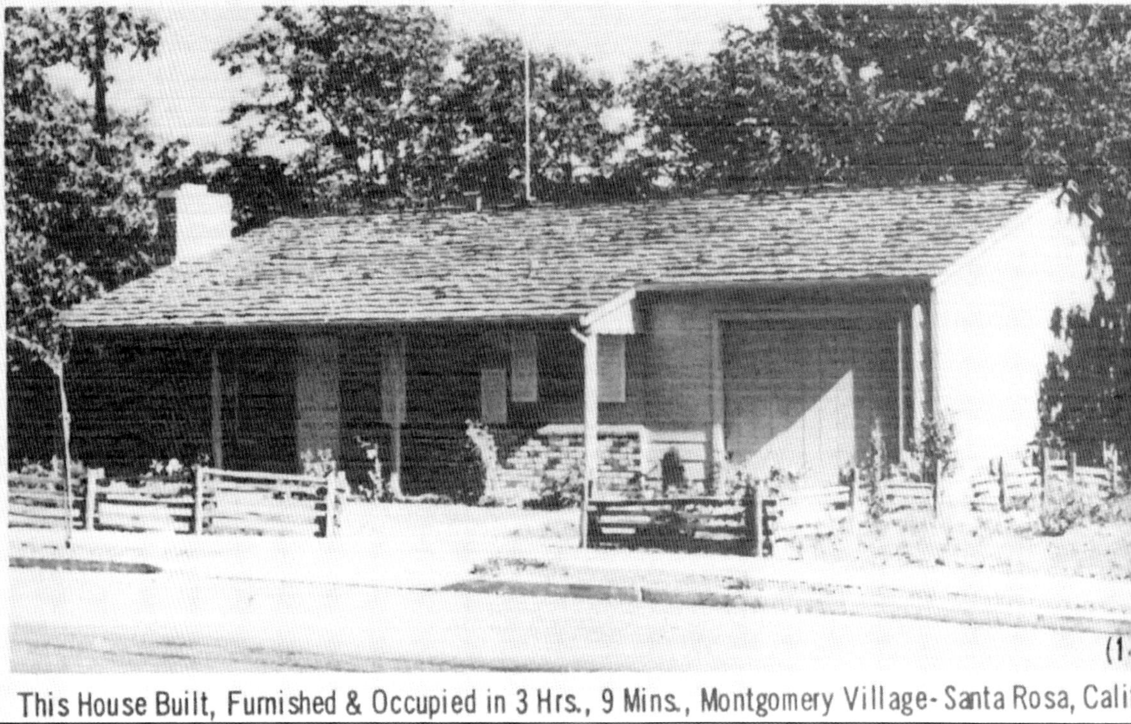

MONTGOMERY VILLAGE, C. 1950. This promotional postcard was used by Codding Enterprises to advertise their new residential and shopping center area in Montgomery Village. In this post-war period, new affordable homes were in great demand, and builders and developers competed to attract the attention of potential buyers. This card was mailed to Pennsylvania in 1954 and reads, "the shopping center is different from any you have ever seen."

Five

Commercial and Landmark Buildings

Commercial buildings have always been a popular subject for picture postcards. Towns are proud of their buildings, such as courthouses, post offices, or libraries, because they provide proof of a solid base for any community. Retail establishments, hotels, and banks have used postcards to advertise their presence and to solicit business. Moreover, people buying and mailing postcards want to show where they have been and what they have seen.

This section aims to select a cross-section of Santa Rosa's buildings. Some of these buildings have long been lost to fires, earthquakes, or progress. Others have changed drastically over the years, and still others survive. These postcards will provide another window to the way things were.

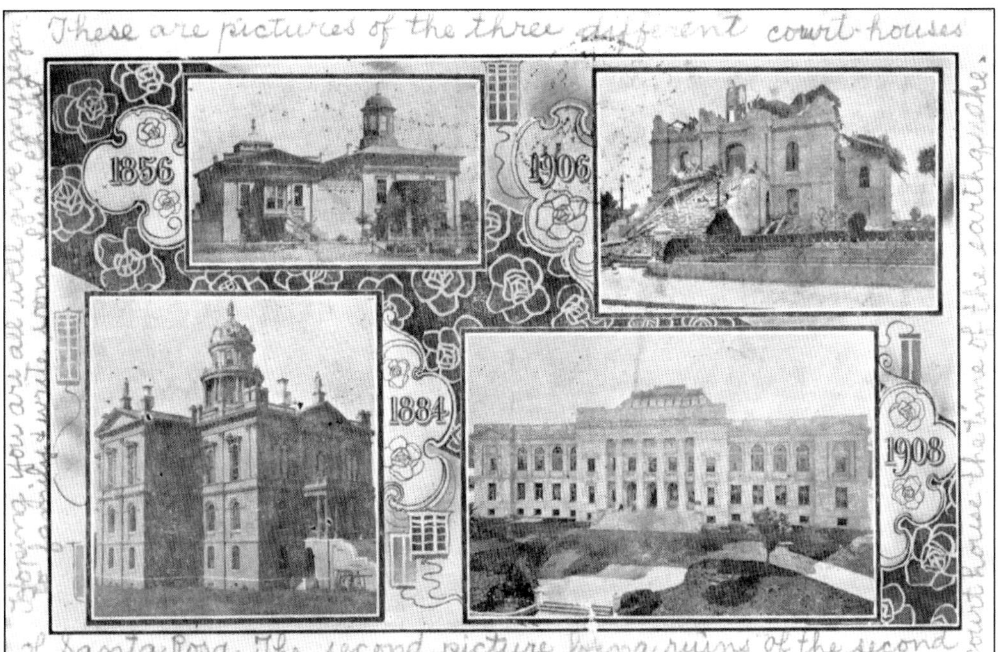

Sonoma County Courthouses, c. 1910. This is the only postcard located picturing the first courthouse in Santa Rosa. This small one-story building was constructed in 1856 and located on the northwest corner of Fourth Street and Mendocino Avenue across from an open plaza.

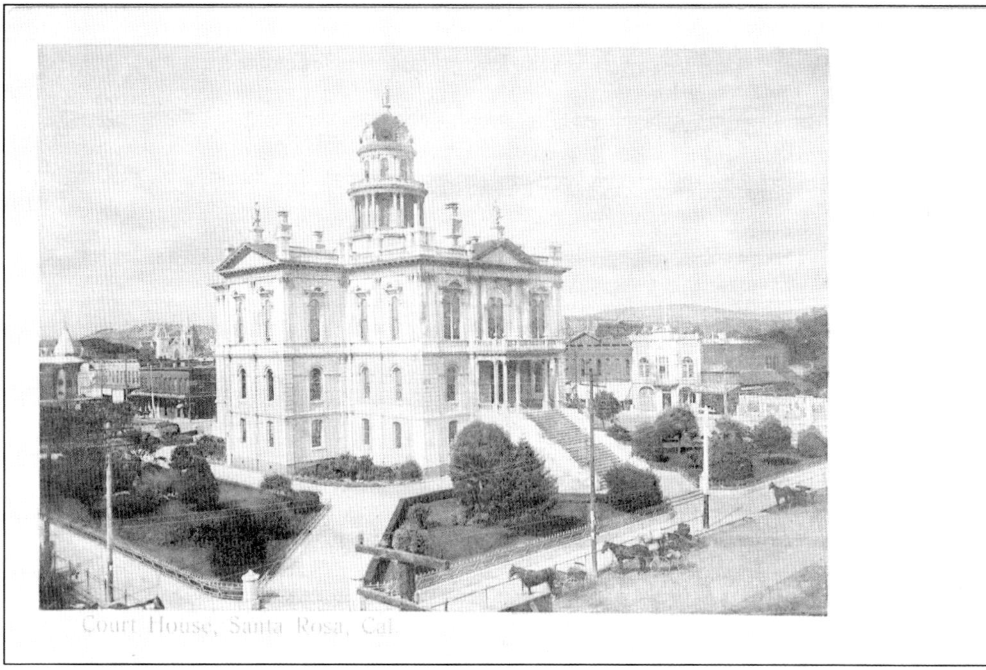

COURTHOUSE, C. 1905. This is the second courthouse in Santa Rosa. The imposing brick structure was completed in 1884 in the center of the plaza. It was the hub of all county government activity until it was destroyed in the 1906 earthquake.

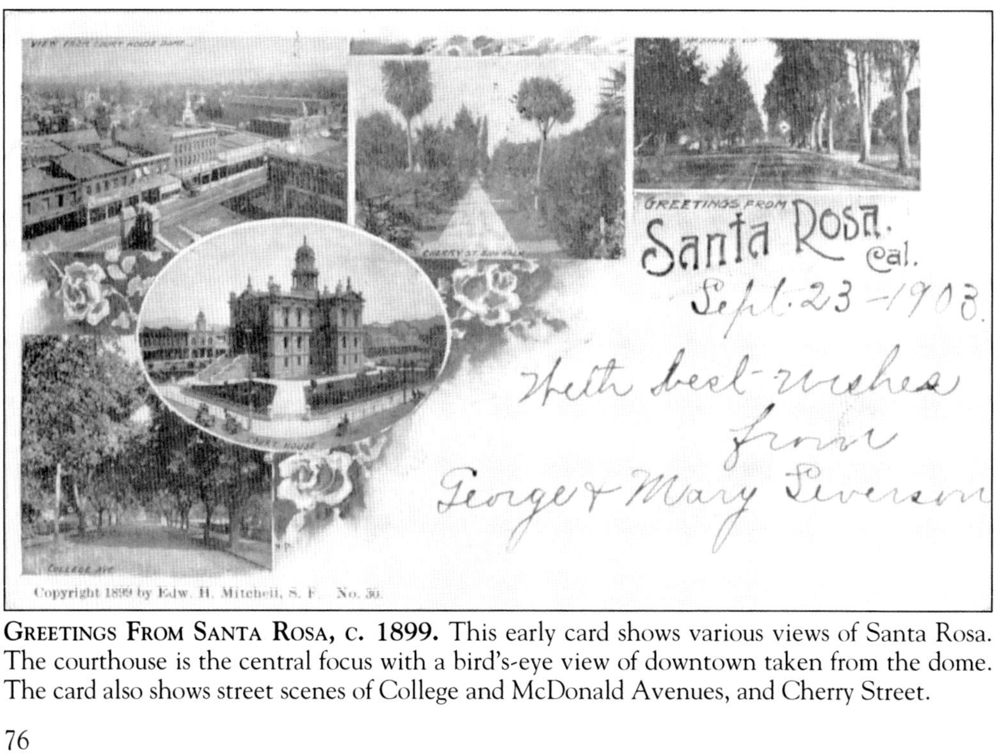

GREETINGS FROM SANTA ROSA, C. 1899. This early card shows various views of Santa Rosa. The courthouse is the central focus with a bird's-eye view of downtown taken from the dome. The card also shows street scenes of College and McDonald Avenues, and Cherry Street.

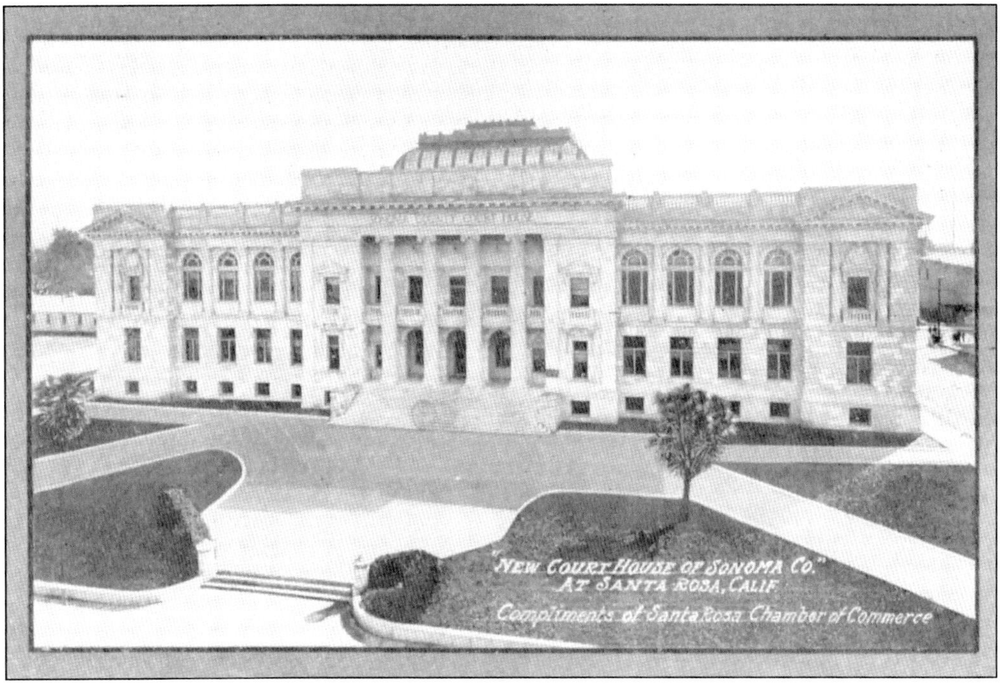

NEW COURTHOUSE OF SONOMA COUNTY, C. 1910. The Chamber of Commerce gave out this small postcard showing the newly completed courthouse in 1910. Construction on this impressive stone building began in 1908.

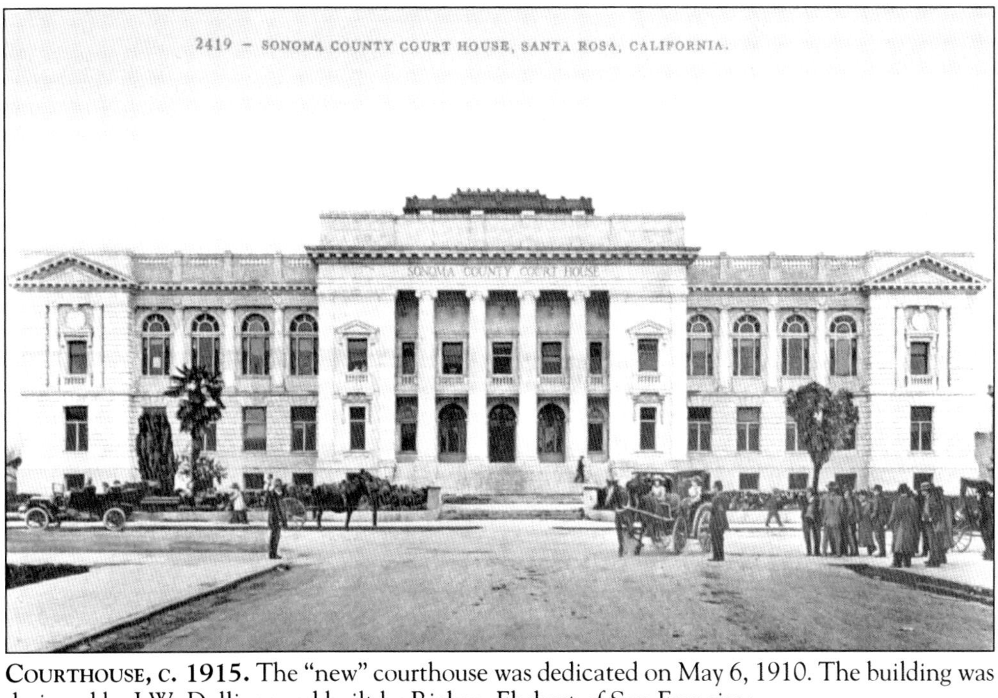

COURTHOUSE, C. 1915. The "new" courthouse was dedicated on May 6, 1910. The building was designed by J.W. Dolliver and built by Rickon-Ehrhart of San Francisco.

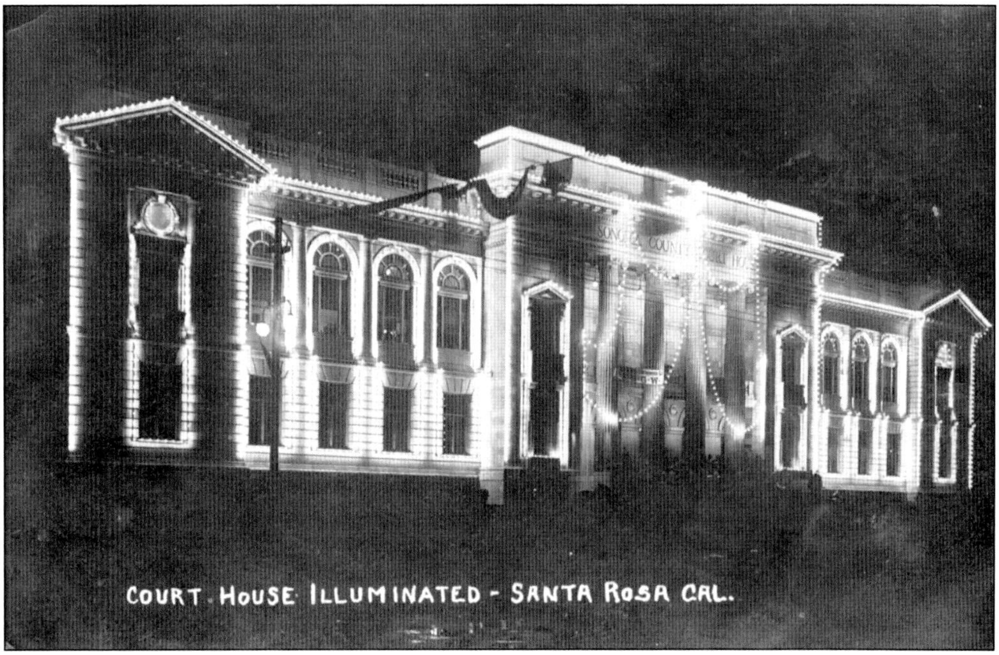

ILLUMINATED COURTHOUSE, 1912. The courthouse is ablaze with lights for the 1912 Rose Carnival.

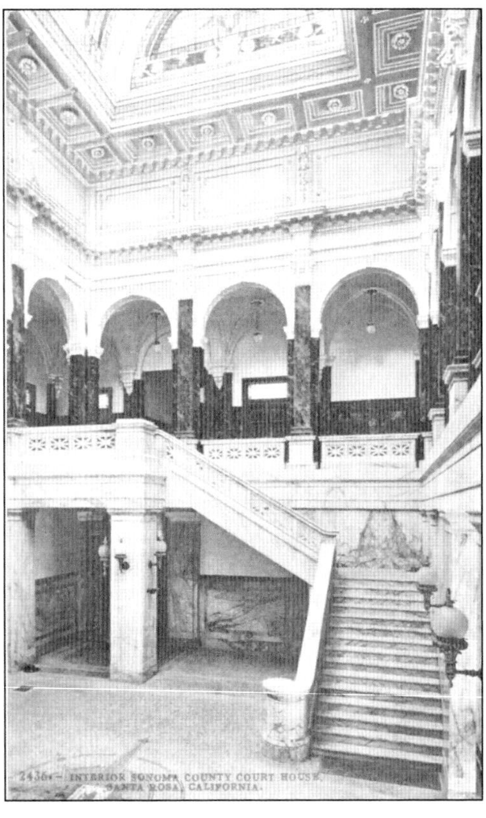

COURTHOUSE INTERIOR, C. 1925. No expense was spared to make the new courthouse the pride of Santa Rosa. Beautiful marble staircases and columns, stained-glass skylights, and large bronze wall lamps were intended to impress the courthouse visitor.

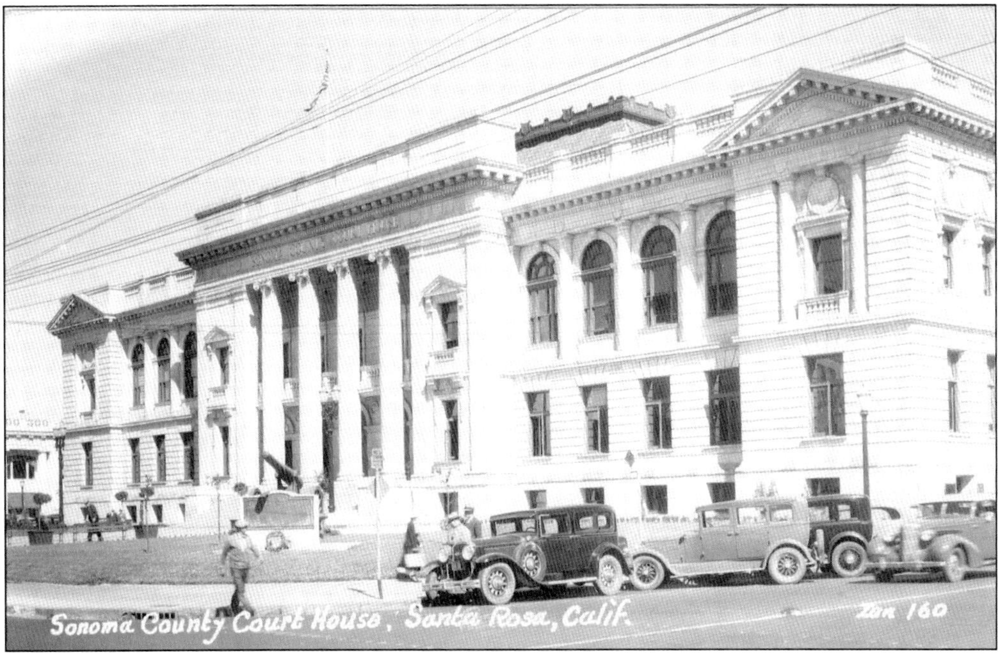

Courthouse, c. 1935. This photocard shows the courthouse from the intersection of Exchange Avenue and Fourth Street. Notice the large cannon mounted behind the bronze monument to Sheriff James Petry. Petry was killed in a shootout with gangsters and his death caused the infamous lynching in 1920 in the Santa Rosa Rural Cemetery.

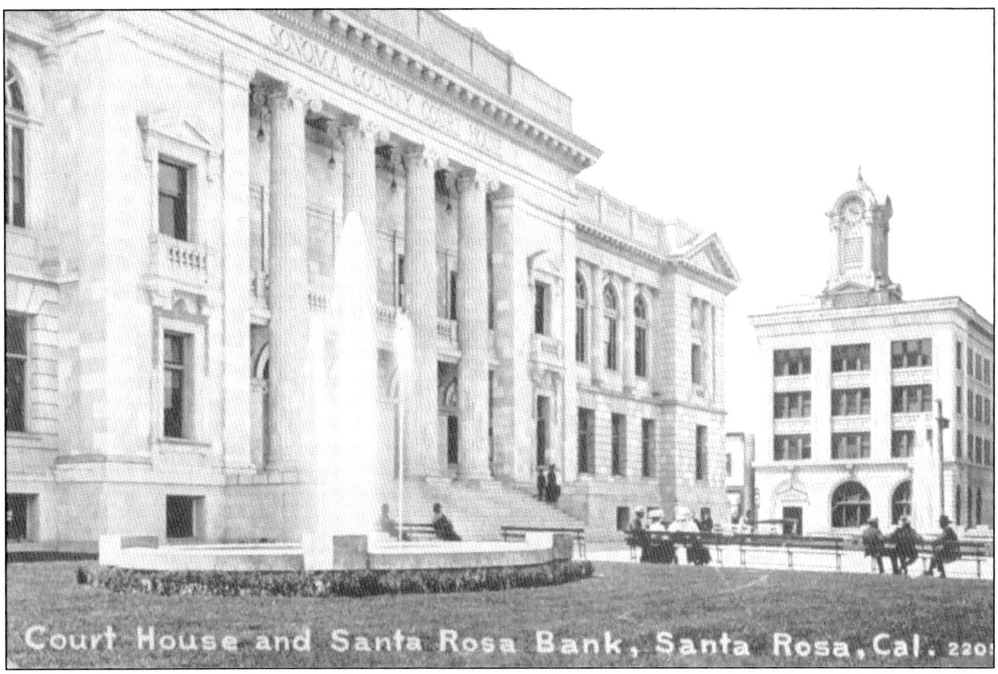

Courthouse and Santa Rosa Bank, c. 1921. The Home-Coming Festival of September 1921 was advertised on the back of this card. It shows an earlier view of the courthouse and the Santa Rosa Bank Building, which became the Bank of Italy in 1917.

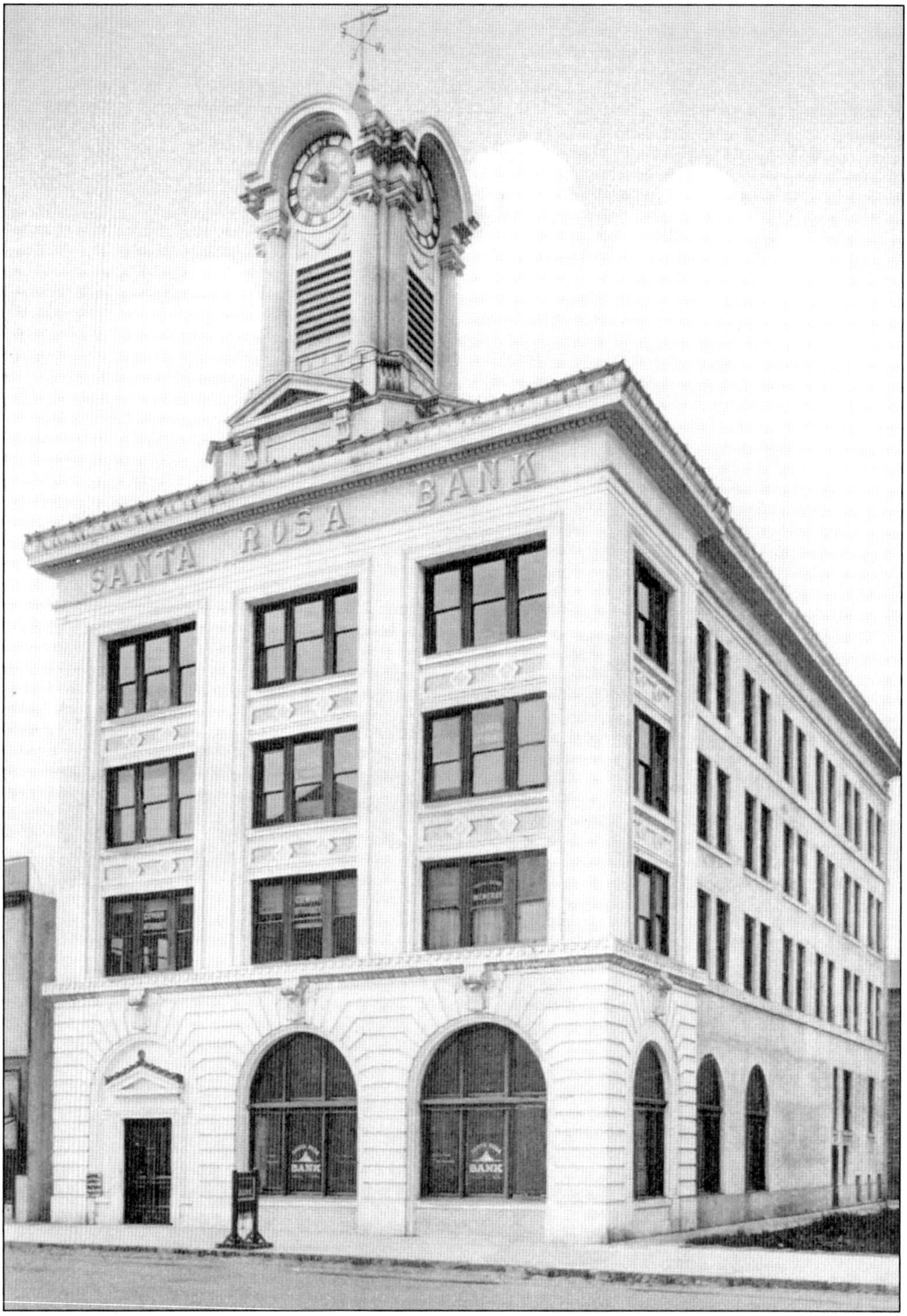

Santa Rosa Bank Building, c. 1906. This imposing building was constructed in 1906 after the earthquake. A beautiful building in the Renaissance Revival style, it has been and continues to be a major landmark in downtown Santa Rosa.

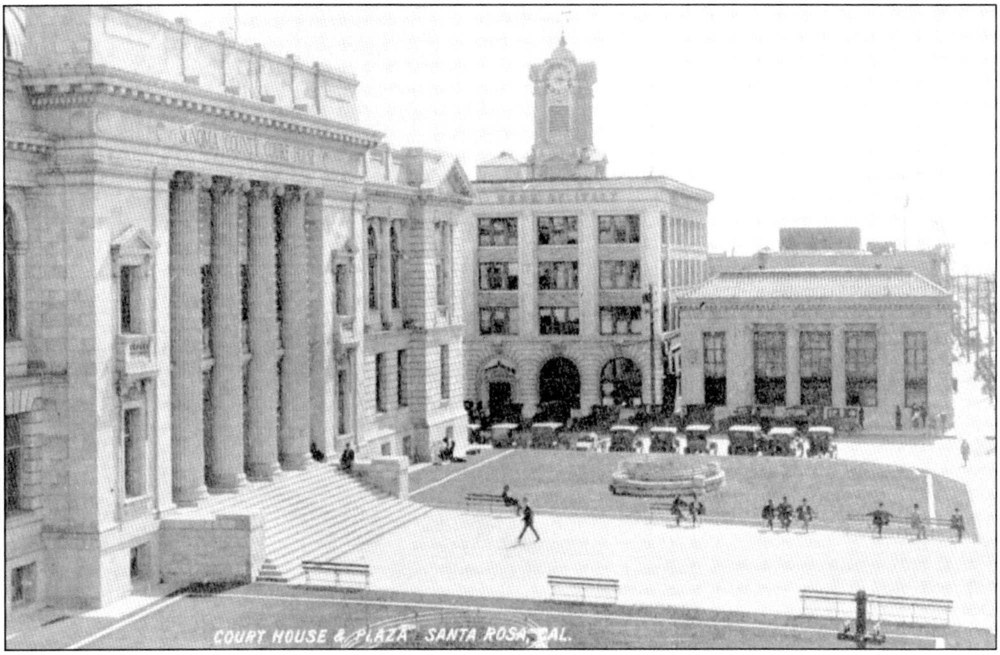

COURTHOUSE AND PLAZA, c. 1920. The Santa Rosa Bank Building now housed the Bank of Italy, a change which occurred in 1917.

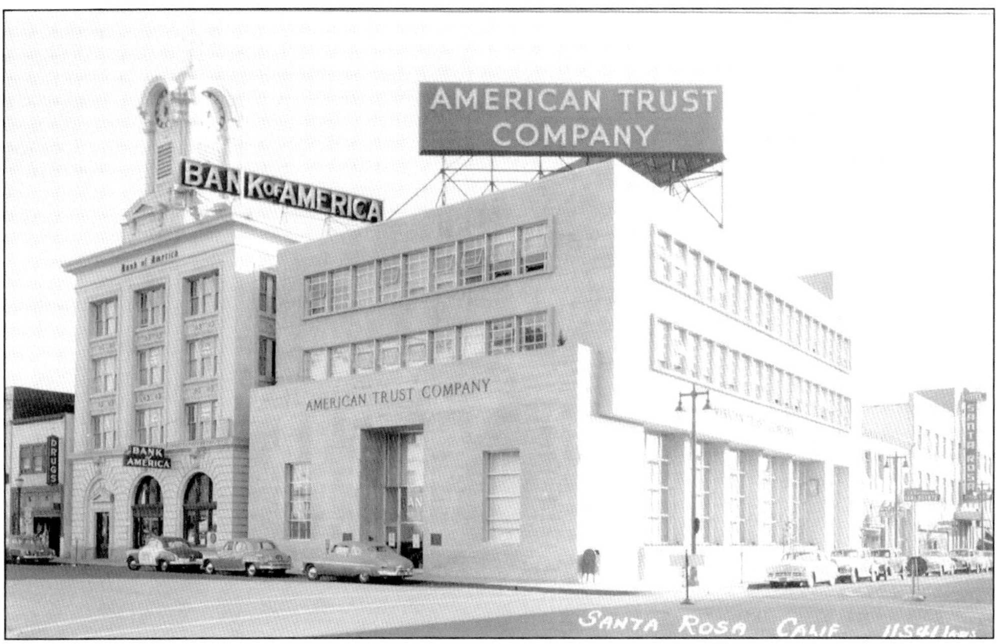

BANK OF AMERICA AND AMERICAN TRUST COMPANY, c. 1950. This photocard shows the former Santa Rosa Bank Building as the Bank of America. The building was used by Crocker Bank until 1968. It is known today as the Empire Building.

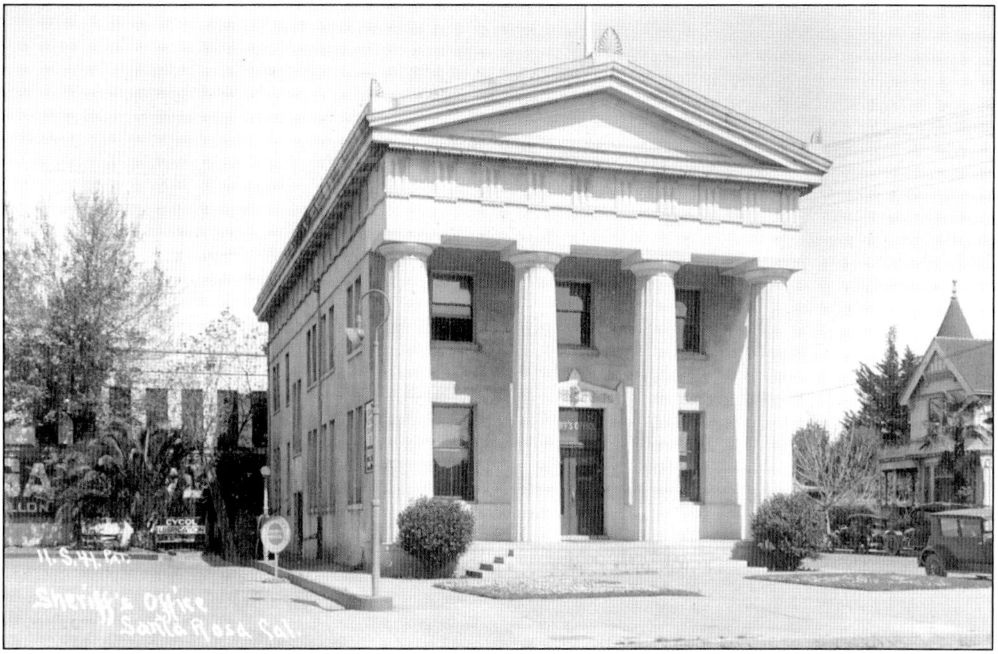

SHERIFF'S OFFICE, C. 1930. The Sheriff's Office was located at the corner of Hinton Avenue and Third Street. This building was lost to redevelopment in the 1960s.

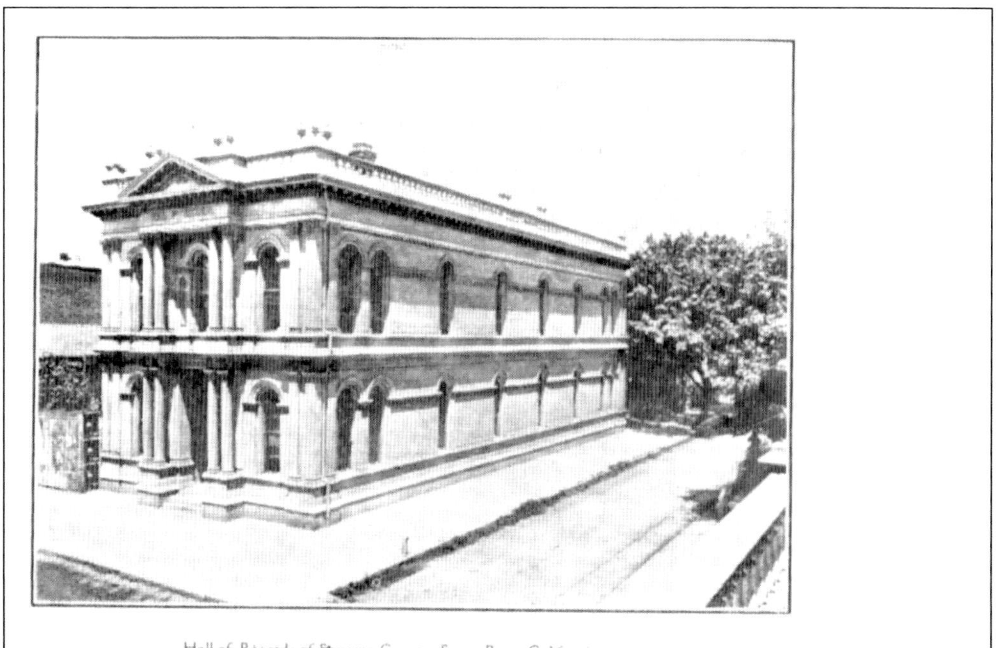

HALL OF RECORDS, C. 1900. The Hall of Records was constructed in 1871 on Fourth Street just to the west of the original 1856 courthouse. This building was destroyed in the 1906 earthquake.

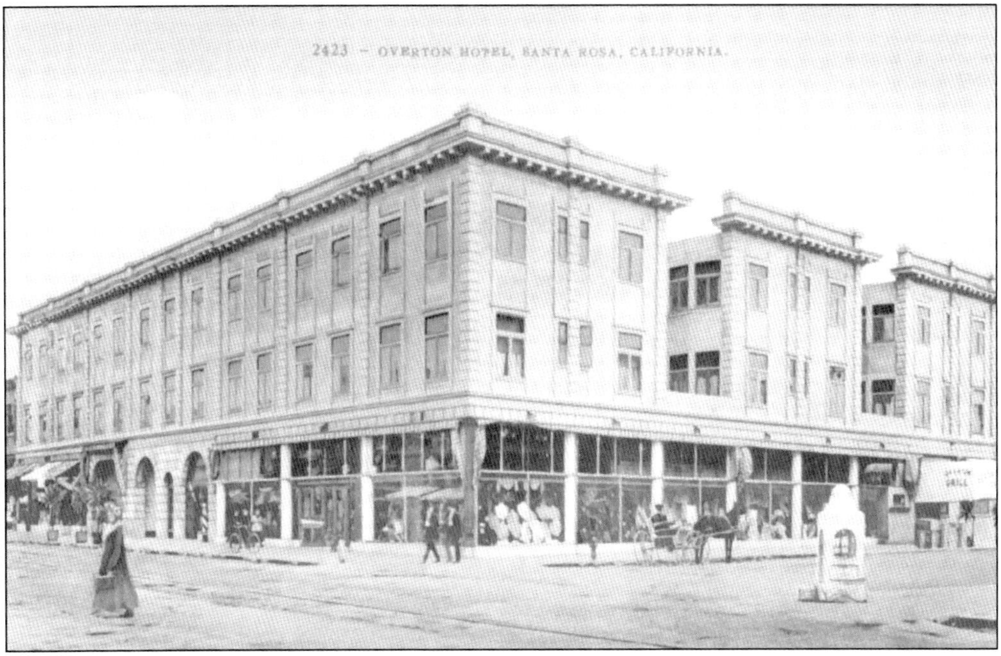

Overton Hotel, c. 1915. The Overton Hotel, built in 1906, was located at 508 Fourth Street. This hotel and the Occidental Hotel replaced many of the smaller brick hotels lost in the 1906 earthquake.

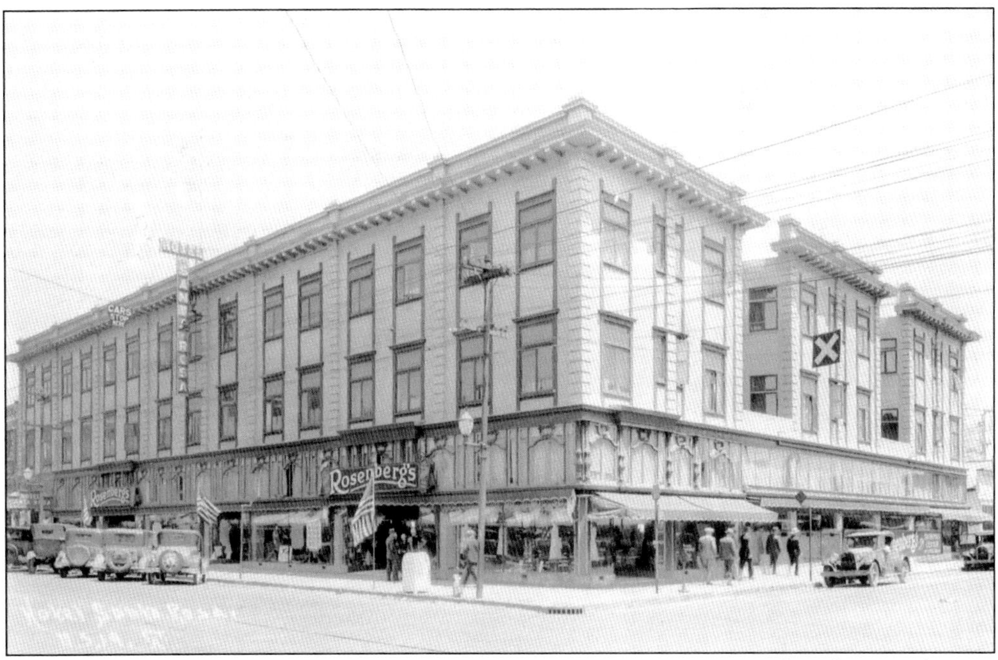

Hotel Santa Rosa, c. 1930. This photocard shows the Overton Hotel as the Hotel Santa Rosa and Rosenberg's Department Store. Rosenberg's was destroyed by fire in 1936. A sign on the far right advertises, "Rosenberg's—The Shopping Center of Santa Rosa."

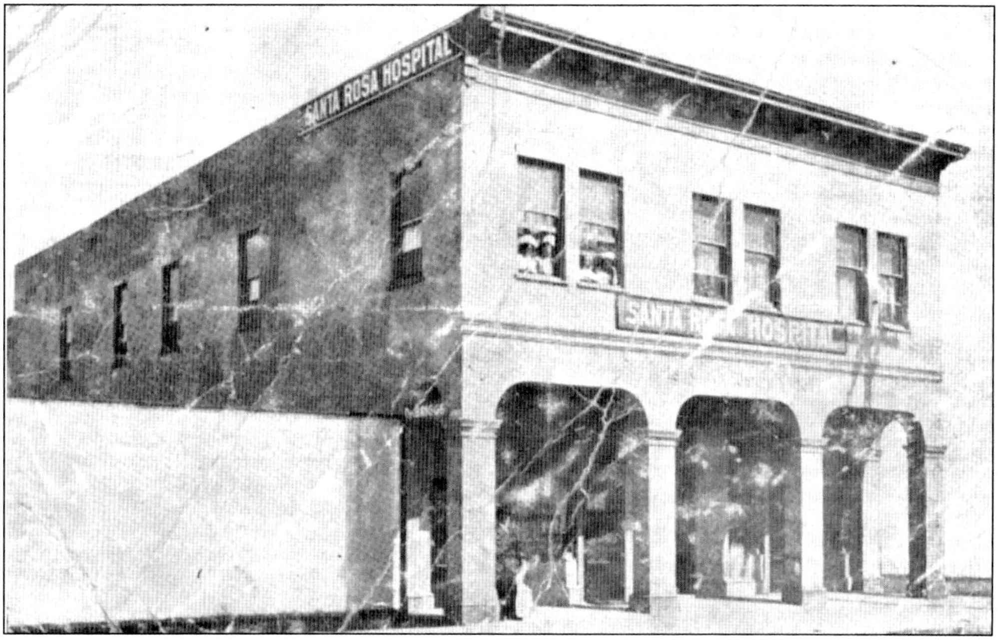

SANTA ROSA HOSPITAL, C. 1905. The Santa Rosa Hospital was located at 741 Humboldt Street.

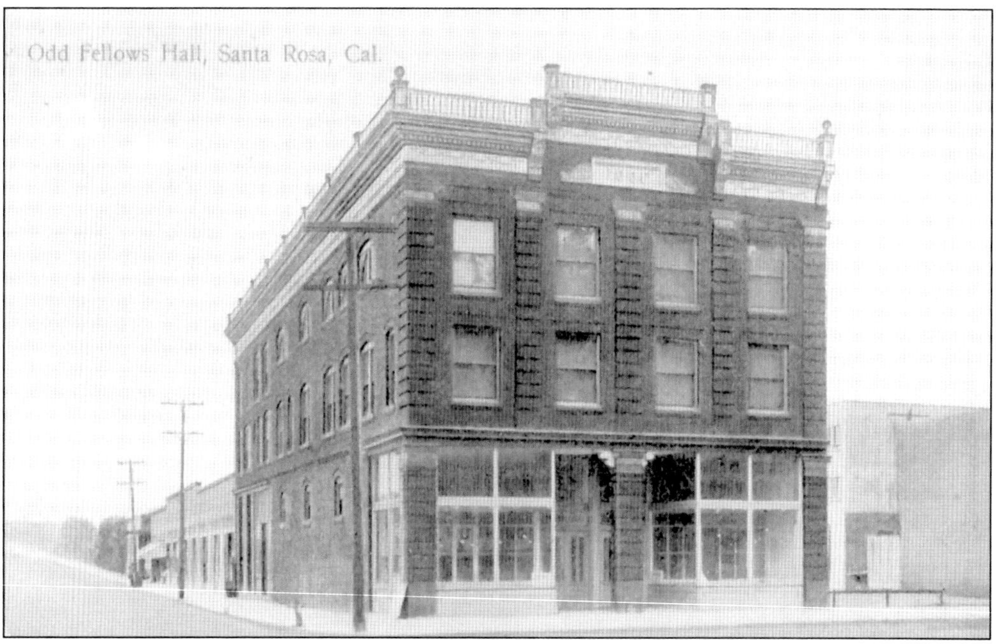

ODD FELLOWS HALL, C. 1915. The International Order of Odd Fellows Hall was located at Exchange Avenue and Third Street.

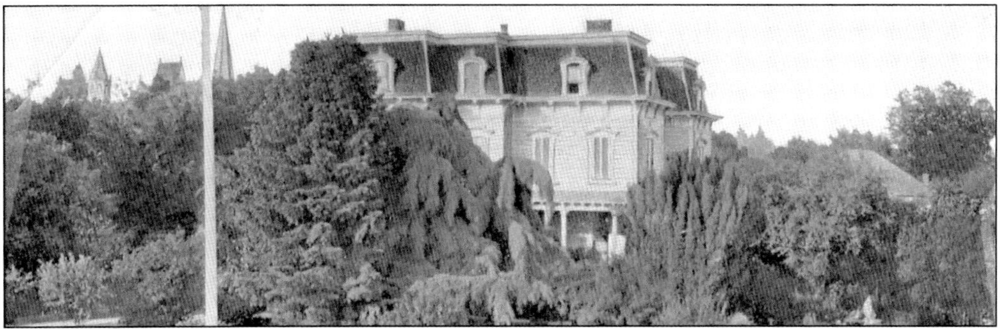

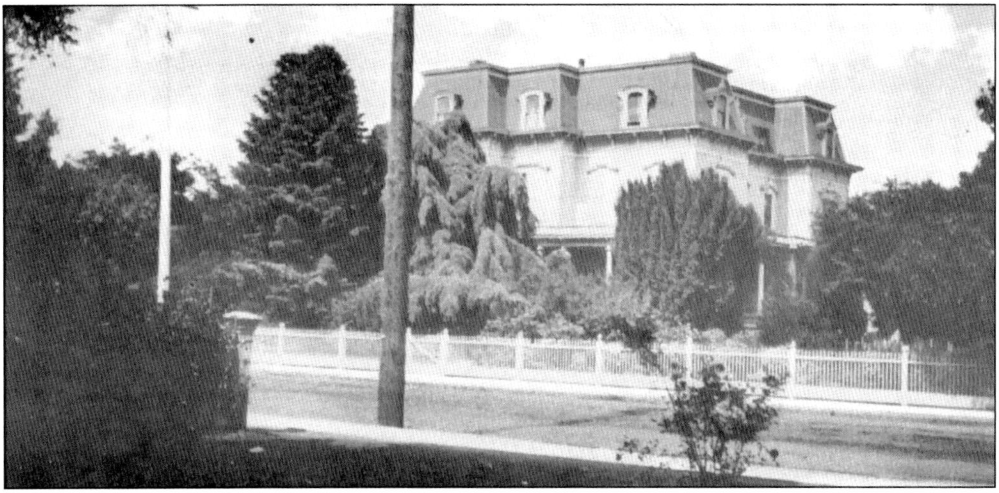

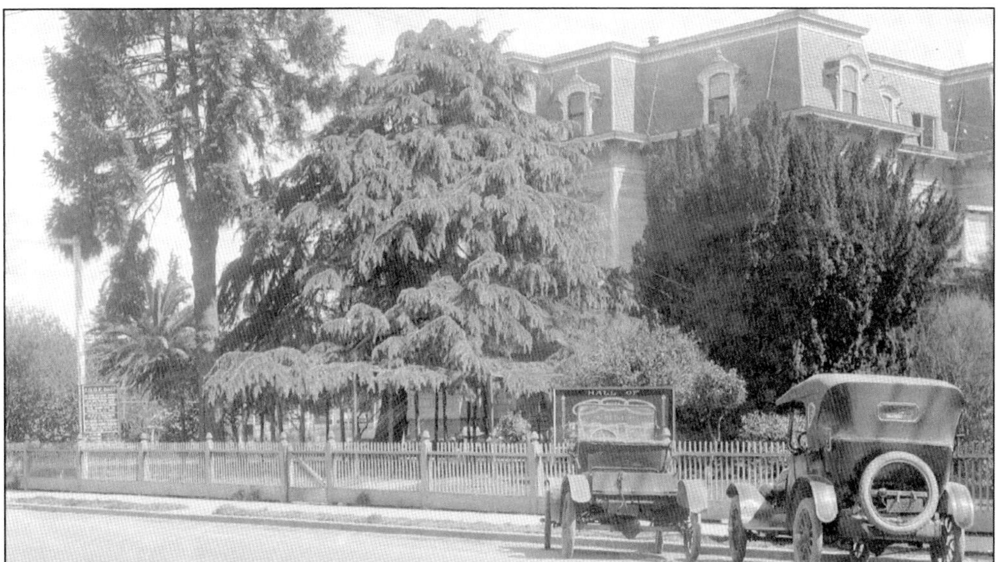

THREE VIEWS OF 426 MENDOCINO AVENUE. These three postcards show the same beautiful mansard roof building: (top) as the Riley House, (middle) as the Hotel Lebanon, and (bottom) as IOOF Lodge No. 53. This building is a mystery! The dates of construction and demolition are uncertain; we only know that it had many uses and is no longer there.

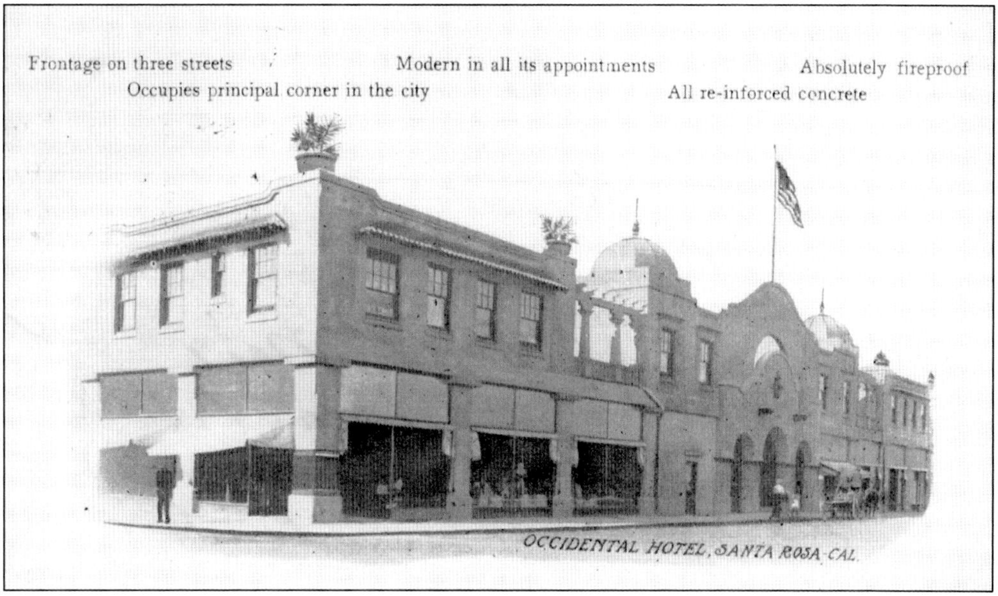

Occidental Hotel, c. 1910. An advertising postcard for the Occidental Hotel clearly states that it is all reinforced concrete and fireproof. The Occidental, located at Fourth and B Streets, was built in 1906 over the site where a prior hotel was destroyed in the great earthquake and seven people lost their lives.

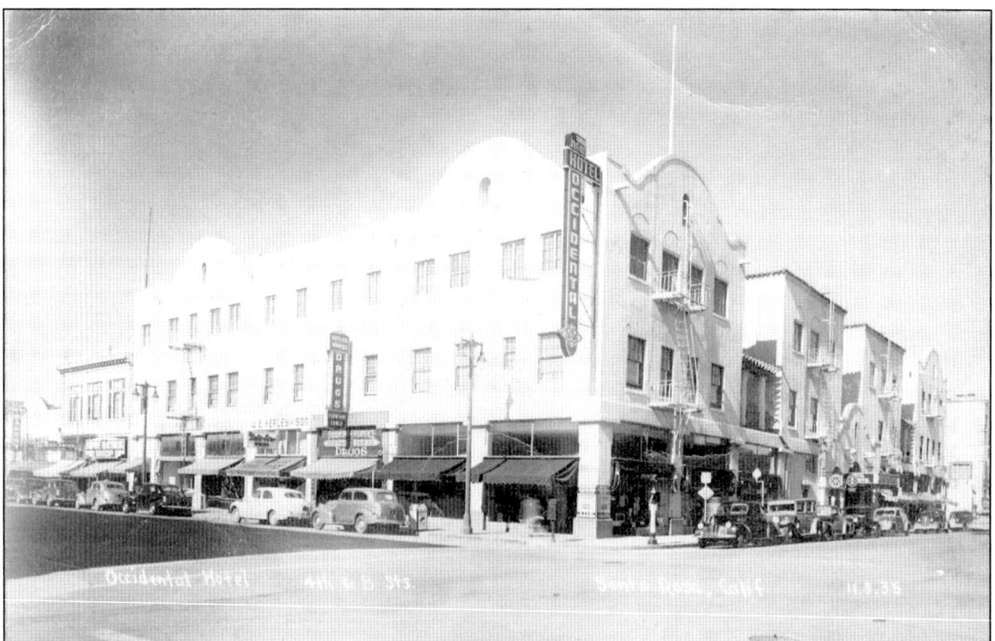

Occidental Hotel, c. 1940. This photocard shows a later Occidental Hotel with an additional story and a much different facade.

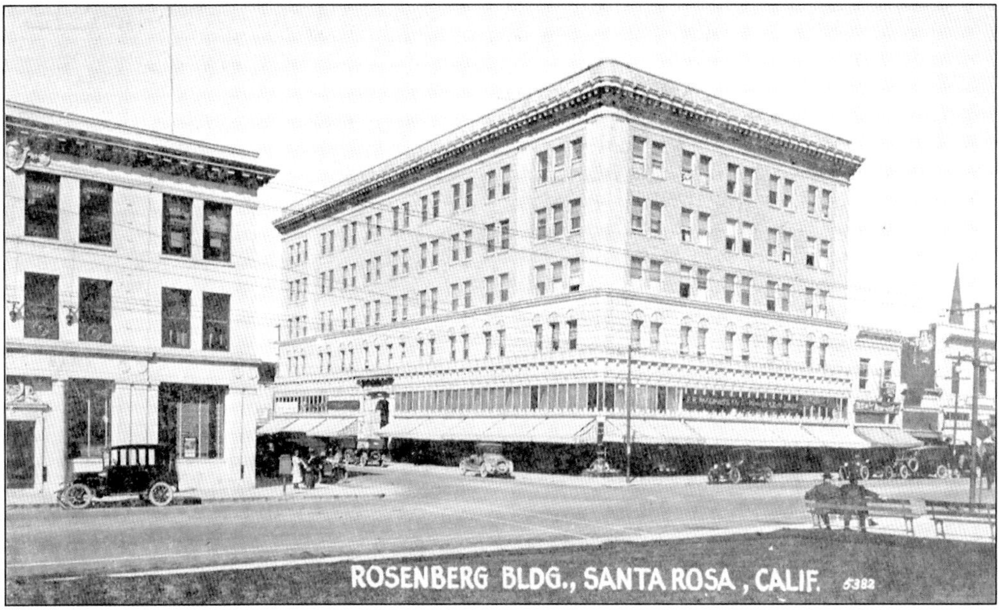

ROSENBERG BUILDING, C. 1925. The Rosenberg Office Building was built in 1921 at the corner of Fourth Street and Mendocino Avenue. This building, always an important landmark in the courthouse square area, remains in use today.

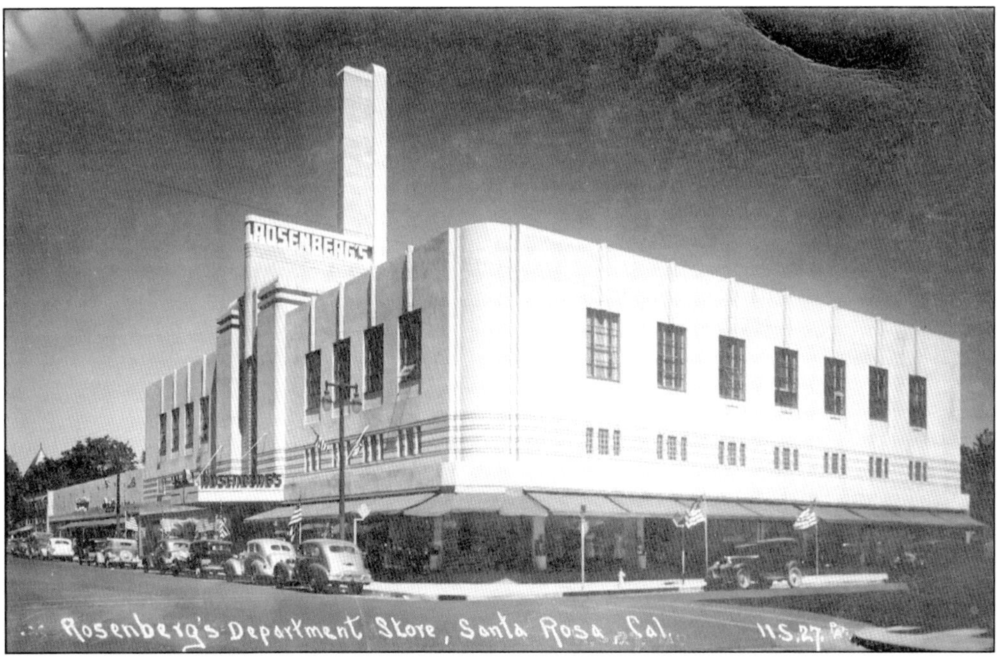

ROSENBERG DEPARTMENT STORE, C. 1940. The second Rosenberg Department Store was built in 1937 in the Art Deco or Art Moderne style. Rosenberg's had been in business in Santa Rosa since 1896. This wonderful building replaced their prior store, which burned in 1936.

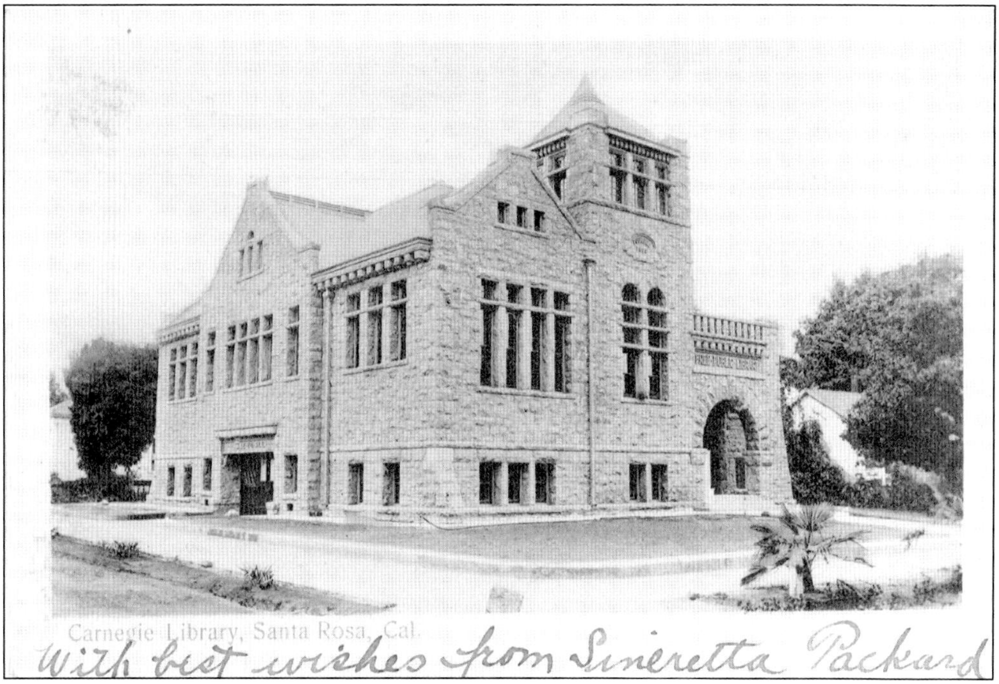

CARNEGIE LIBRARY, C. 1905. This postcard shows the Carnegie Library, which was constructed in 1904 at Fourth and E Streets, the location of the present library. This view shows the pre-earthquake height of the tower.

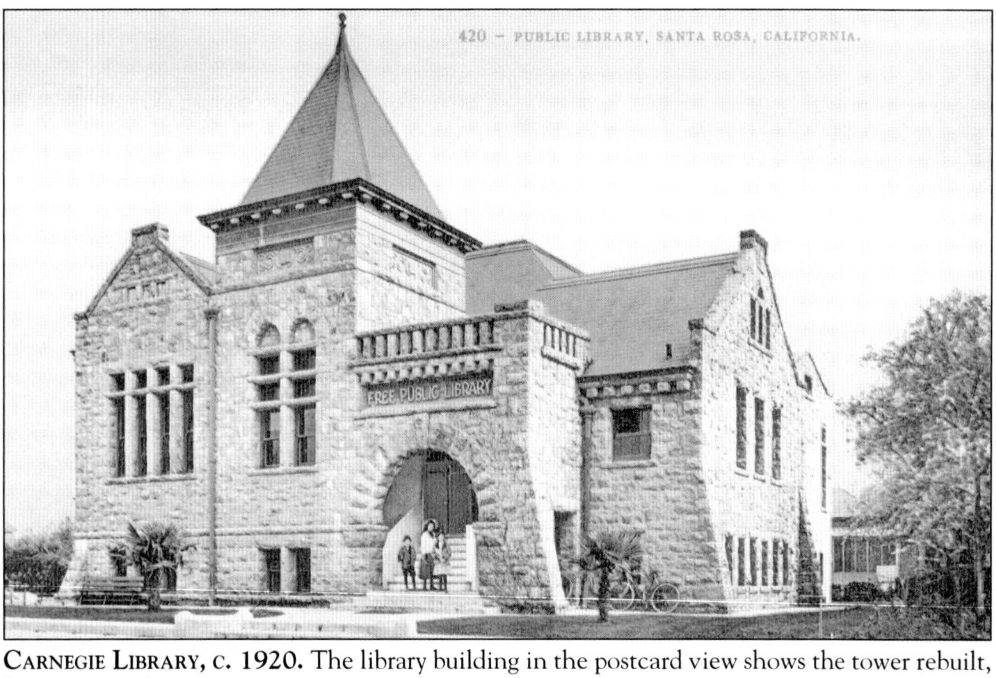

CARNEGIE LIBRARY, C. 1920. The library building in the postcard view shows the tower rebuilt, but one story lower.

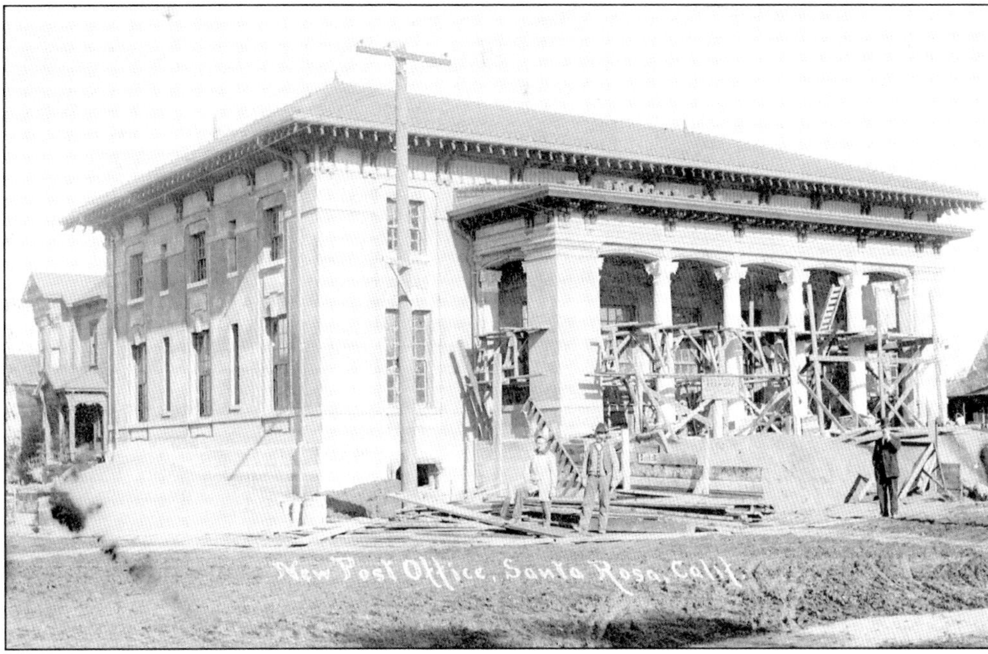

POST OFFICE, C. 1909. The post office was one of the first 12 buildings constructed in California by the federal government. Located at Fifth and A Streets, the structure was completed in 1909.

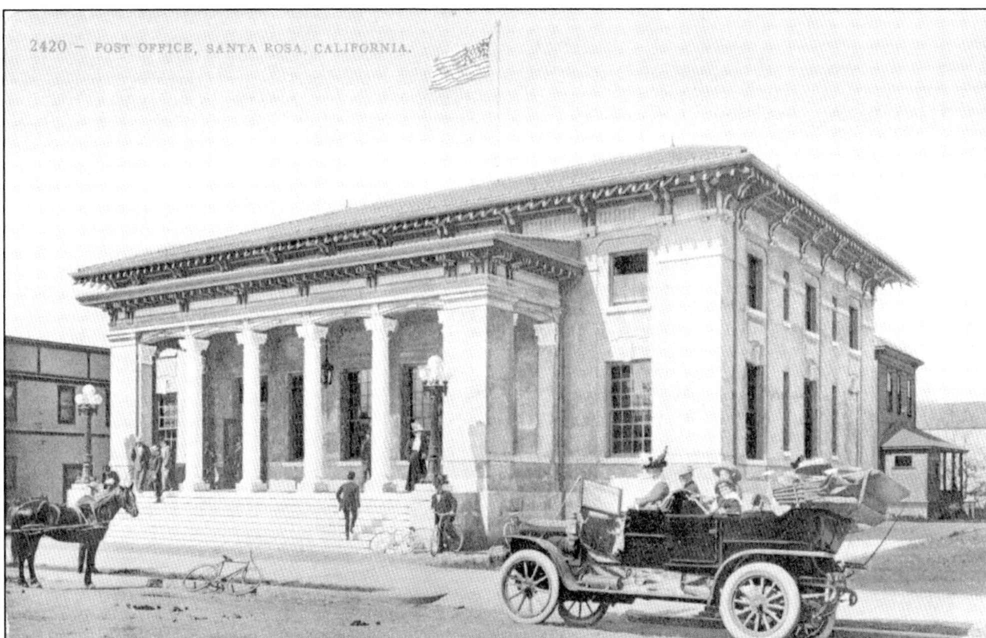

POST OFFICE, C. 1915. The post office was moved to its current address on Seventh Street in 1979. Since then it has been the home of the Sonoma County Museum.

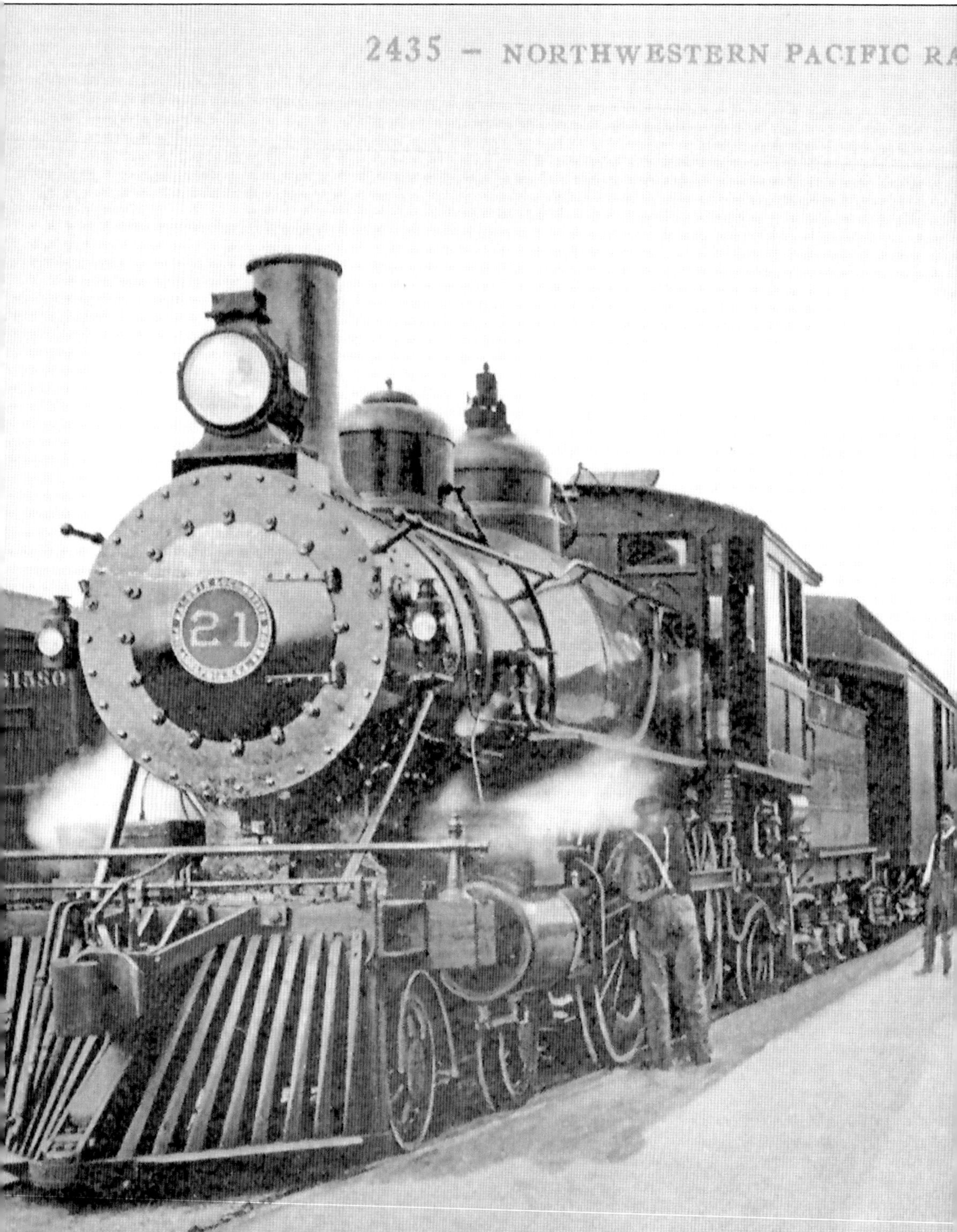

NORTHWESTERN PACIFIC RAILROAD DEPOT, c. 1915. This postcard shows Northwestern Pacific Locomotive No. 21 at the depot located at 9 Fourth Street. The building of Santa Rosa Woolen

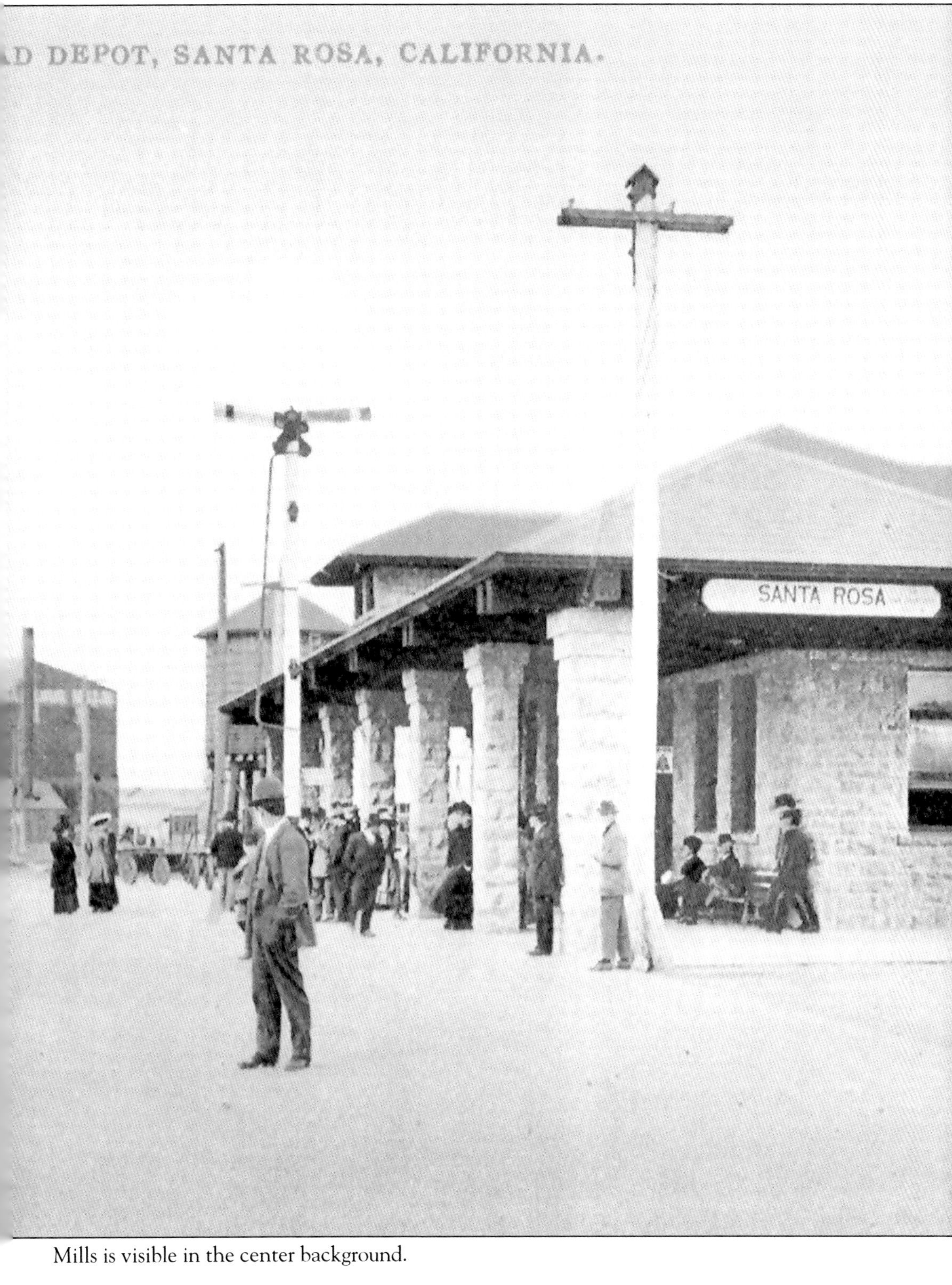

Mills is visible in the center background.

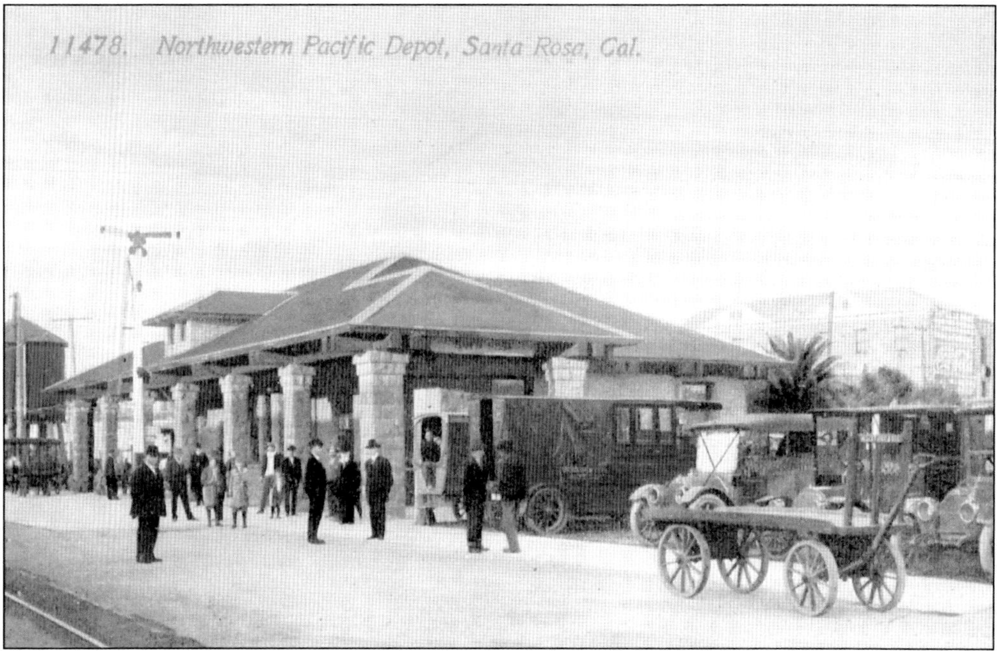

NWP Depot, c. 1919. The bustling depot building was built in 1904 from local native stone. The multi-story, stone building of Hotel LaRose is visible in the background.

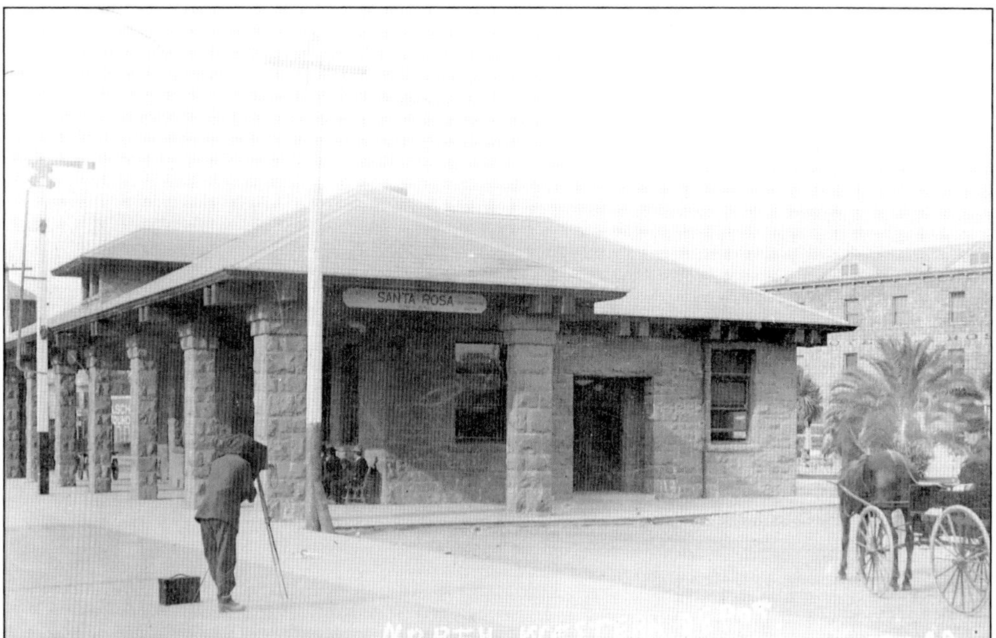

NWP Depot, c. 1915. This photocard shows a local photographer taking a picture of this often-photographed building. The photo he took was probably intended for a postcard as well. This beautifully restored depot bursts with activity again with its new occupants, the Santa Rosa Visitors Bureau and the NWP Rail Museum.

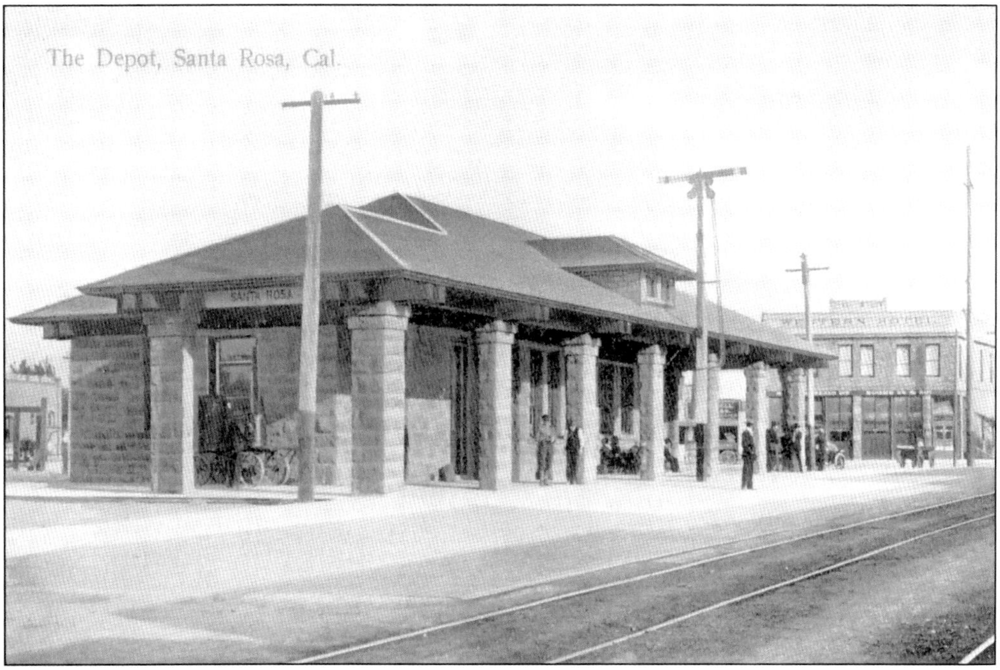

The Depot, c. 1920. This is another view of the NWP Depot looking south toward the Western Hotel. The stone hotel, constructed in 1903, suffered only minor damage in the 1906 earthquake.

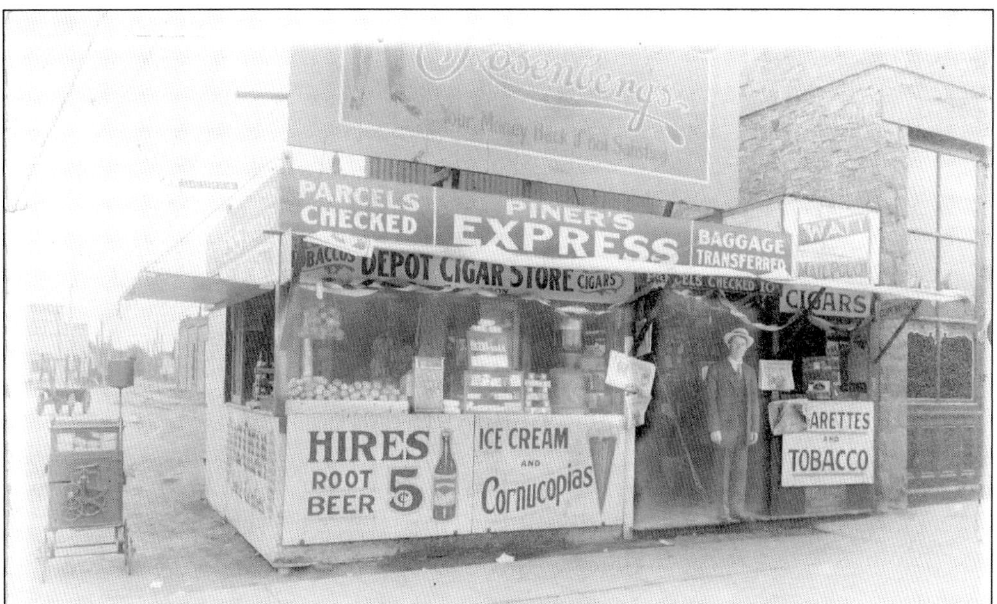

Piner's Express, c. 1920. This great photocard shows Piner's Express located next to the Western Hotel. This establishment took care of everything for the railroad traveler. One could have baggage transferred, have a root beer and a smoke, and pick up the current newspaper!

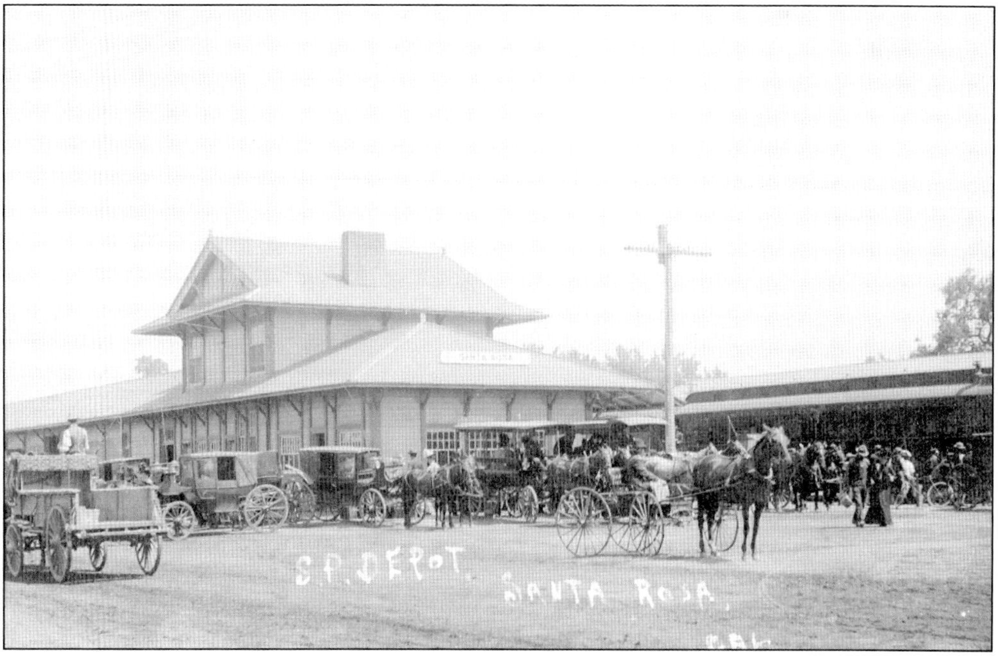

SOUTHERN PACIFIC DEPOT, c. 1900. This photocard shows the Southern Pacific Depot located at 804 North Street. Every horse-drawn buggy and hack in town was there to meet the passenger train.

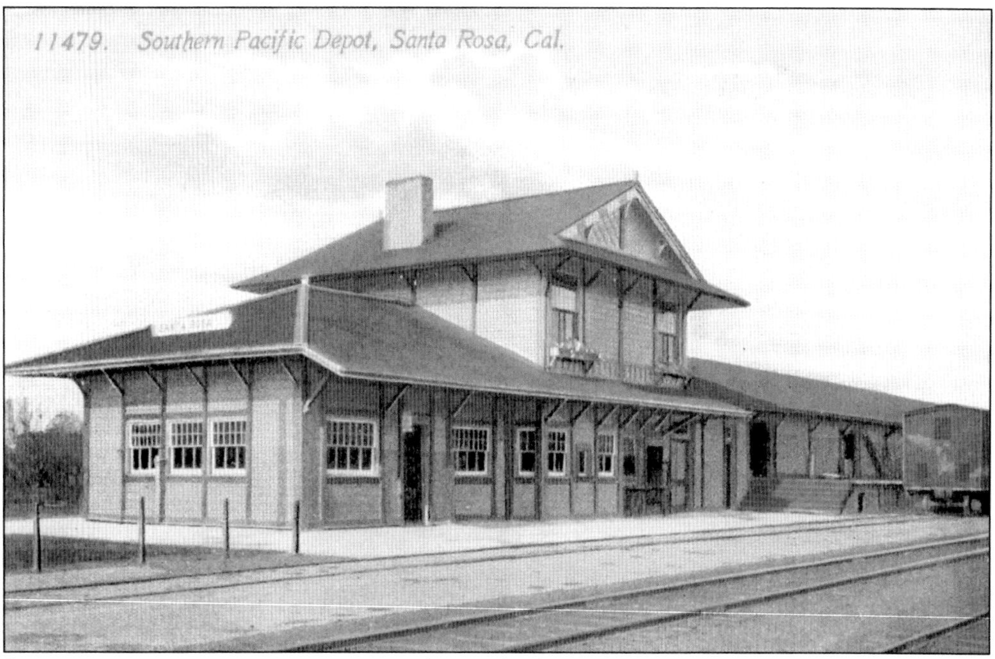

SOUTHERN PACIFIC DEPOT, c. 1910. In this trackside view of the SP Depot, one can see flower boxes in the second-story windows and the long platform for handling freight.

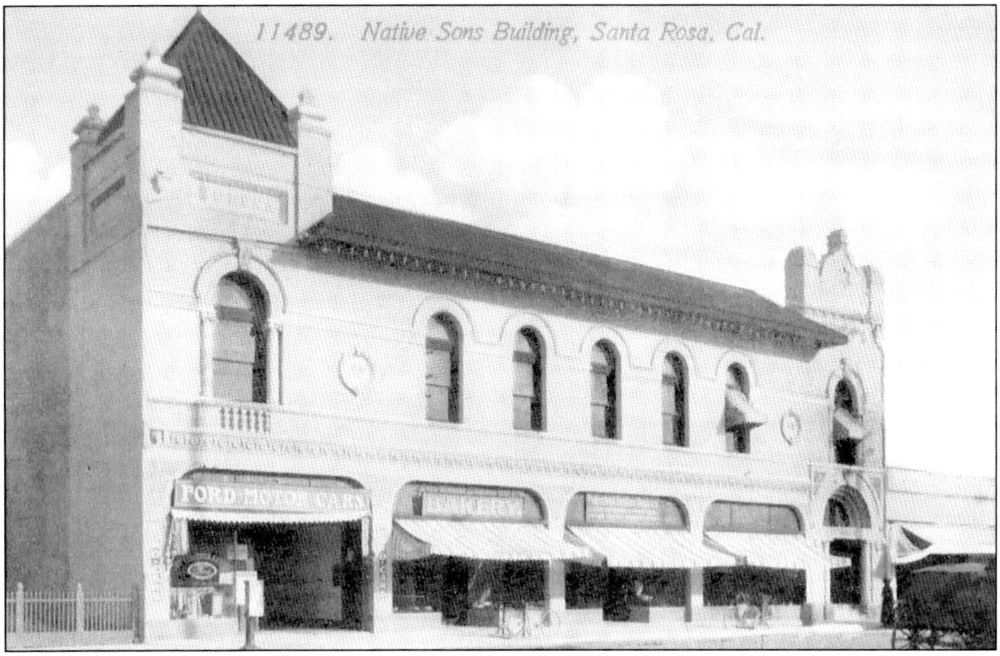

NATIVE SONS OF THE GOLDEN WEST BUILDING, C. 1915. The Native Sons Building, located on Mendocino Avenue at Fifth Street, was completed in 1907. It is the only structure built for a fraternal organization that is still standing in Santa Rosa today.

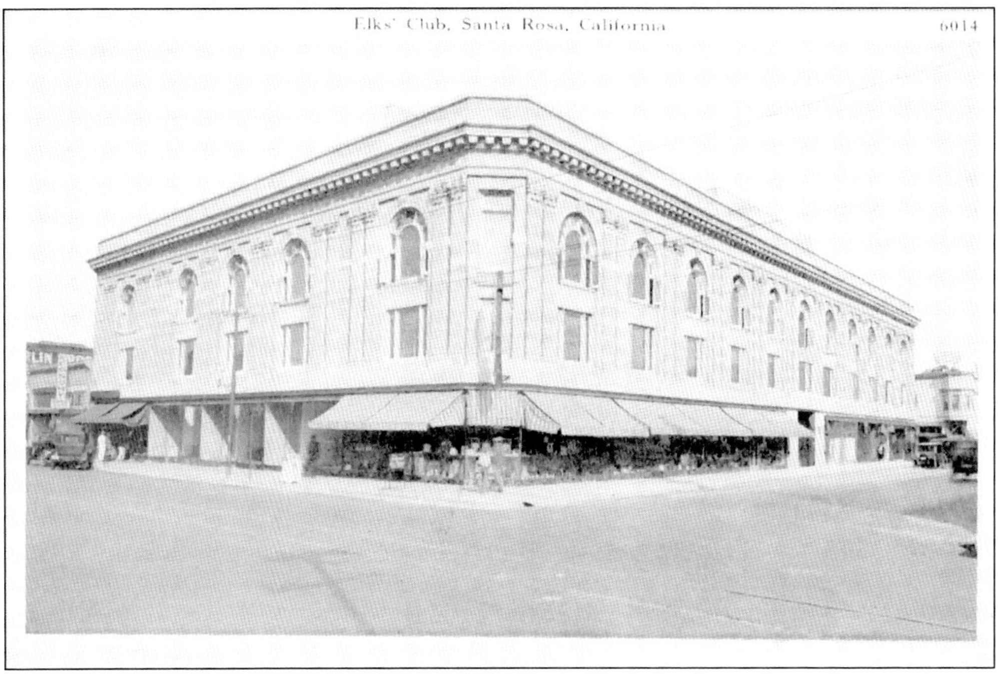

ELKS CLUB, C. 1920. The Elks Club was built on the southwest corner of Fourth and B Streets. It was another building lost to redevelopment in the 1960s.

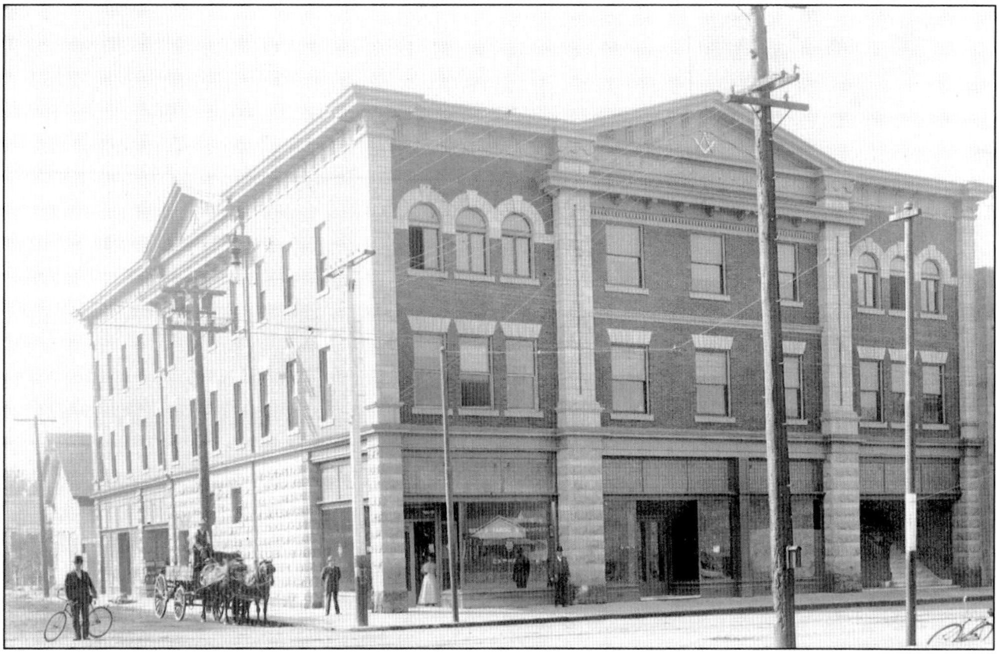

Masonic Building, c. 1910. This photocard shows the Masonic Building, located at the corner of Fourth and D Streets. The office in the corner of the building housed the Wells Fargo and Company Express.

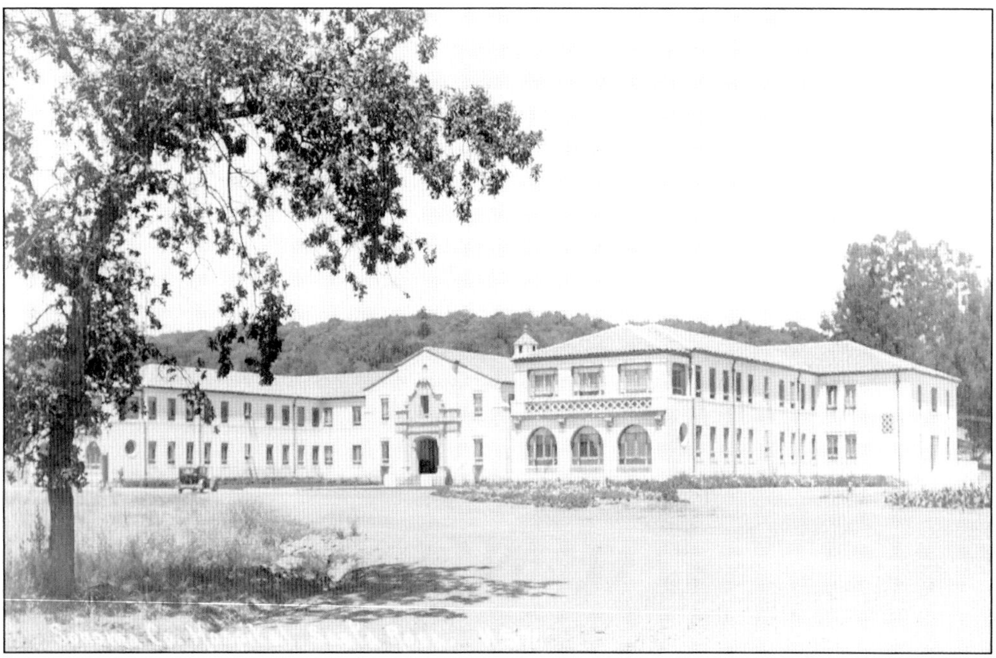

Sonoma County Hospital, c. 1930. The Sonoma County Hospital was erected in the Depression Era, the early 1930s, with Public Works Administration funds.

Six

HOLIDAY GREETINGS FROM SANTA ROSA

The postcards in this chapter are, of course, the most beautiful in color and design. Unfortunately, black and white imagery cannot do these justice. Two postcards in this chapter were printed in Germany, and the remaining nine were printed by one publisher in San Francisco, probably in about 1910. Each of the nine cards is a different design. It is likely they were all printed at the same time for the Christmas holiday.

We wonder why we have never seen any other holidays depicted on Santa Rosa postcards. What about Easter greetings, or Independence Day, or Thanksgiving? Maybe you've got one or two cards in your collection that we didn't know about!

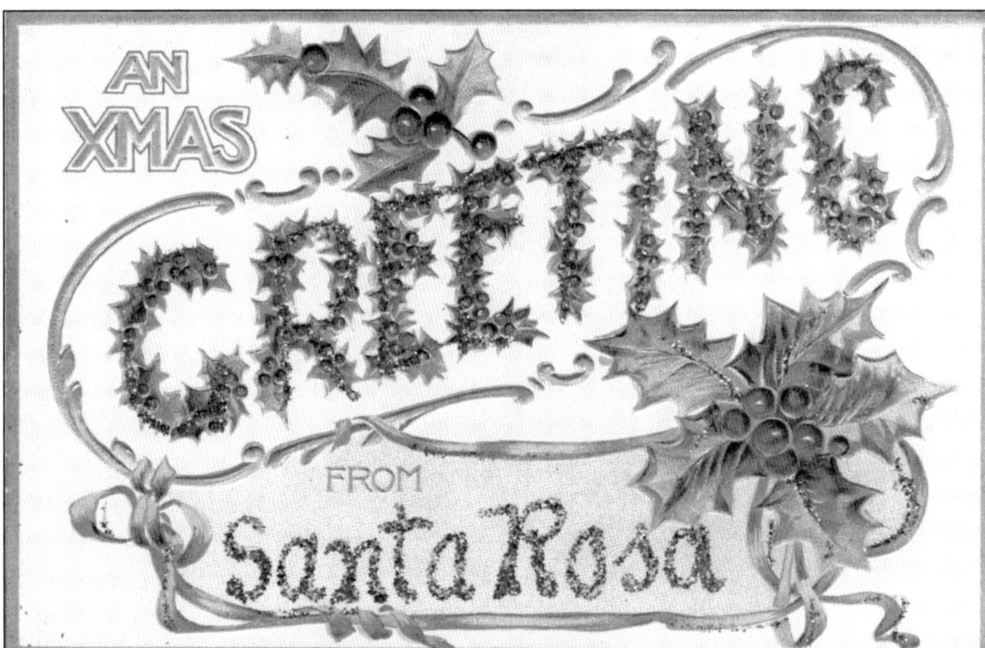

A CHRISTMAS GREETING, C. 1910.

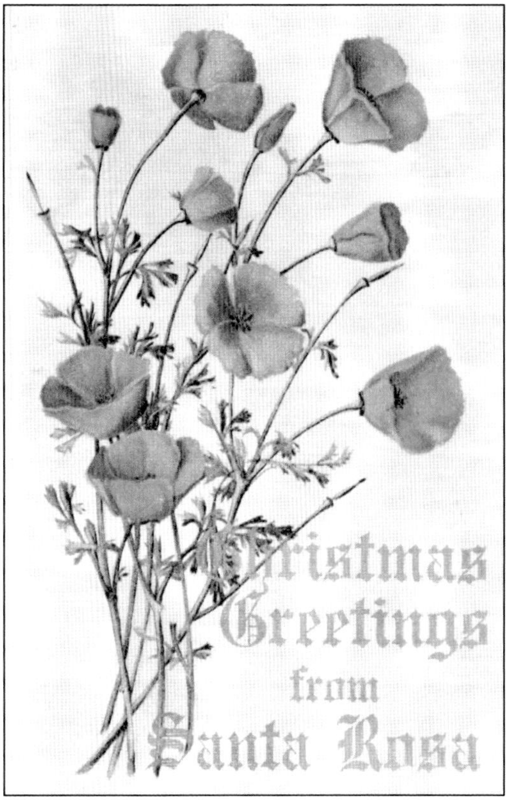

CALIFORNIA POPPY GREETING CARD.

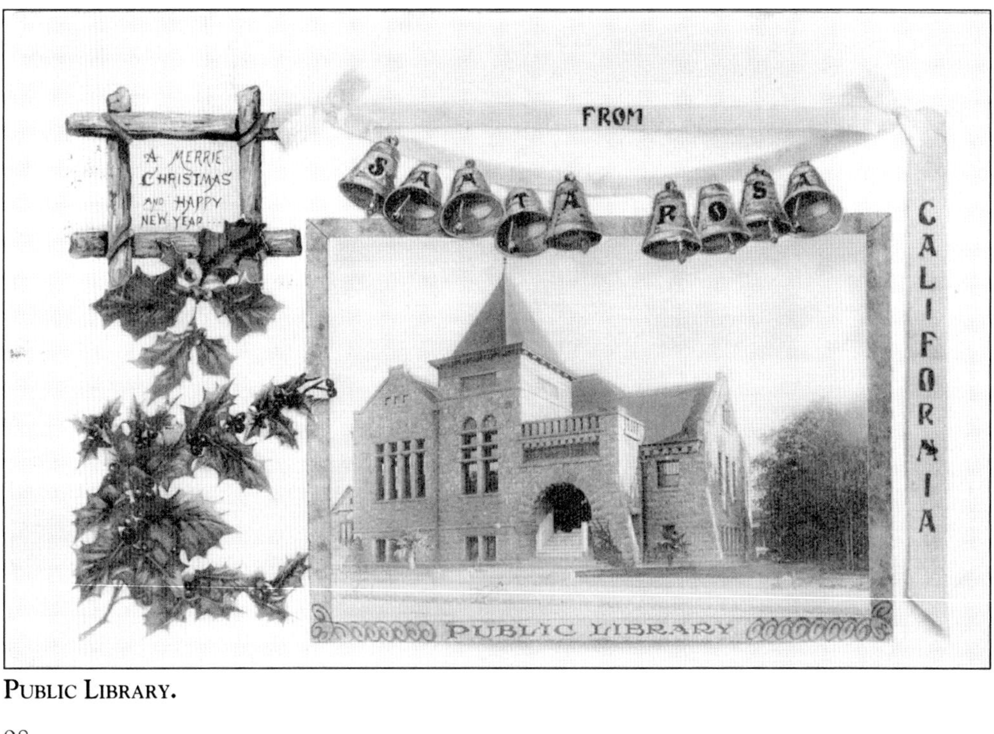

PUBLIC LIBRARY.

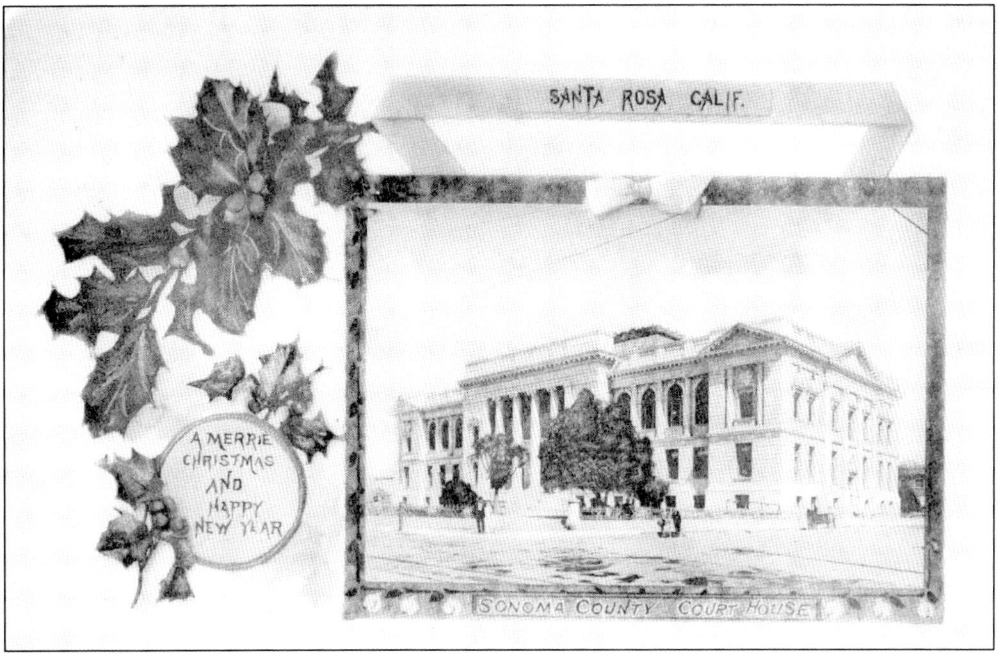

SONOMA COUNTY COURTHOUSE.

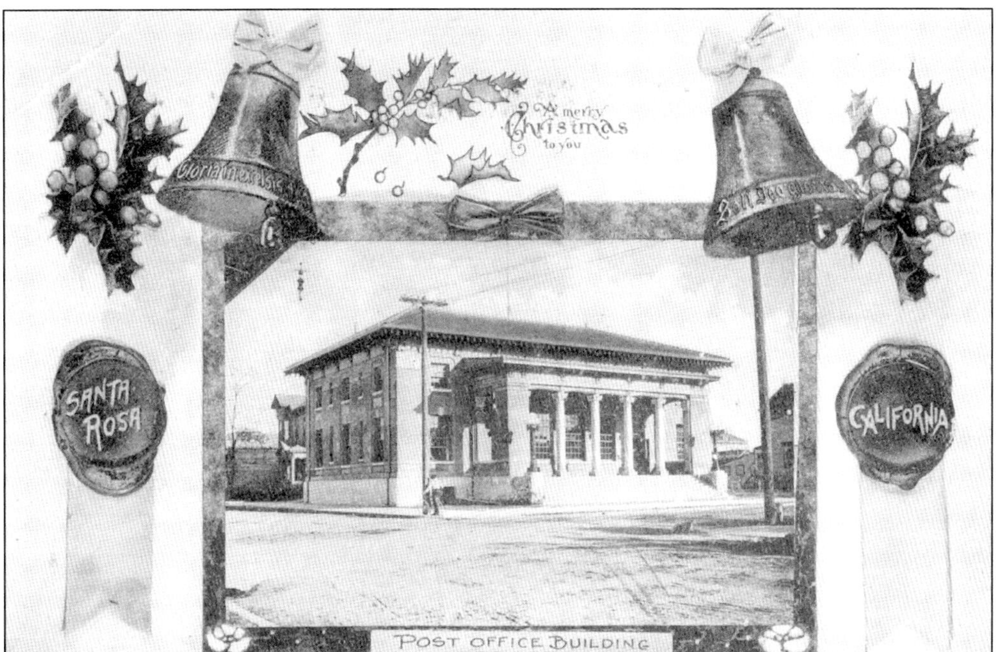

POST OFFICE BUILDING.

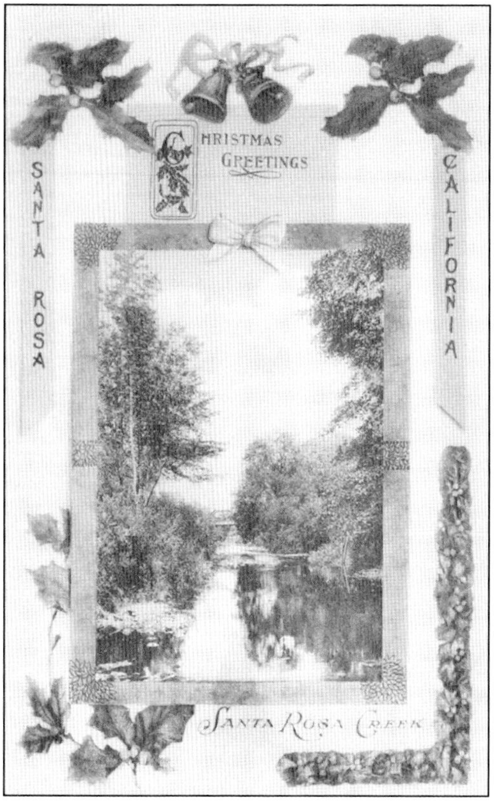

SANTA ROSA CREEK.

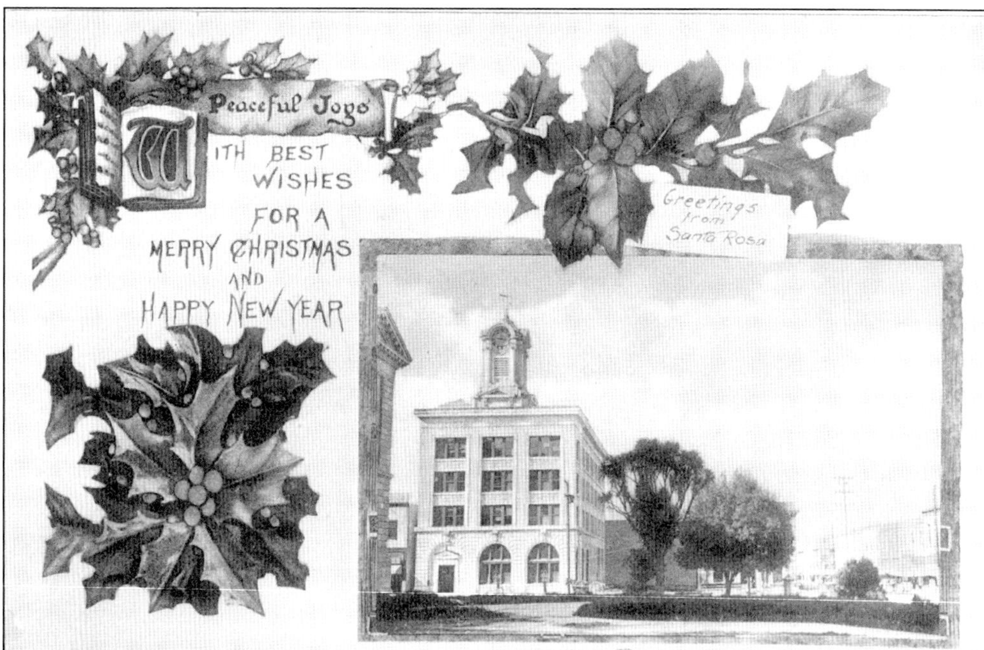

SANTA ROSA BANK.

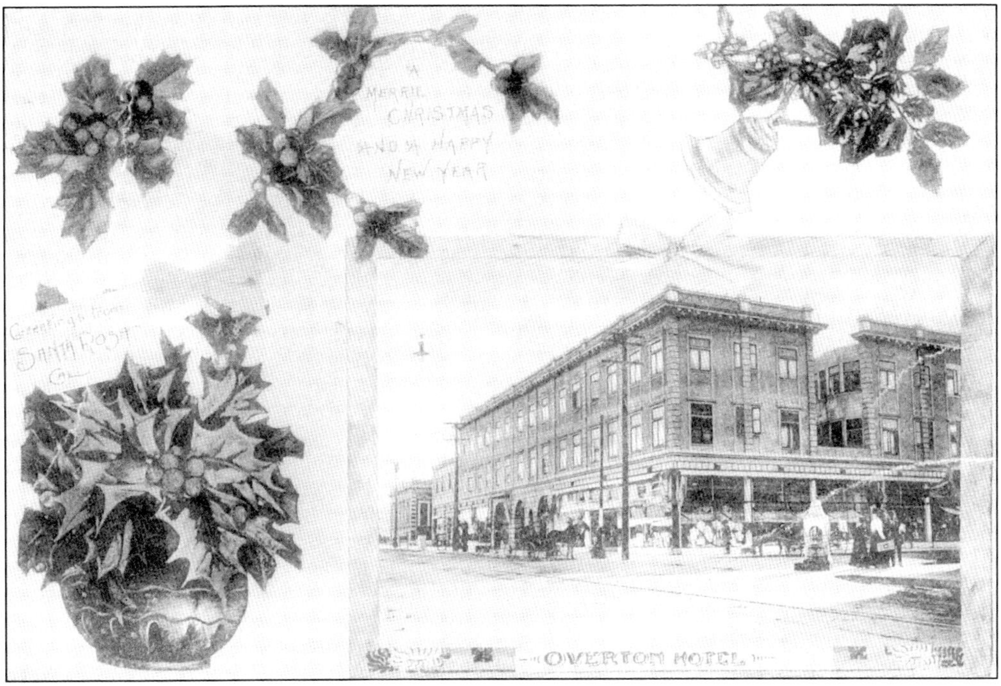

OVERTON HOTEL.

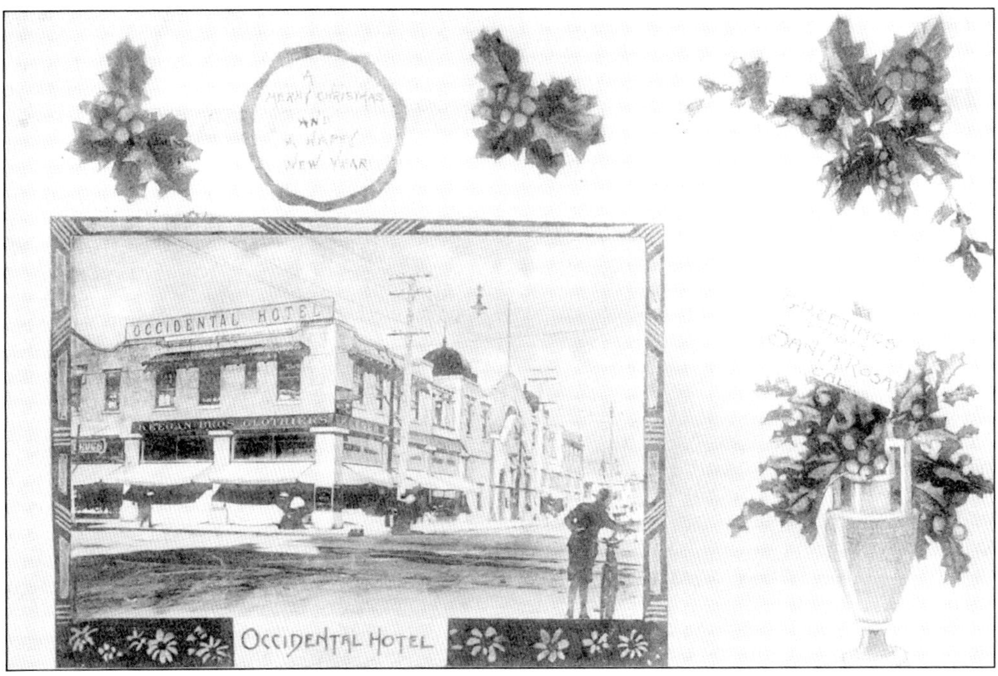

OCCIDENTAL HOTEL.

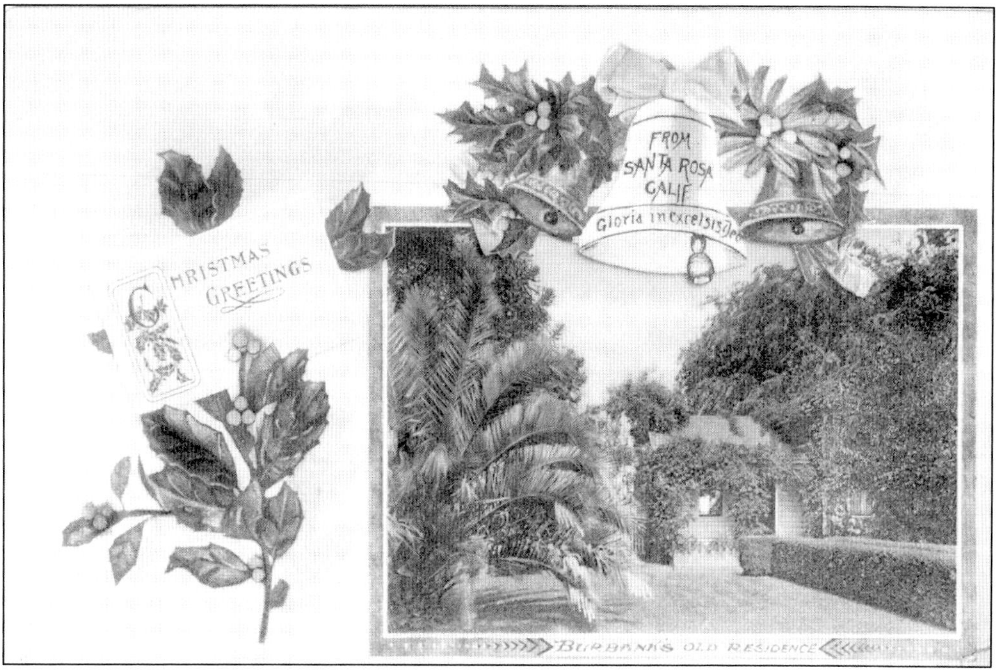

BURBANK'S OLD RESIDENCE.

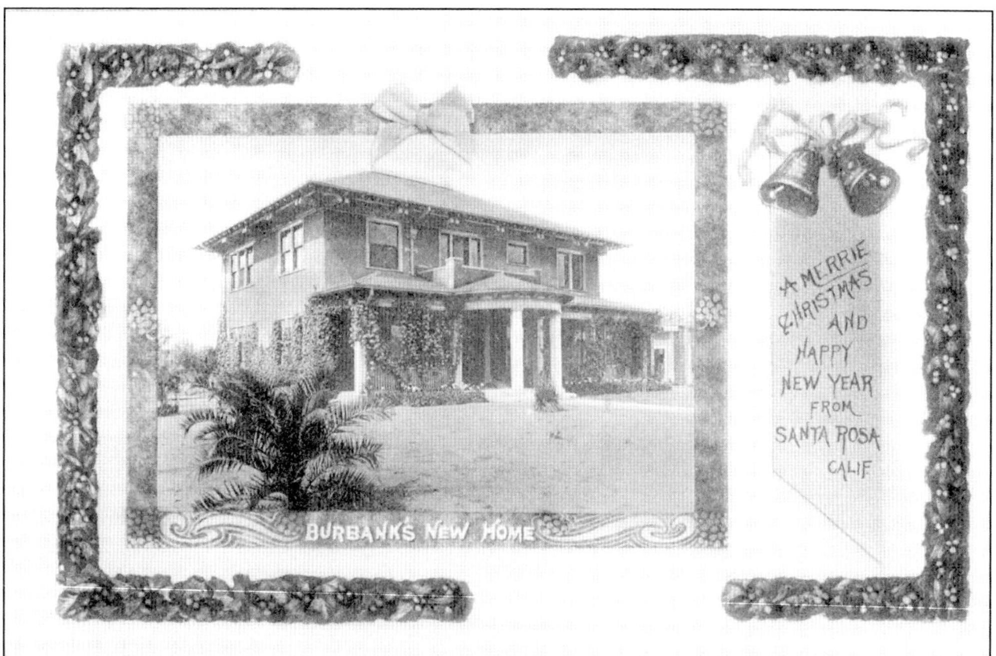

BURBANK'S NEW HOME.

Seven

The Great Earthquake of 1906

Just before dawn at 5:13 on Wednesday morning, April 18, 1906, a disastrous earthquake measuring 8.3 on the Richter scale struck Northern California. The destruction in downtown Santa Rosa was almost complete, and very few buildings escaped some damage. Most brick structures were either totally destroyed or damaged beyond repair. The courthouse was toppled, and Fourth Street appeared to be a war zone. Frame structures generally survived with less damage; at least they could be repaired.

The death toll in Santa Rosa was the highest per capita of any city in Northern California. Many people died in the various brick hotels that were located in the center of town. Some people trapped in the collapse of buildings perished in the ensuing fires that raged through the downtown area. The destruction of the firehouse and damage to water mains made fighting the fires an almost impossible job.

The earthquake's aftermath became the subject of many period postcards. This selection will provide the reader with an idea of the complete destruction that the town center endured. The rebuilding over the next several years completely changed the face of Santa Rosa.

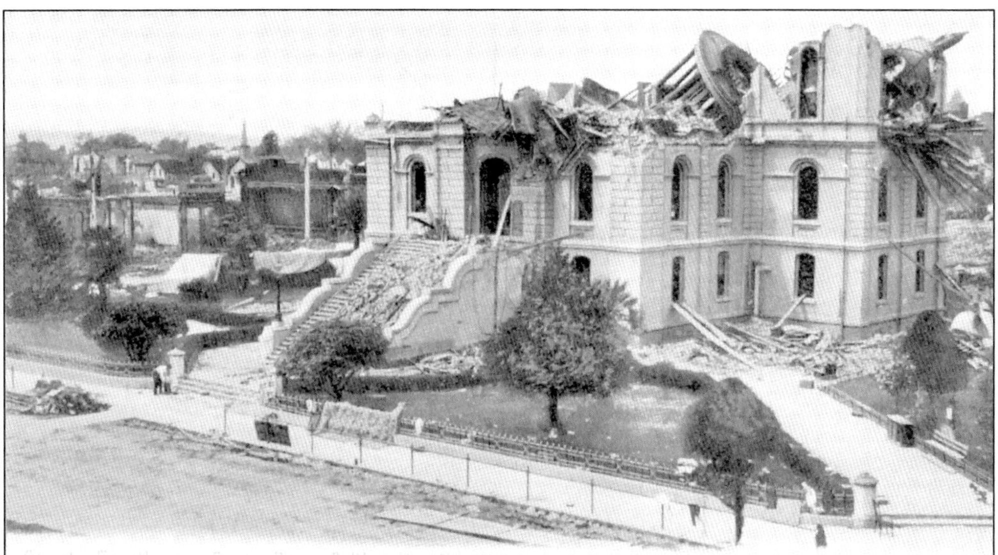

Santa Rosa Courthouse. This view of the courthouse from Fourth Street shows the total destruction of the building.

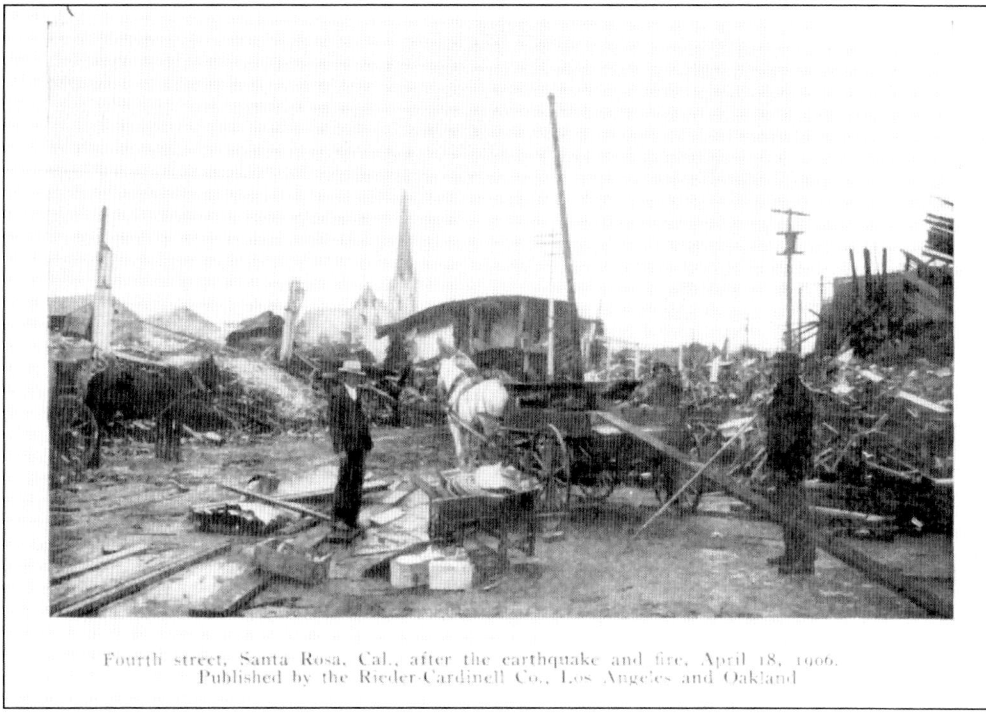

FOURTH STREET. Looking east on Fourth Street, the Methodist Episcopal Church steeple is visible in the background. The man in the foreground is believed to be Luther Burbank.

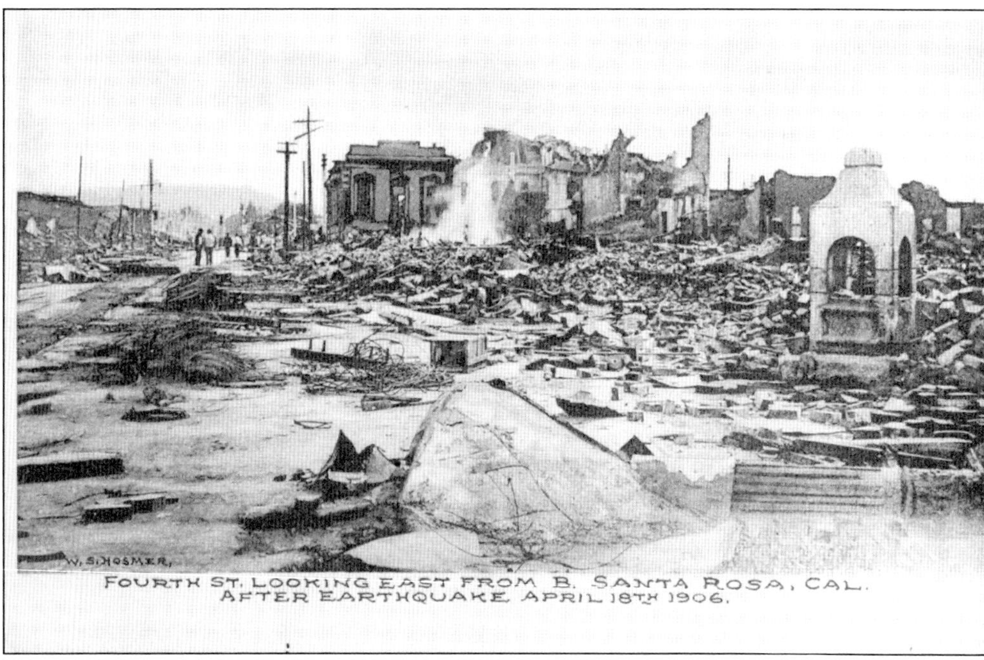

FOURTH STREET. This scene looks east from B Street.

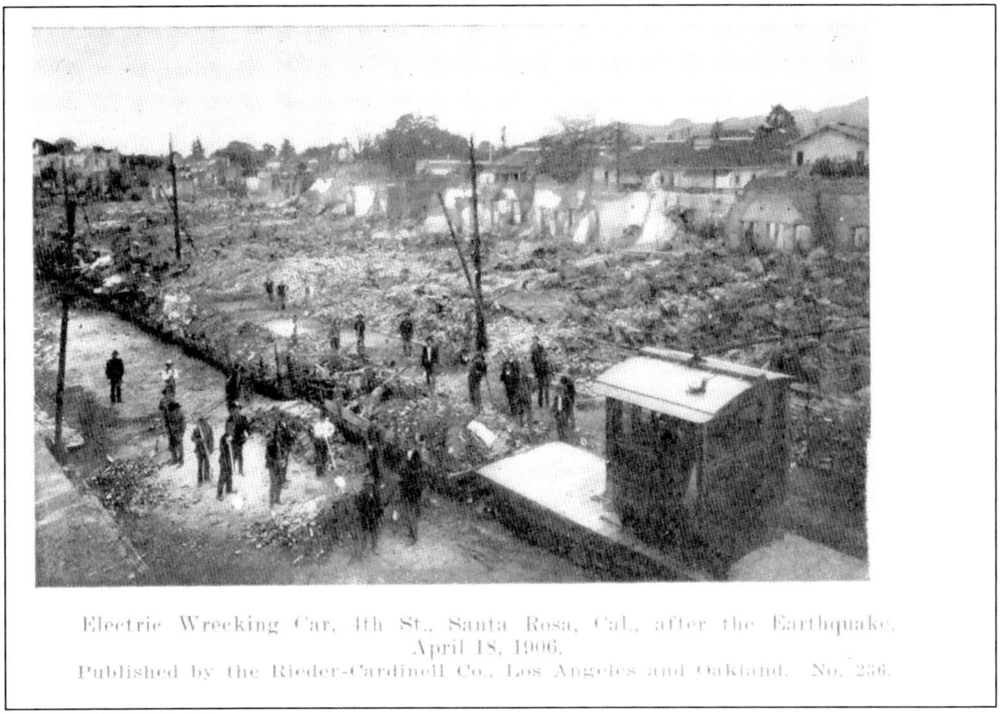

FOURTH STREET. A wrecking crane on the trolley tracks was used to help remove debris.

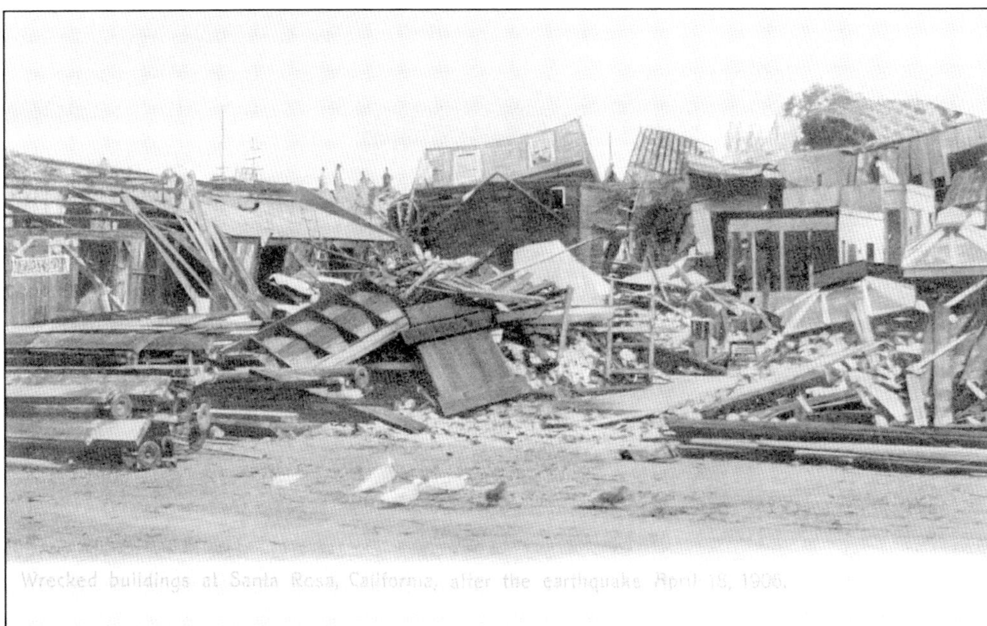

BUILDINGS DESTROYED. The damage to frame buildings can be seen in this card.

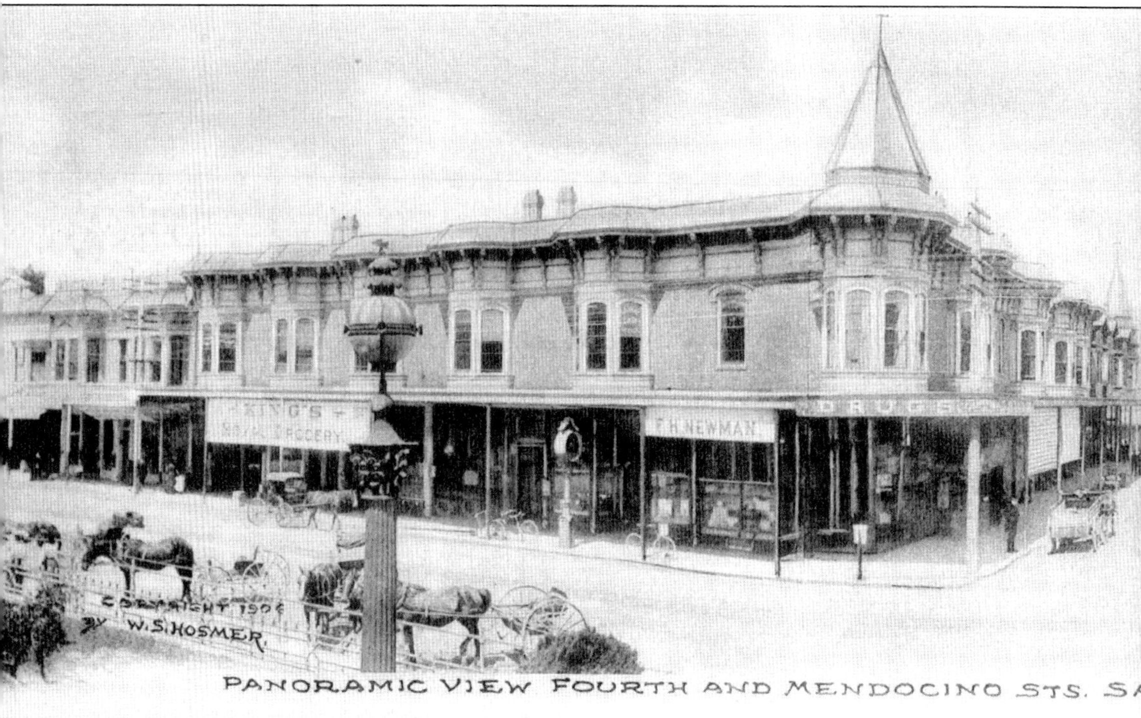

Before and After Views. These double postcards show a panoramic view of the intersection

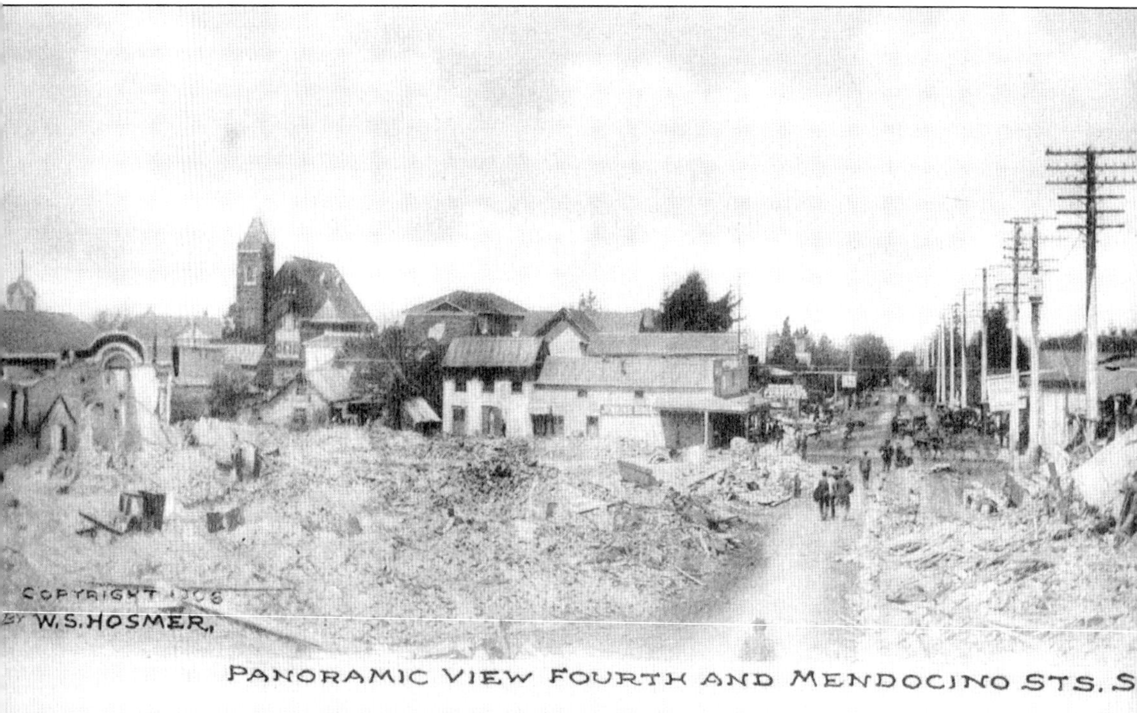

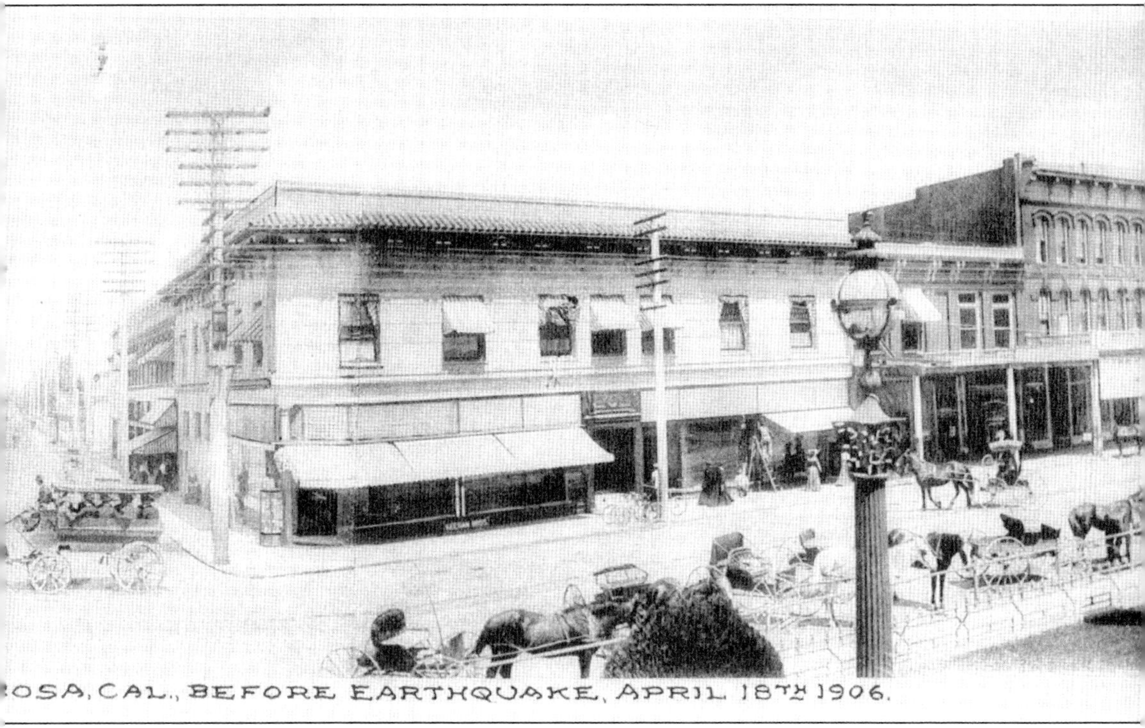

of Fourth Street and Mendocino Avenue before and after the earthquake.

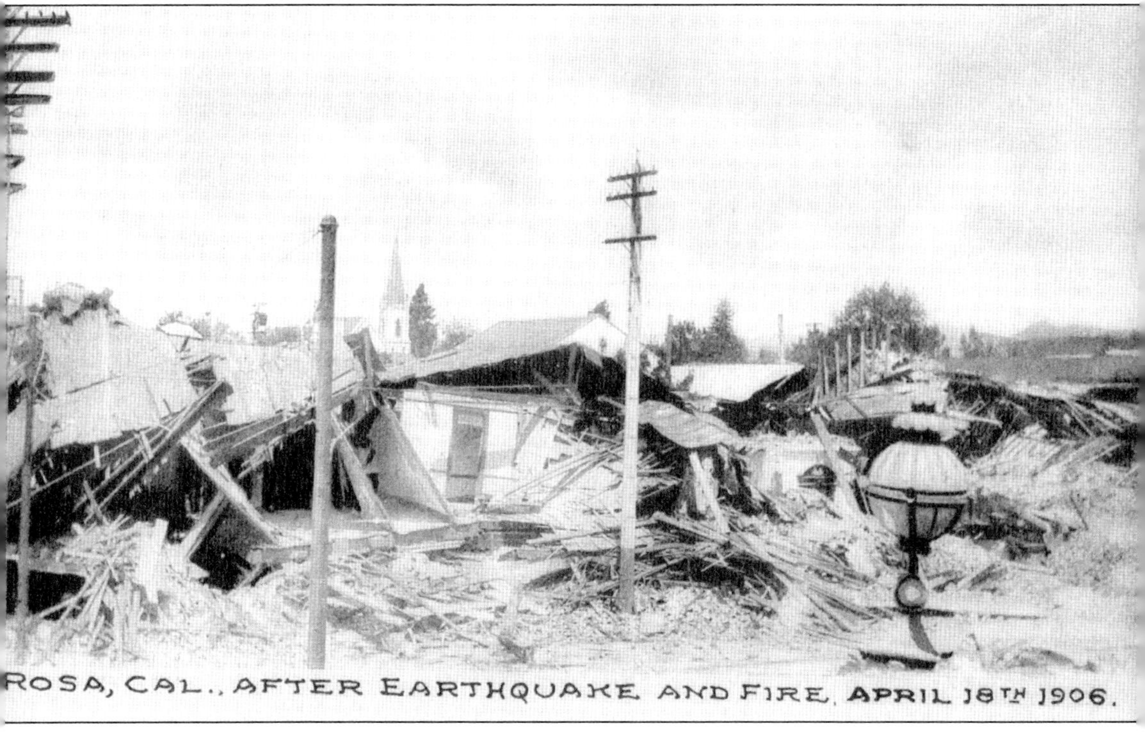

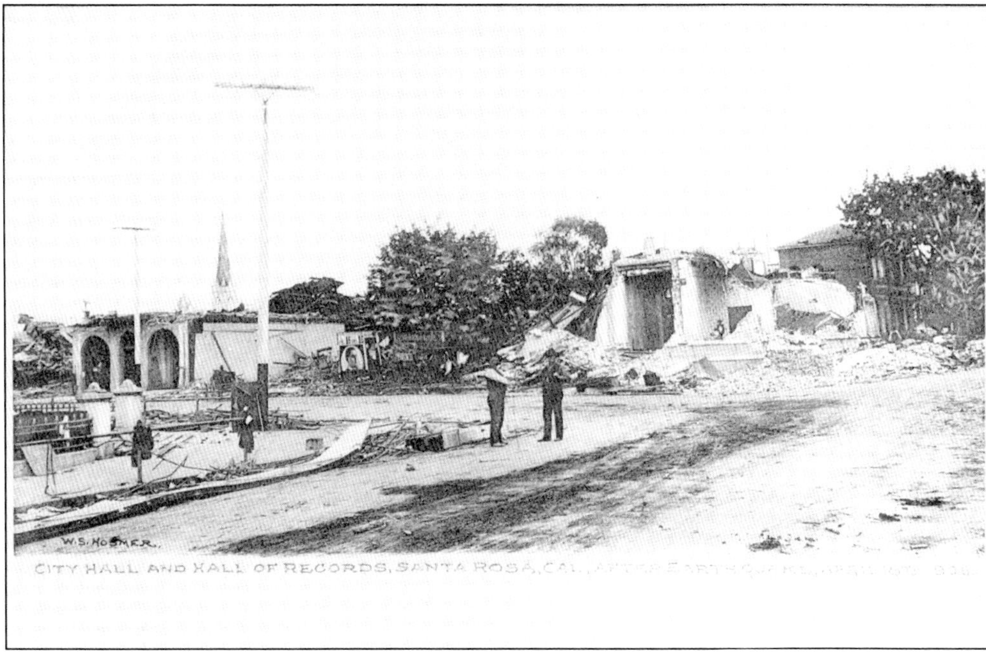

CITY HALL AND HALL OF RECORDS. This view of the intersection of Third Street and Hinton Avenue shows the damage to city hall and the Hall of Records.

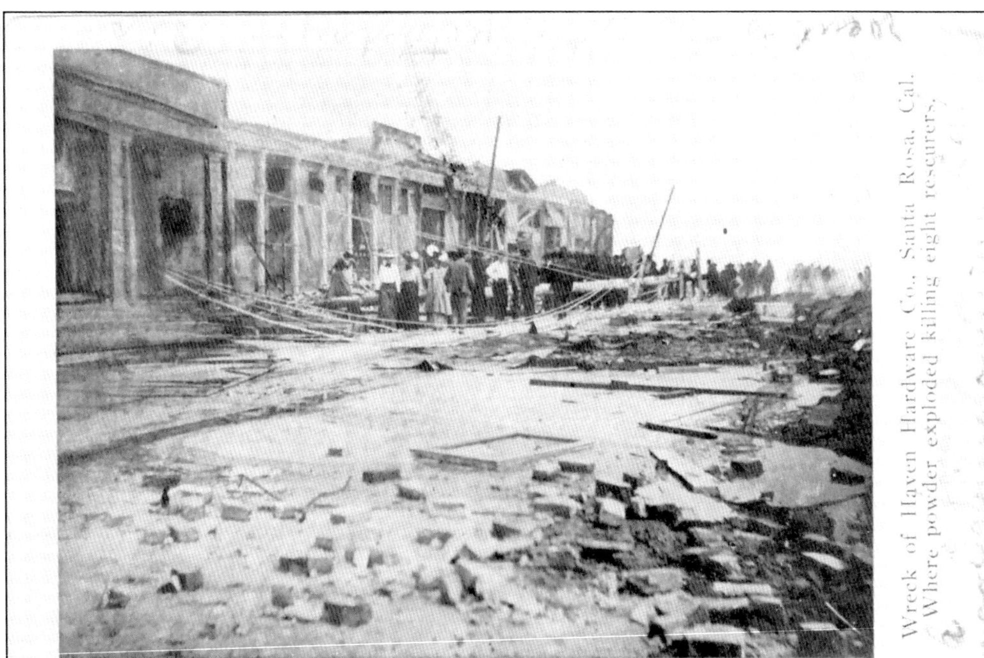

HAVEN HARDWARE COMPANY. This retail store was located at 420 Fourth Street. We attempted to verify the account of eight people killed in an explosion at this building, but were unable to do so.

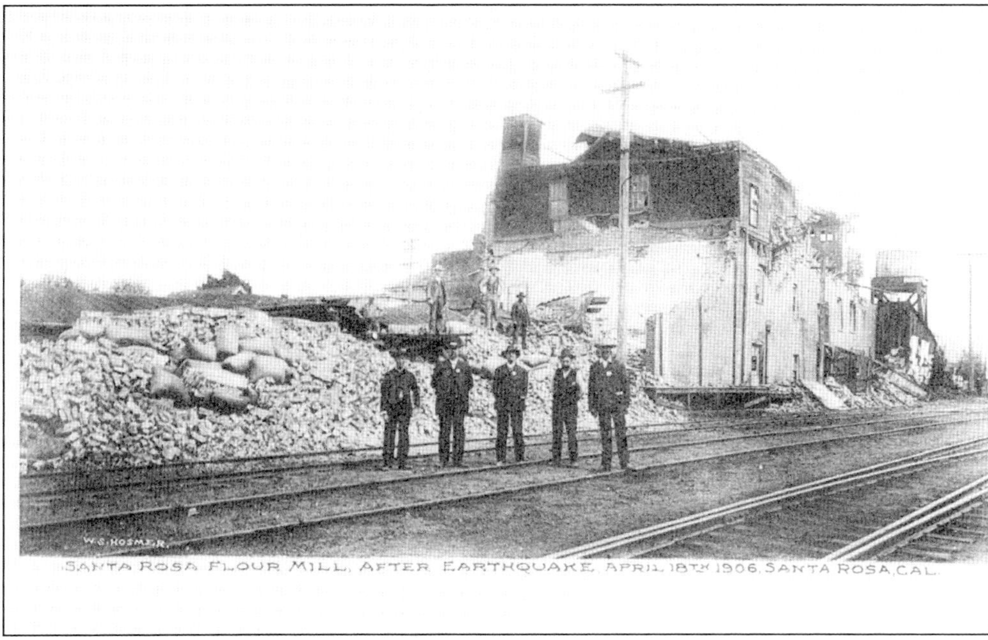

SANTA ROSA FLOUR MILL. The flour mill was located on Wilson Street, between Sixth and Seventh Streets.

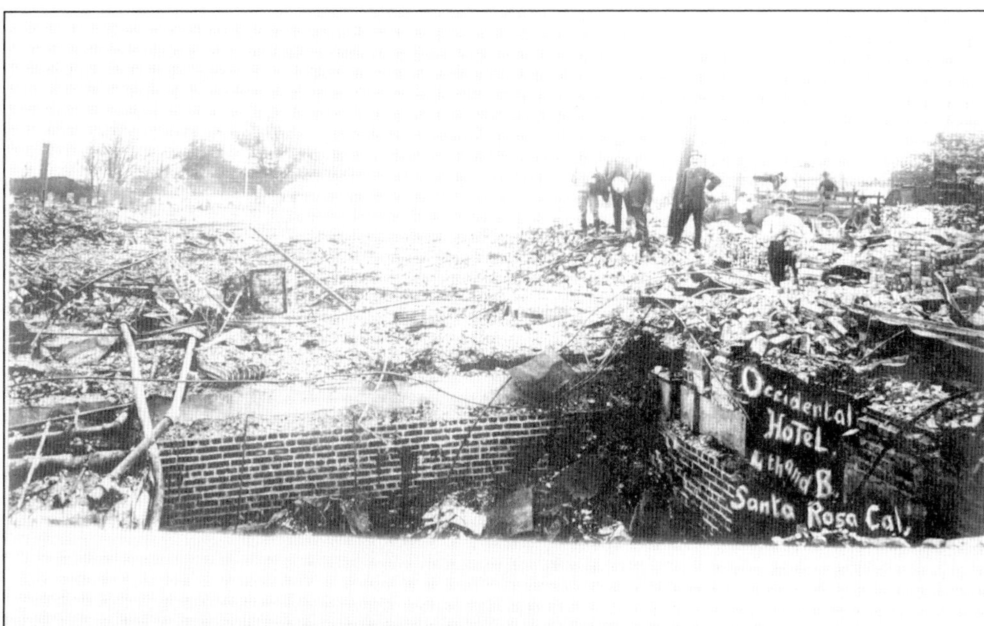

OCCIDENTAL HOTEL. The Occidental Hotel, located at Fourth and B Streets, was in complete ruins after the earthquake.

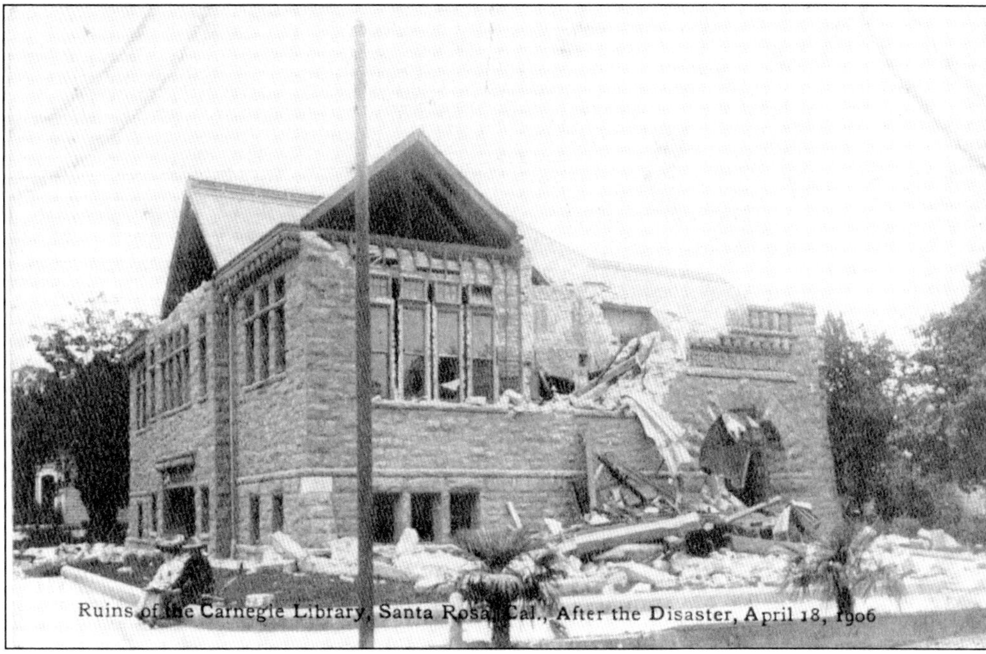

Carnegie Library. This postcard shows the collapsed two-story stone library building.

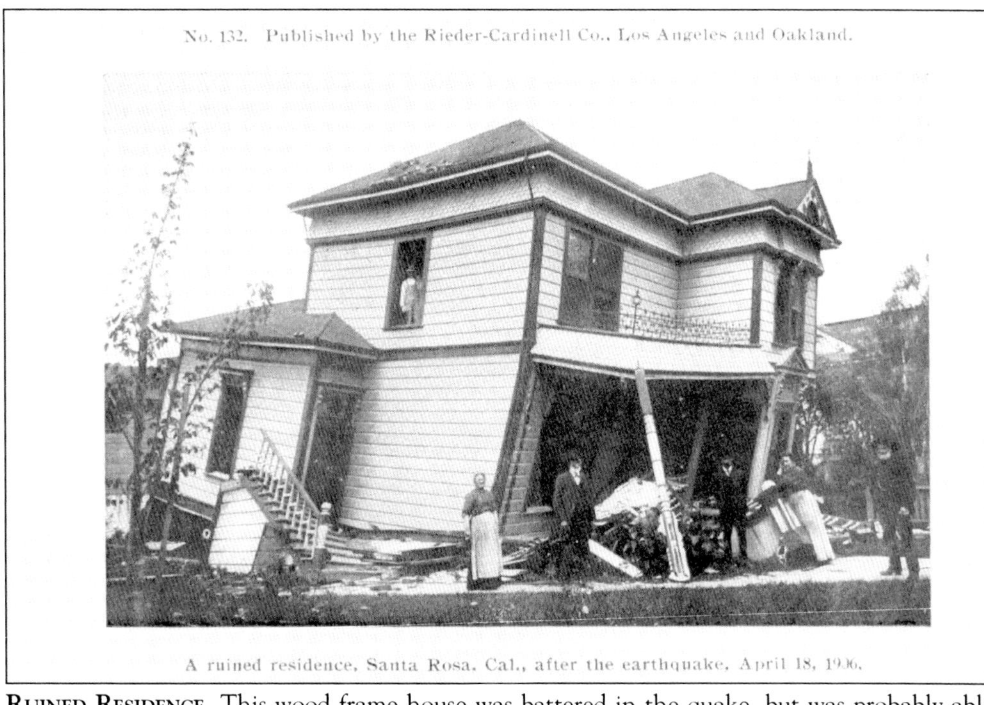

Ruined Residence. This wood-frame house was battered in the quake, but was probably able to be reconstructed.

Eight

Odds and Ends, Plus a Bit of Humor

As the title implies, this is our "catch-all" chapter. In our preparation for this book we looked at a large number of Santa Rosa postcards, and the variety of cards has been unbelievable. There were a number of interesting cards that just didn't fit into the main categories and we wanted to share some of them with you.

We did find that serious postcard collectors are generally not interested in the humorous type of cards, so the group to select from was not as large as we hoped. We have included a few of the better ones for your enjoyment. Many of these comical postcards were preprinted by the publisher leaving a space for a town name to be supplied by the local distributor.

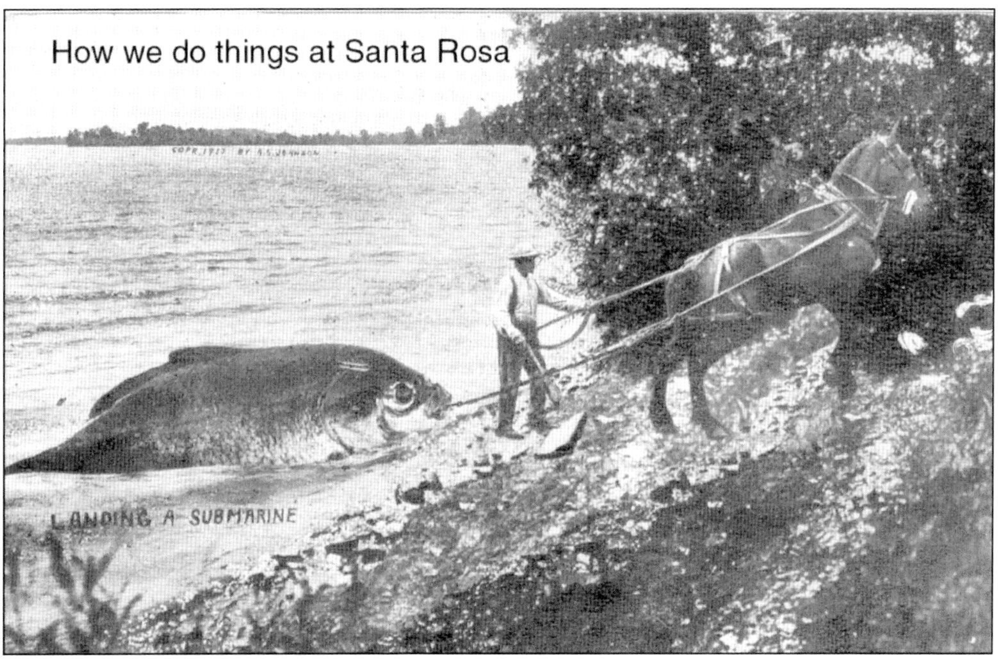

"How We Do Things at Santa Rosa," 1917. This postcard was mailed to Montana in July of 1920. It reads in part, "Dear Daddy, I am sending you this card so you will know what your coming to. I believe you would break your fishing record if you would go fishing here."

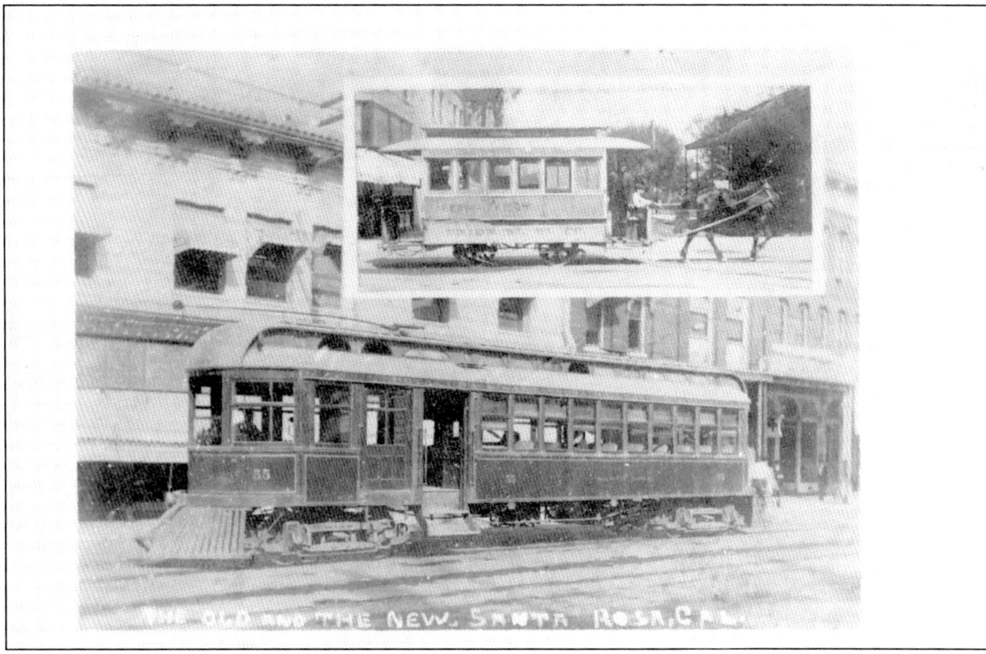

THE OLD AND THE NEW, C. 1905. A horse-drawn streetcar from the Union Street Railway of Santa Rosa appears in this image. In 1903 this company and others combined to form the Petaluma & Santa Rosa Electric Railway, which ran passenger service until 1932.

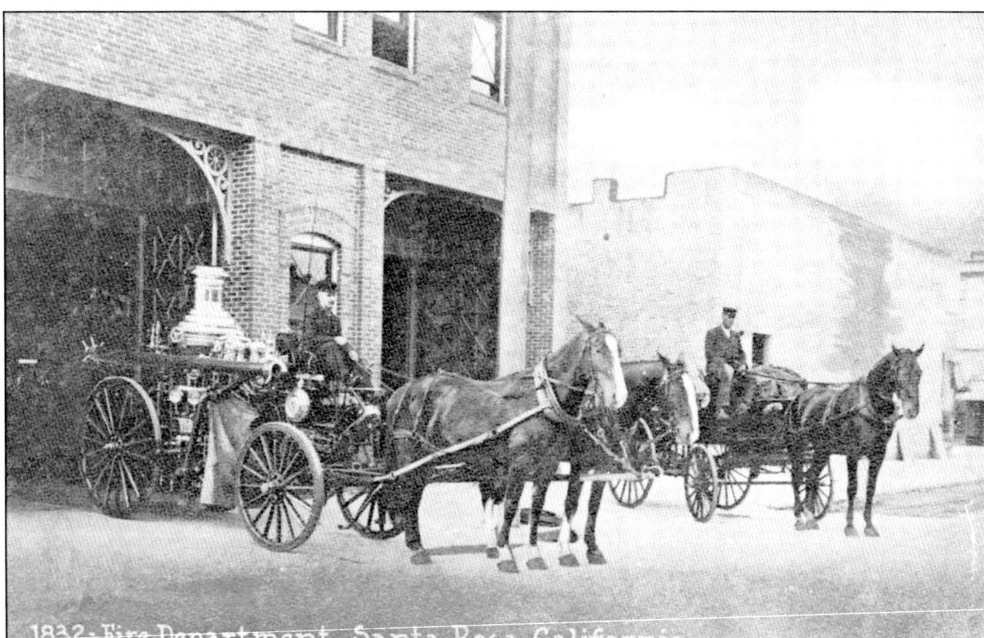

FIRE DEPARTMENT, C. 1905. The main fire station was located on Fifth Street near B Street. The steam pumper No. 2 was purchased in 1904 and is still owned by the Santa Rosa Fire Department. The other vehicle pictured is the Fire Chief's buggy.

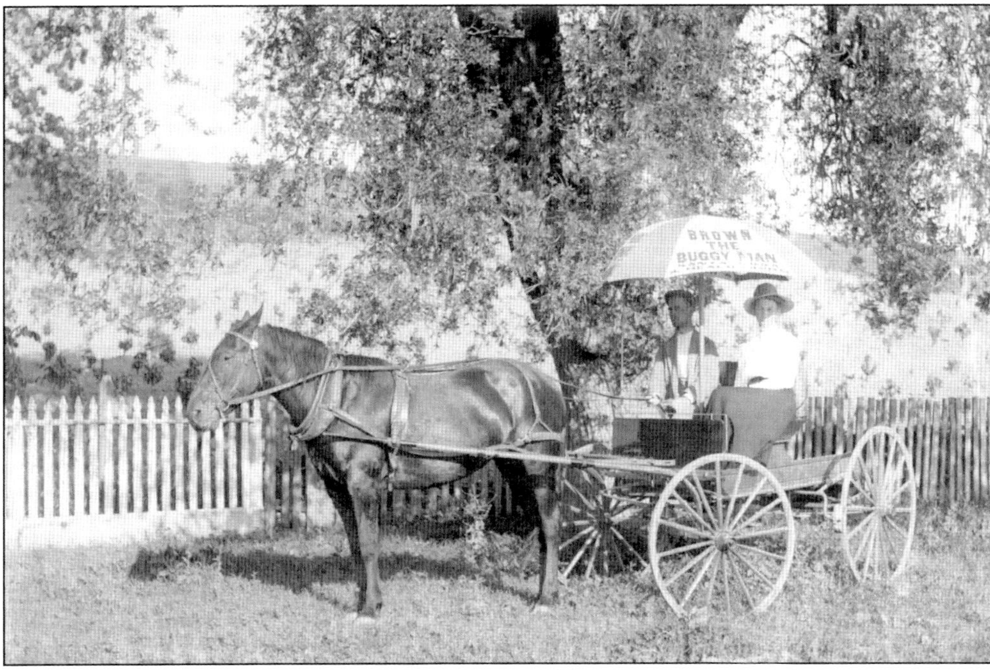

Brown, the Buggy Man, Santa Rosa, c. 1910. This enterprising merchant gave everyone who purchased a buggy from him a free umbrella!

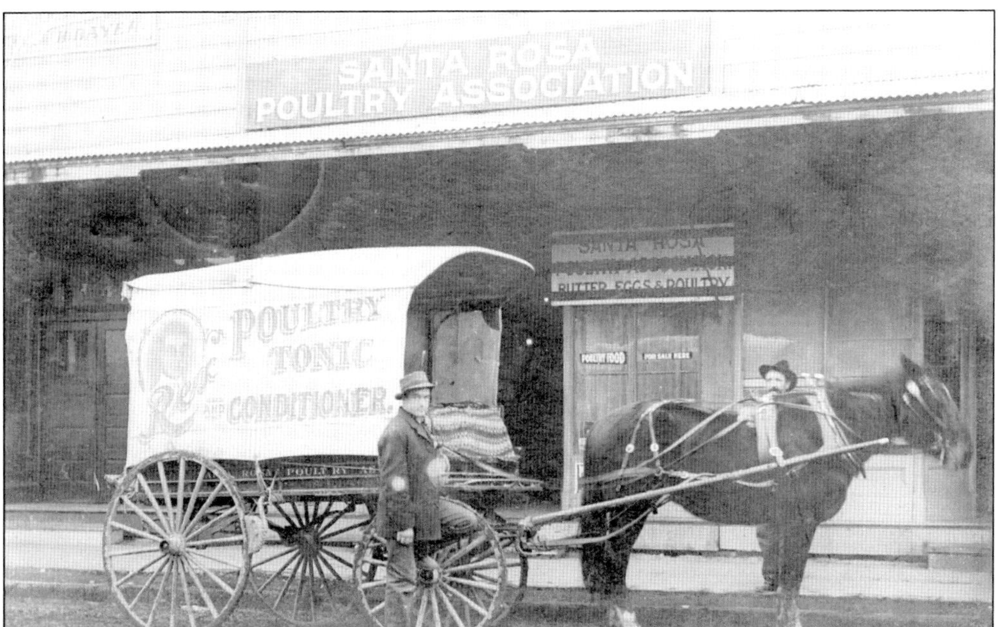

Santa Rosa Poultry Association, c. 1910. The Santa Rosa Poultry Association, located at 313–15 A Street, sold wholesale and retail goods to the poultry industry.

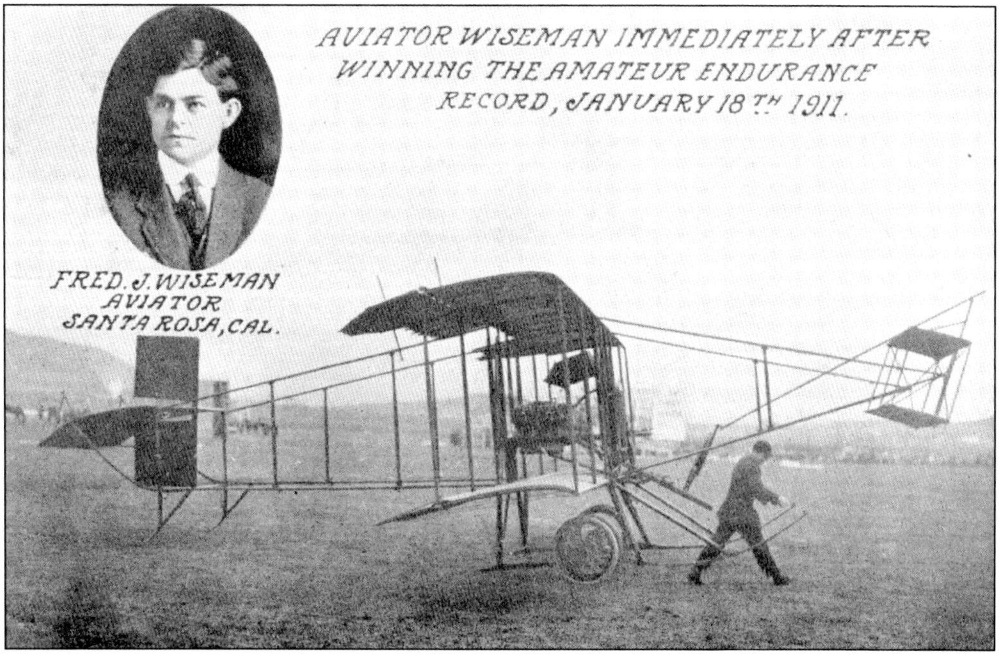

FRED J. WISEMAN, AVIATOR, 1911. Wiseman was the first man to build an "airship" in Sonoma County after visiting the Wright Brothers in Dayton, Ohio, in 1909. He had a short flying career, retiring from the air some ten years later. He said he didn't see any future in flying!

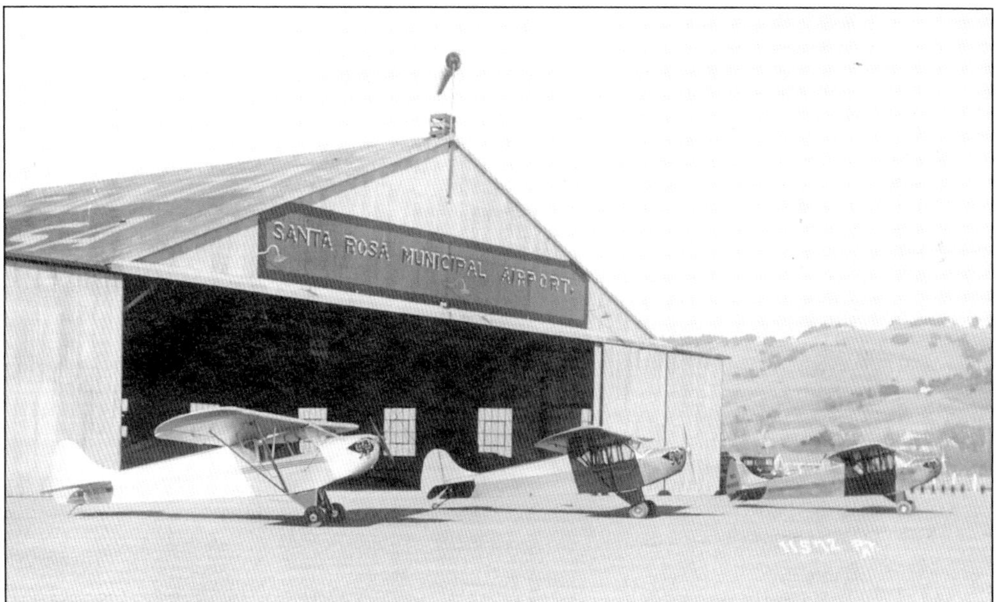

SANTA ROSA MUNICIPAL AIRPORT, C. 1935. This photocard shows the Municipal Airport located on the Fountaingrove Ranch property on the north edge of Santa Rosa. This airport operated until it was replaced by the existing one, on Airport Blvd., originally constructed as an Army Air Corps base in 1941.

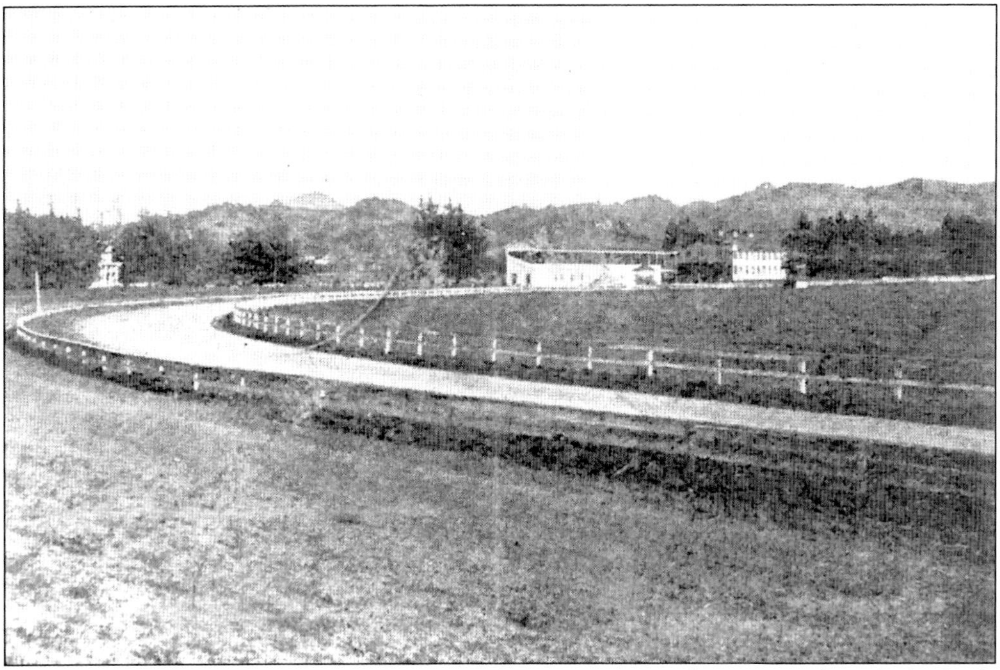

Sonoma County Racetrack, c. 1920. Mailed in 1920, this card is imprinted on the backside as a souvenir of the Sonoma County Fair, compliments of the *Santa Rosa Republican* newspaper. Two years later, in 1922, horse racing was outlawed for a time in California. People lost interest then, and there were no more fairs for 11 years.

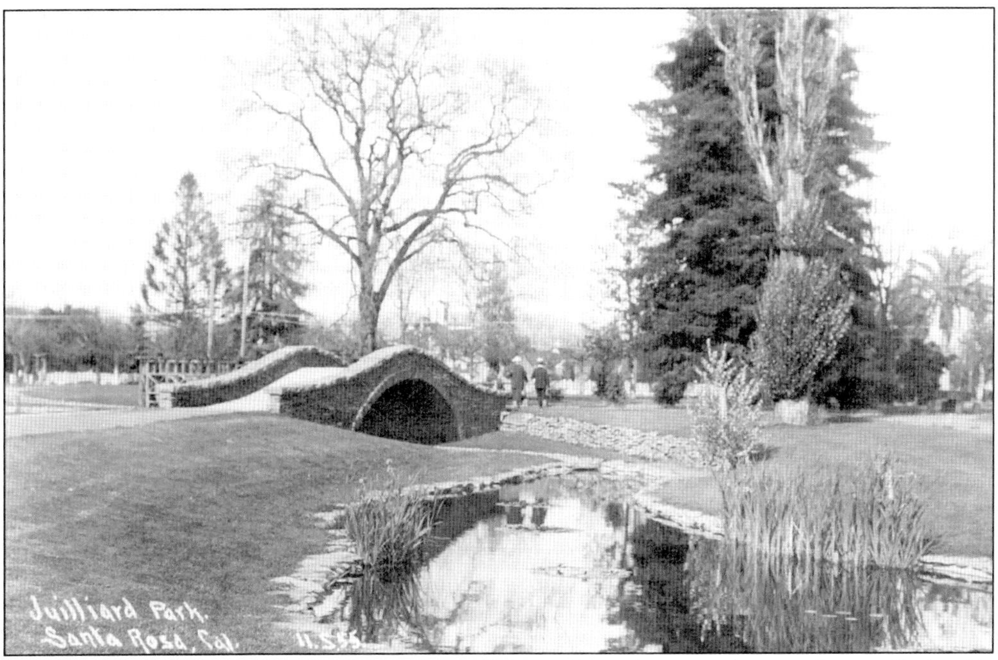

Juilliard Park, c. 1945. Looking east towards Santa Rosa Avenue, the cupola atop Burbank's carriage house appears in the background center of this photocard. Juilliard Park, beautifully designed in 1931, fortunately looks very much the same today.

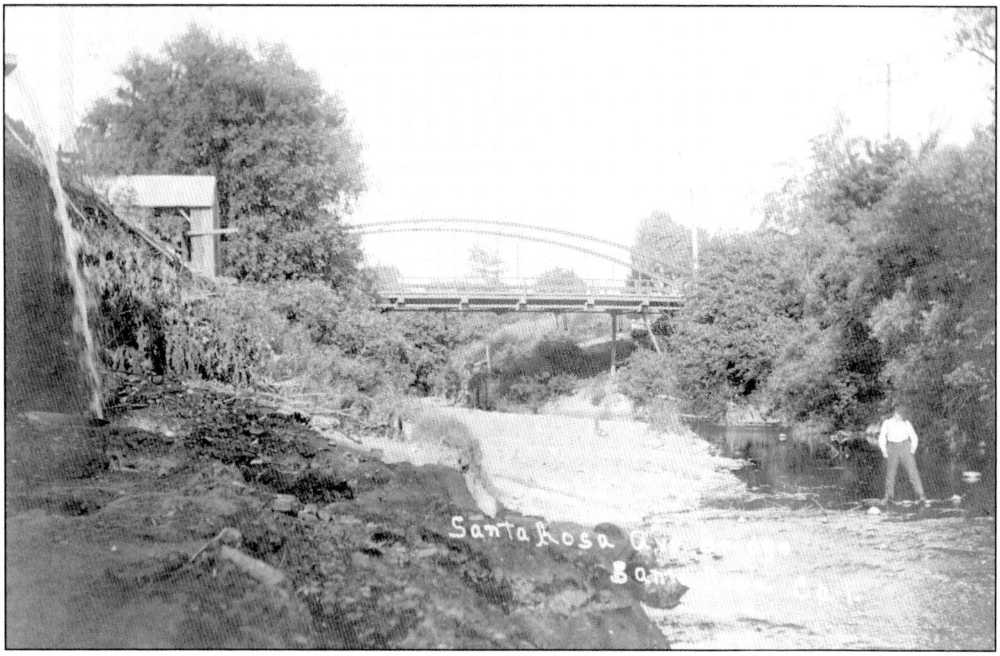

SANTA ROSA AVENUE BRIDGE, C. 1905. The postcards on these two pages show the major bridges over Santa Rosa Creek. The creek in all of these views was a much more beautiful and sizable waterway than we have today.

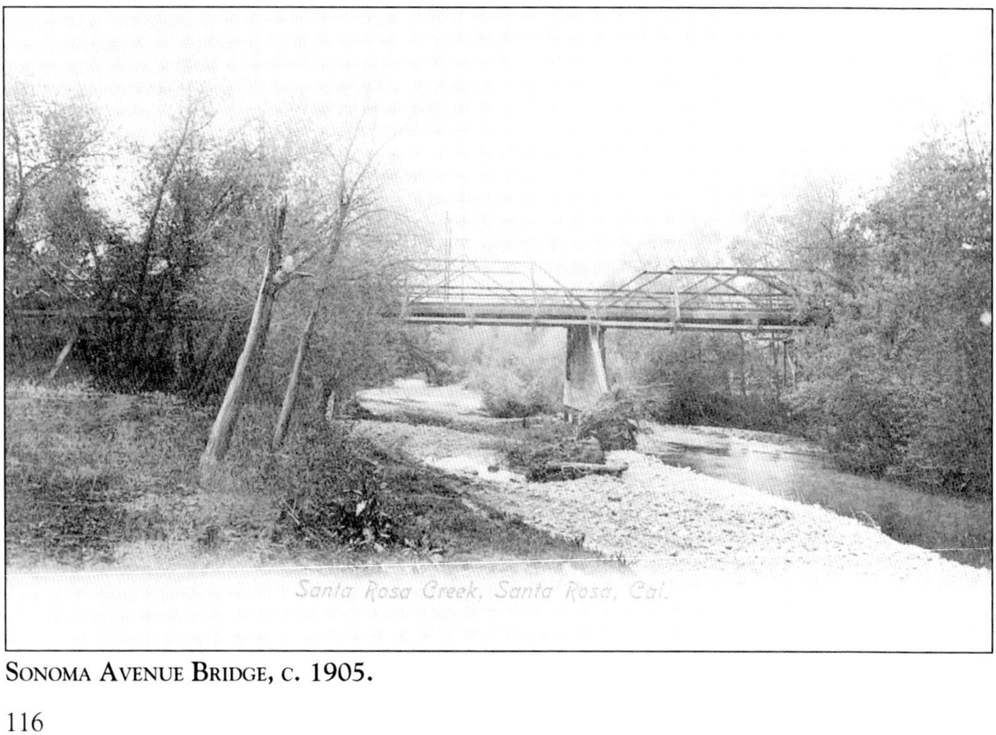

SONOMA AVENUE BRIDGE, C. 1905.

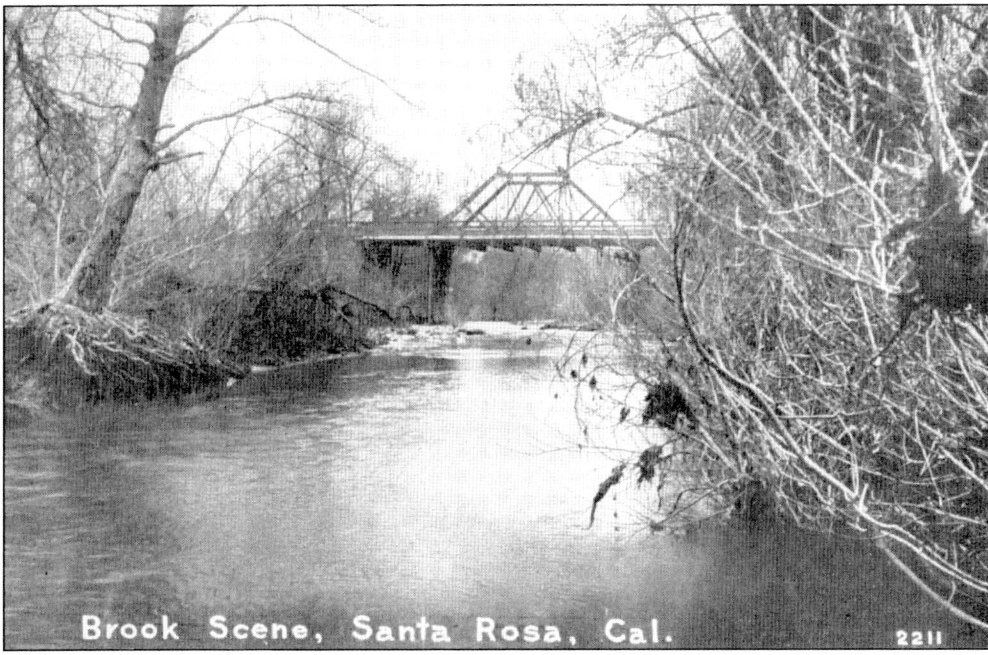

E STREET BRIDGE, C. 1910.

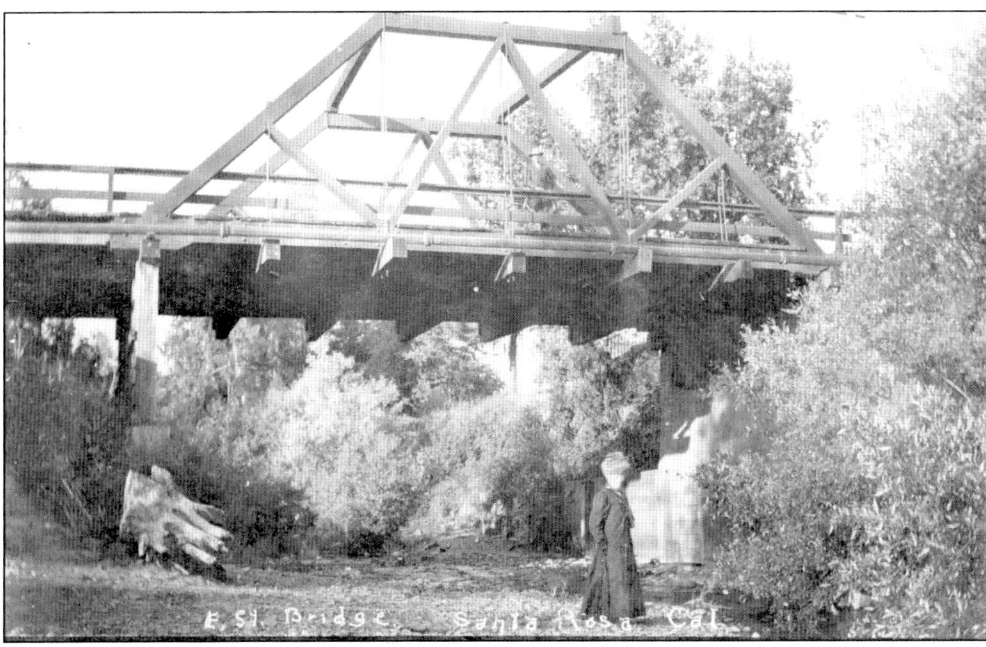

E STREET BRIDGE, CLOSE-UP VIEW, C. 1910.

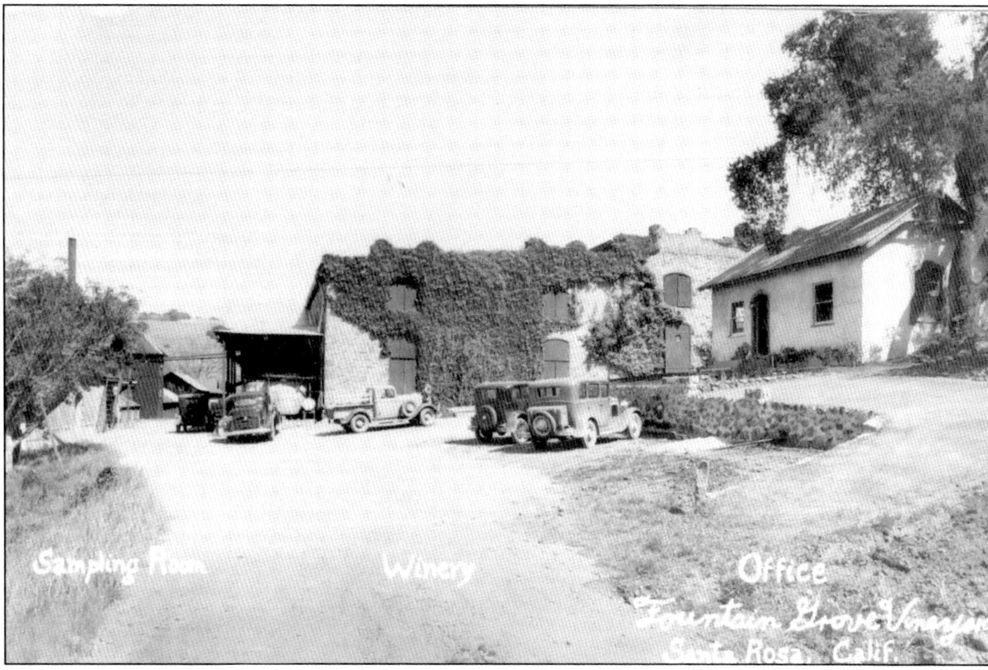

FOUNTAINGROVE VINEYARD, C. 1935. This winery, one of the earliest in Sonoma County, began producing premium wines in the 1870s and continued winemaking for some 75 years.

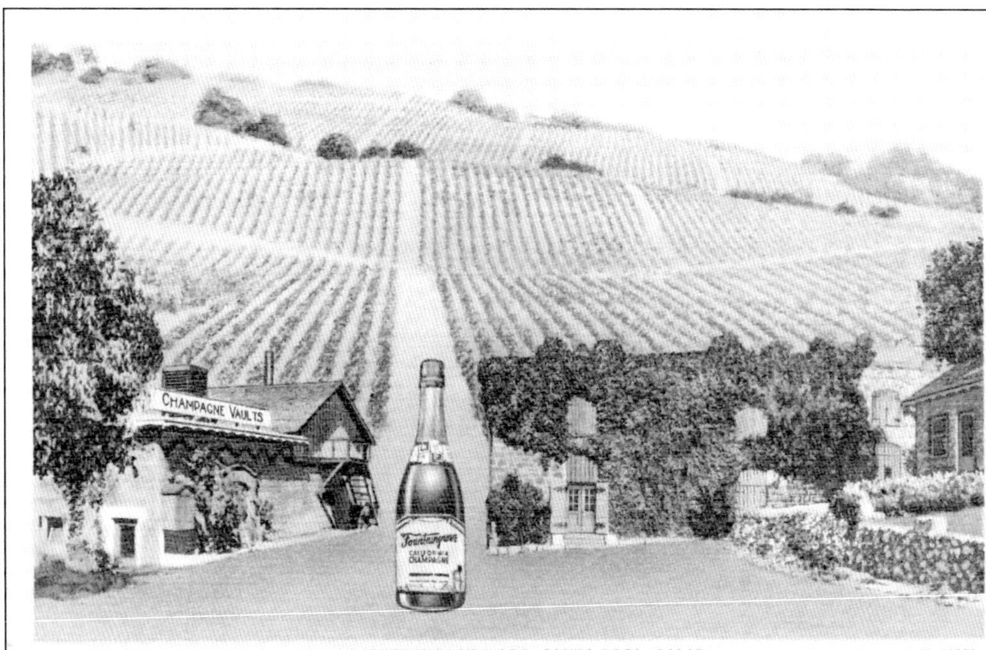

FOUNTAINGROVE VINEYARD, C. 1940. This advertising postcard depicts an artist's romantic version of the Fountaingrove Vineyards and Winery.

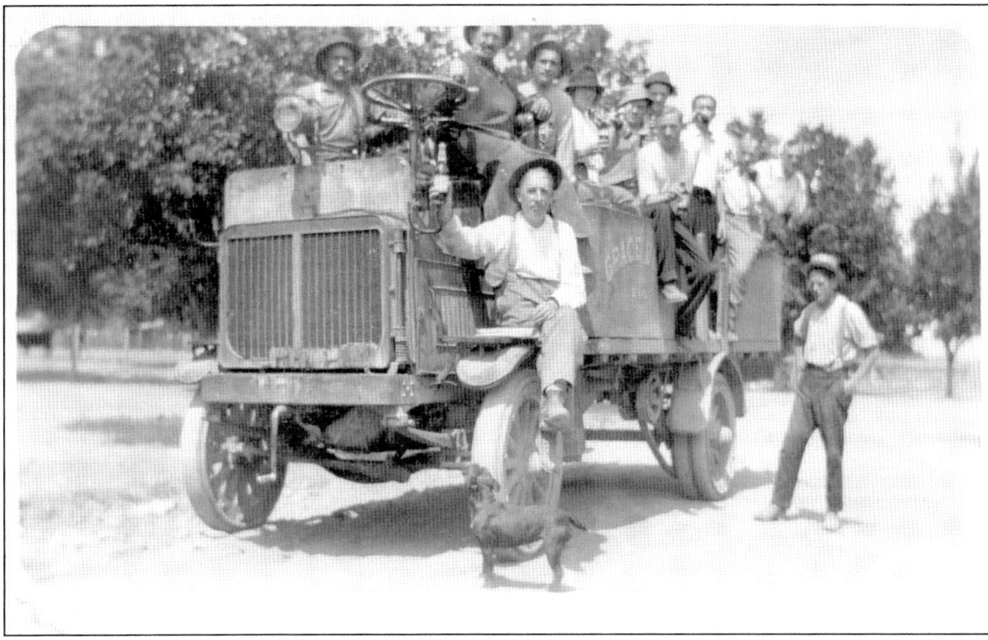

GRACE BROTHERS TRUCK. This great card shows an old Grace Bros. beer truck with folks either having one last drink before prohibition in 1920 or celebrating its repeal in 1932!

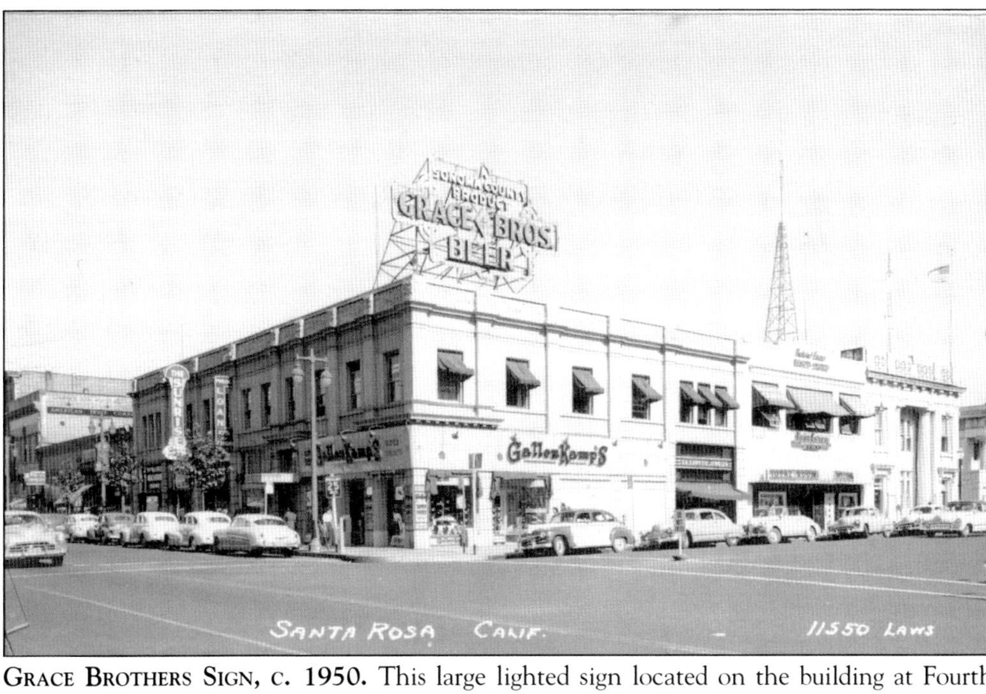

GRACE BROTHERS SIGN, c. 1950. This large lighted sign located on the building at Fourth Street and Hinton Avenue dominated the Santa Rosa skyline for many years.

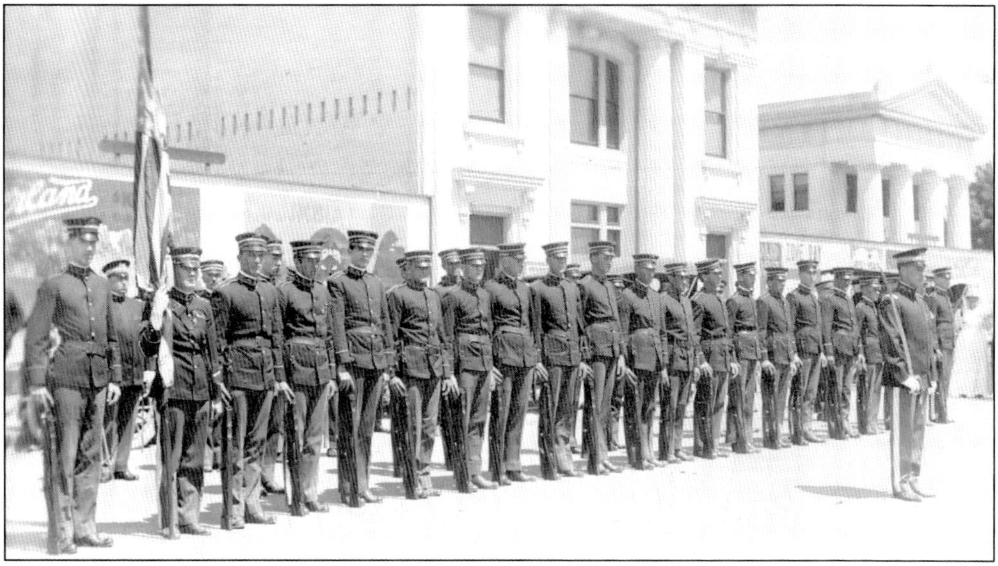

COMPANY E, FIFTH REGIMENT NATIONAL GUARD OF CALIFORNIA, c. 1910. This photocard shows Company E, consisting of Santa Rosa boys lined up for inspection in their parade uniforms in front of the Sheriff's Office and city hall on Hinton Avenue.

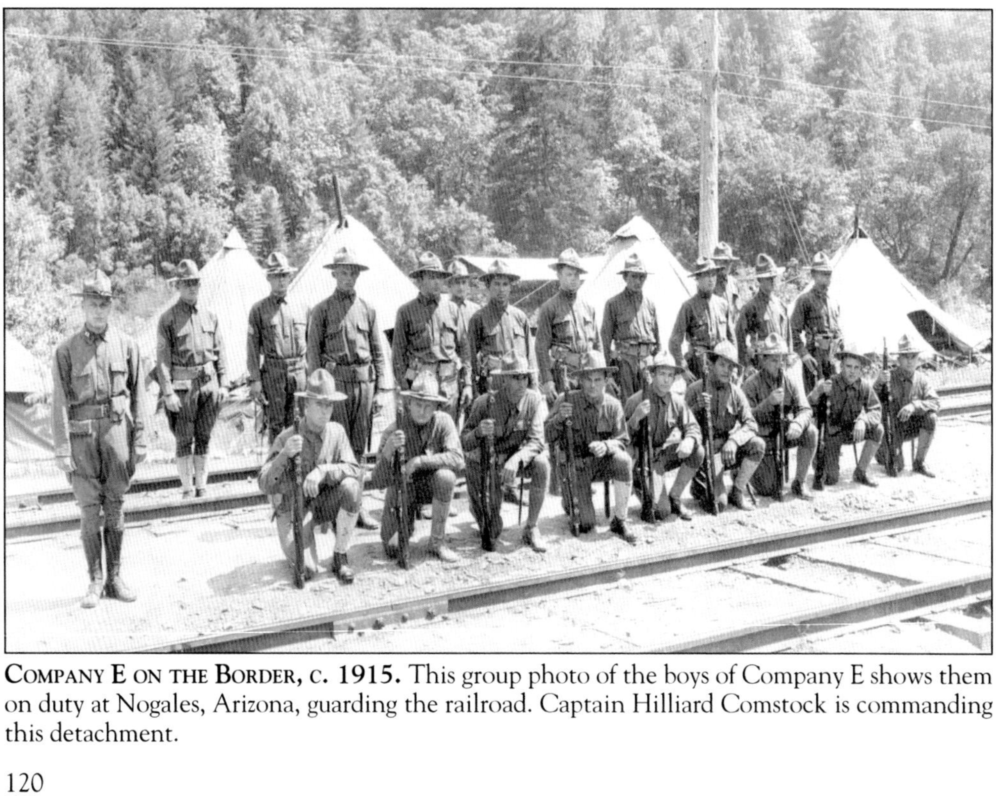

COMPANY E ON THE BORDER, c. 1915. This group photo of the boys of Company E shows them on duty at Nogales, Arizona, guarding the railroad. Captain Hilliard Comstock is commanding this detachment.

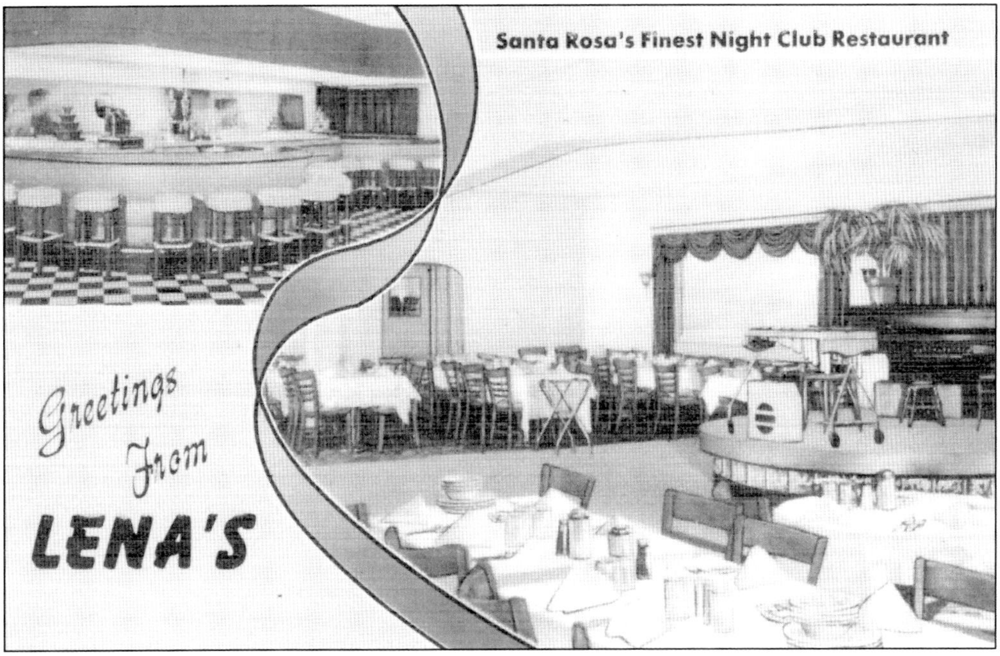

GREETINGS FROM LENA'S, C. 1945. Lena's, an established eatery that began in 1890 and was located at Sixth and Adams Streets, served its last meal in 1996.

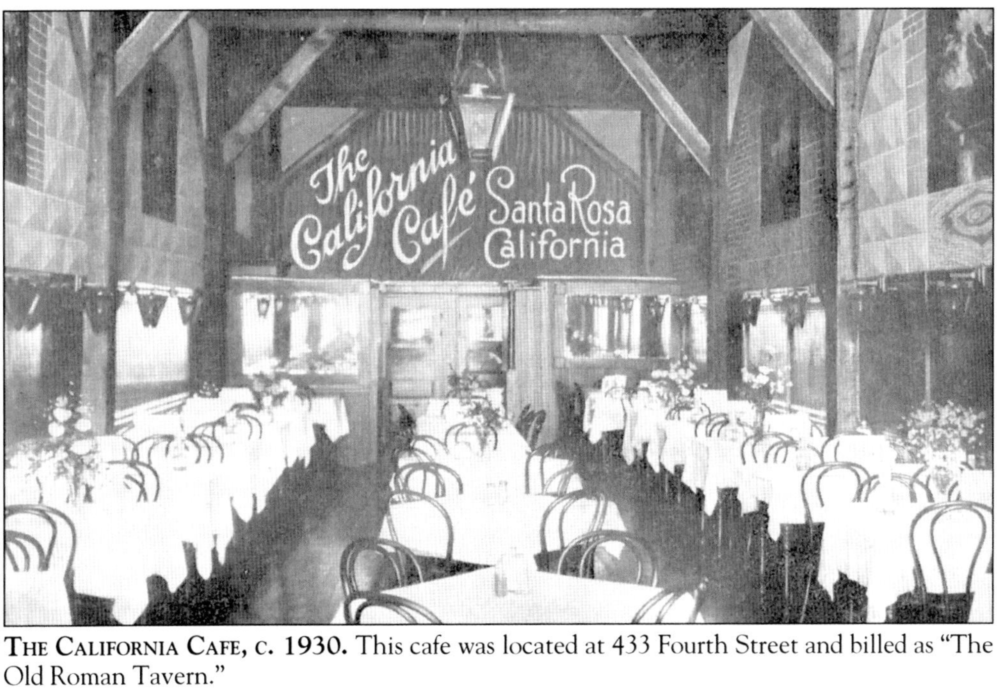

THE CALIFORNIA CAFE, C. 1930. This cafe was located at 433 Fourth Street and billed as "The Old Roman Tavern."

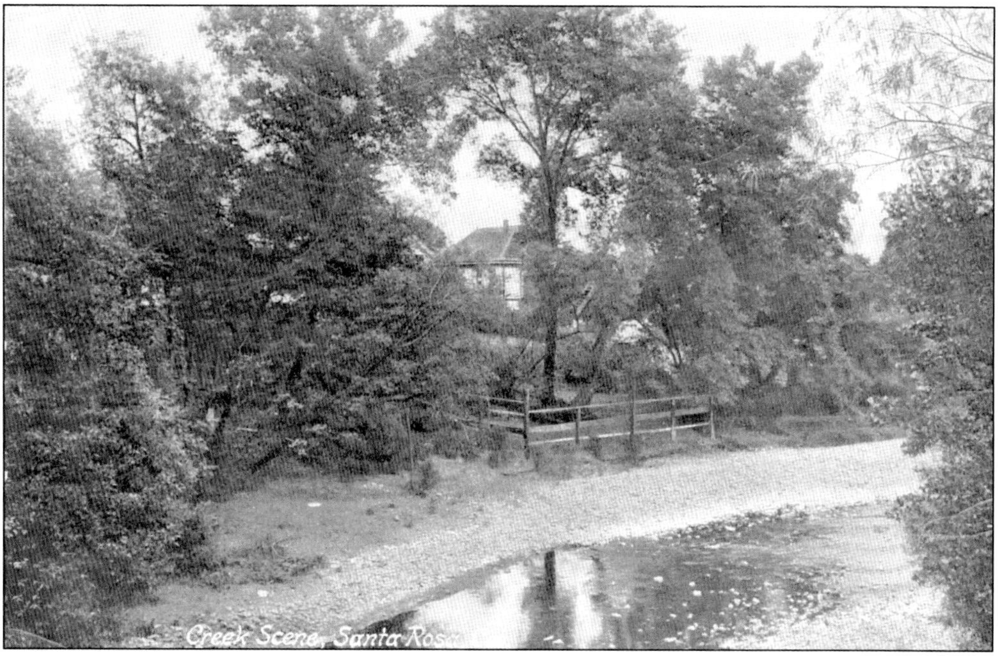

CREEK SCENE, C. 1905. Many cards of this type depict a tranquil time in Santa Rosa's past.

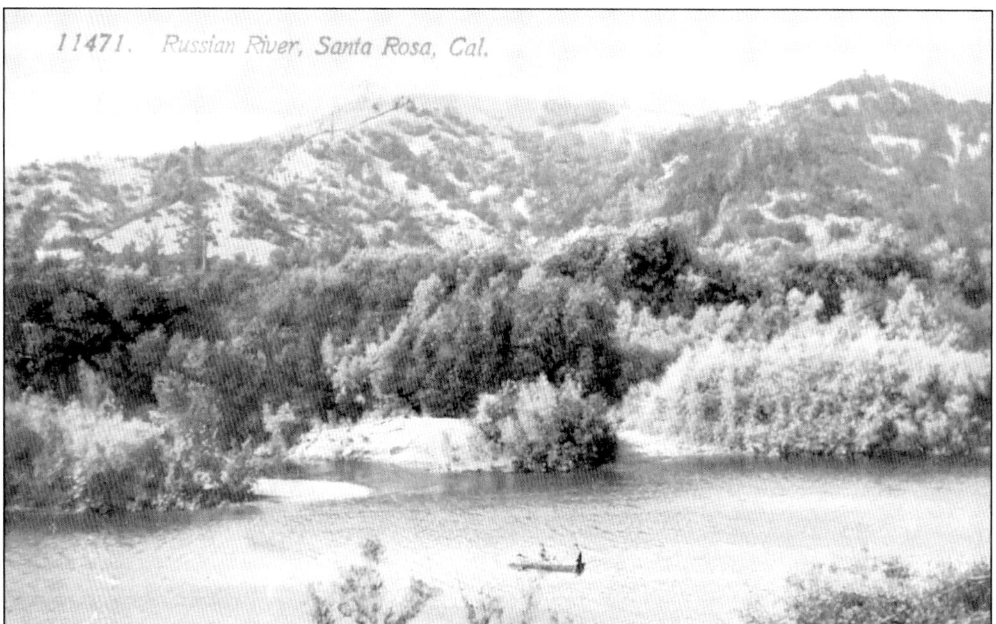

RUSSIAN RIVER, SANTA ROSA, C. 1910. Close, but no cigar! The Russian River was always a tourist destination, especially for San Francisco residents. Santa Rosa was a good 10 miles away from the Russian River, but what the heck, it looks good in print!

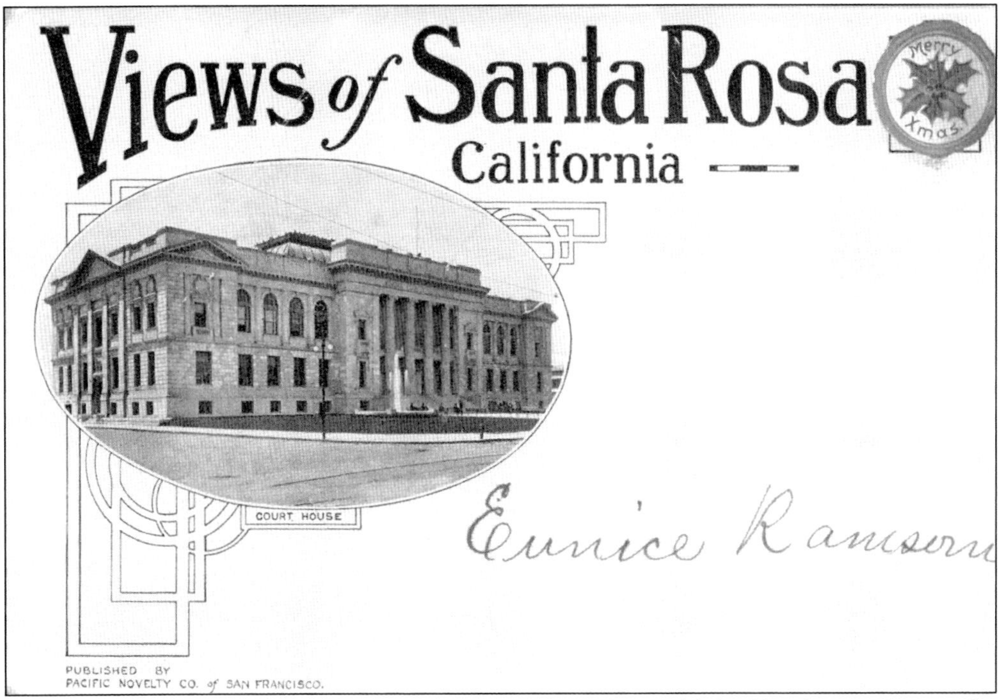

VIEWS OF SANTA ROSA, C. 1910. A postcard mailing packet, published by the Pacific Novelty Company of San Francisco, consisted of 19 different fold-out cards. Most of them have been published elsewhere in this book.

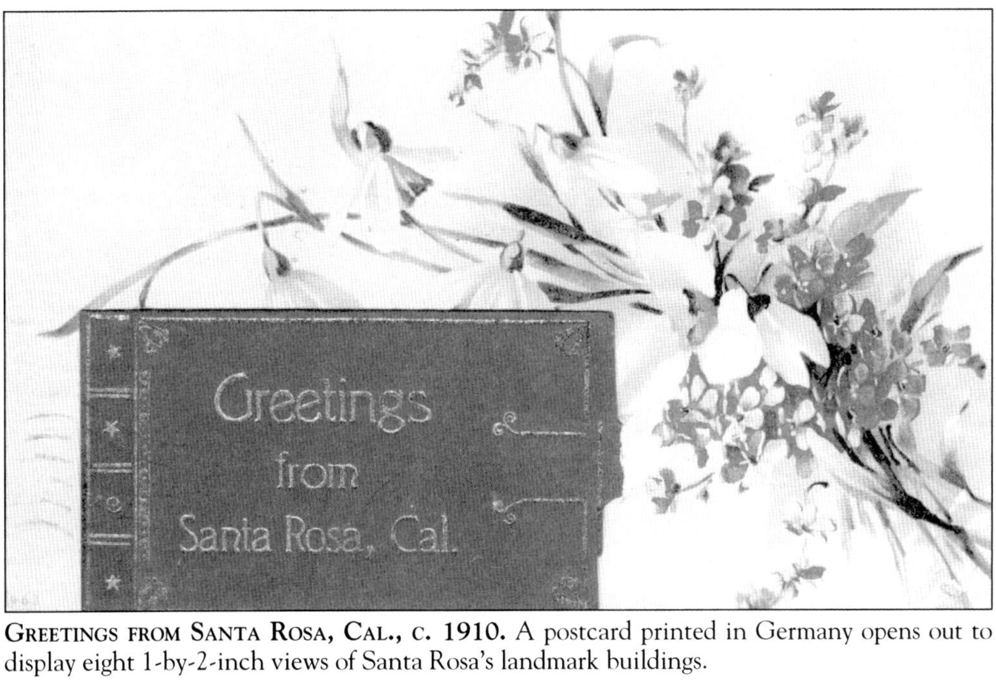

GREETINGS FROM SANTA ROSA, CAL., C. 1910. A postcard printed in Germany opens out to display eight 1-by-2-inch views of Santa Rosa's landmark buildings.

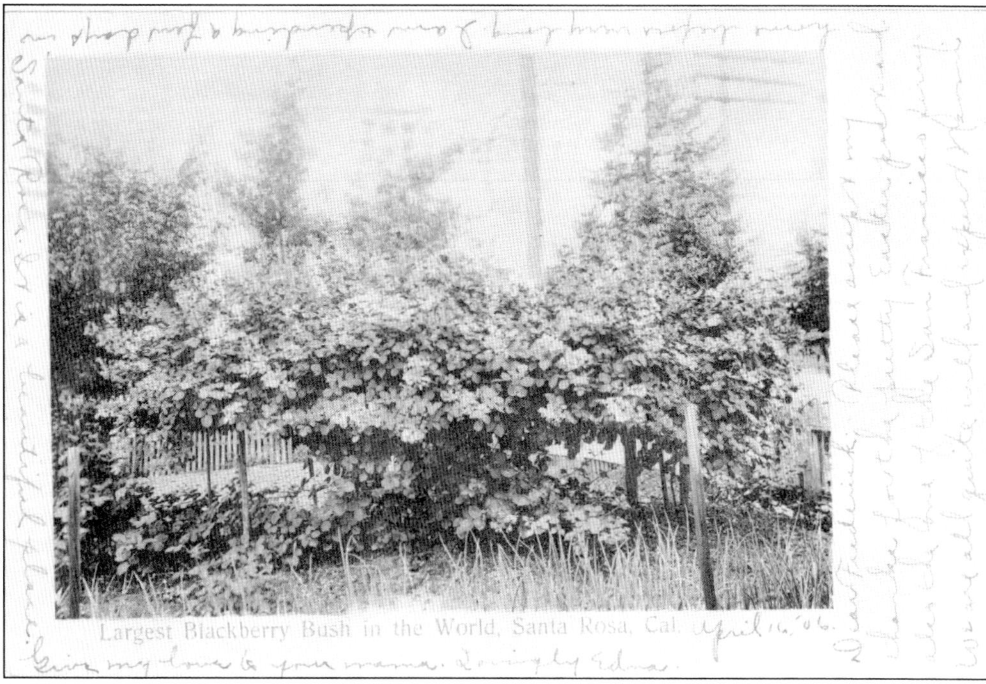

The Largest Blackberry Bush in the World, Santa Rosa, 1906.

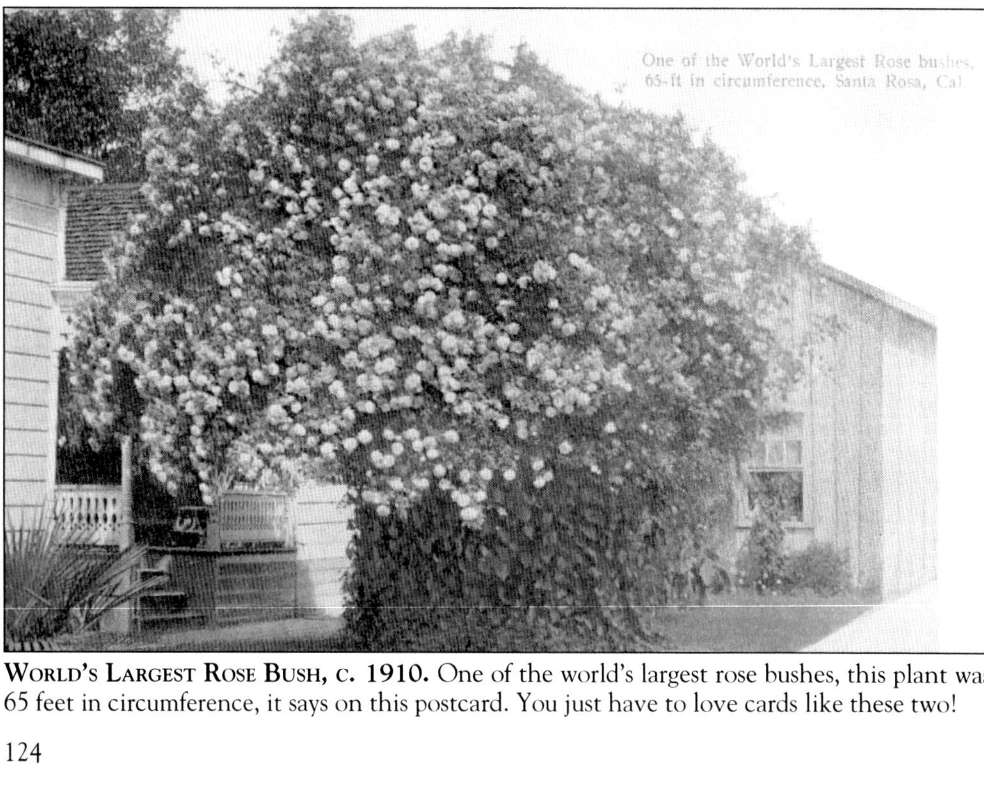

World's Largest Rose Bush, c. 1910. One of the world's largest rose bushes, this plant was 65 feet in circumference, it says on this postcard. You just have to love cards like these two!

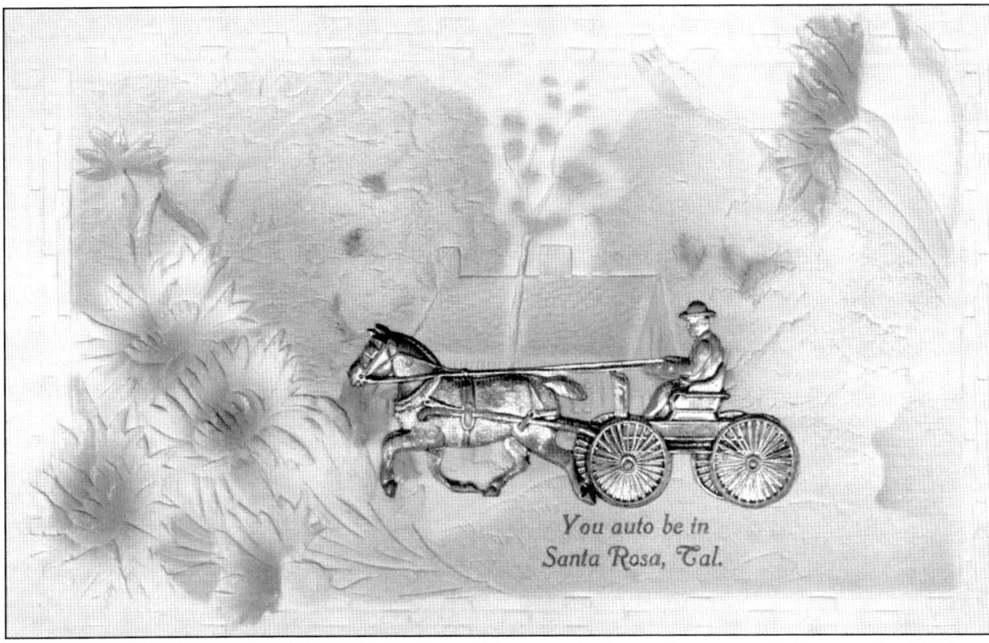

AN EMBOSSED POSTCARD. A heavily embossed figure of a horse, buggy, and driver is highlighted in this postcard.

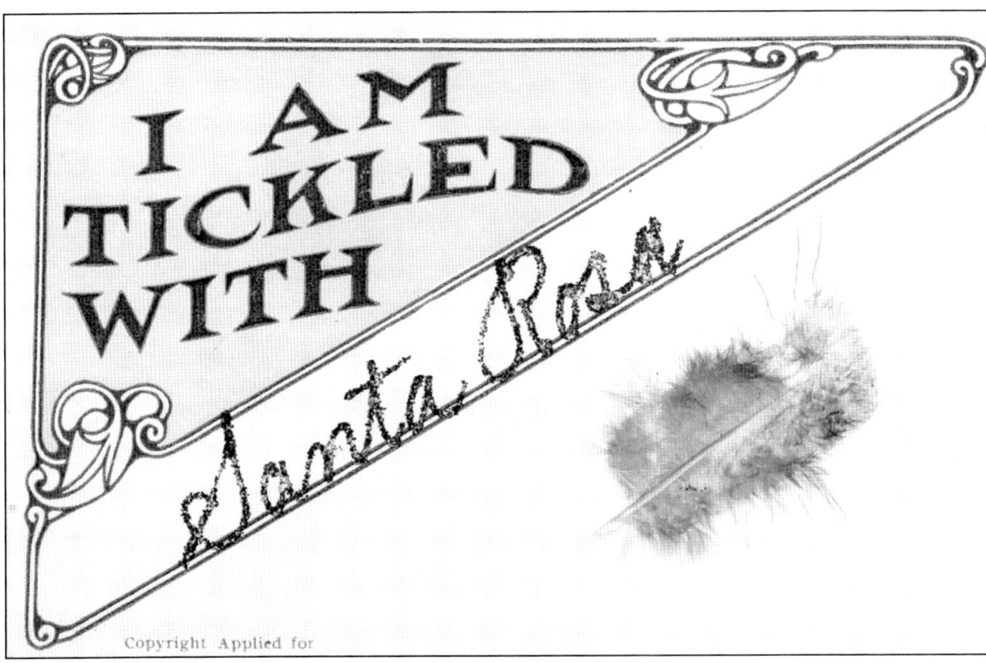

A REAL FEATHER POSTCARD.

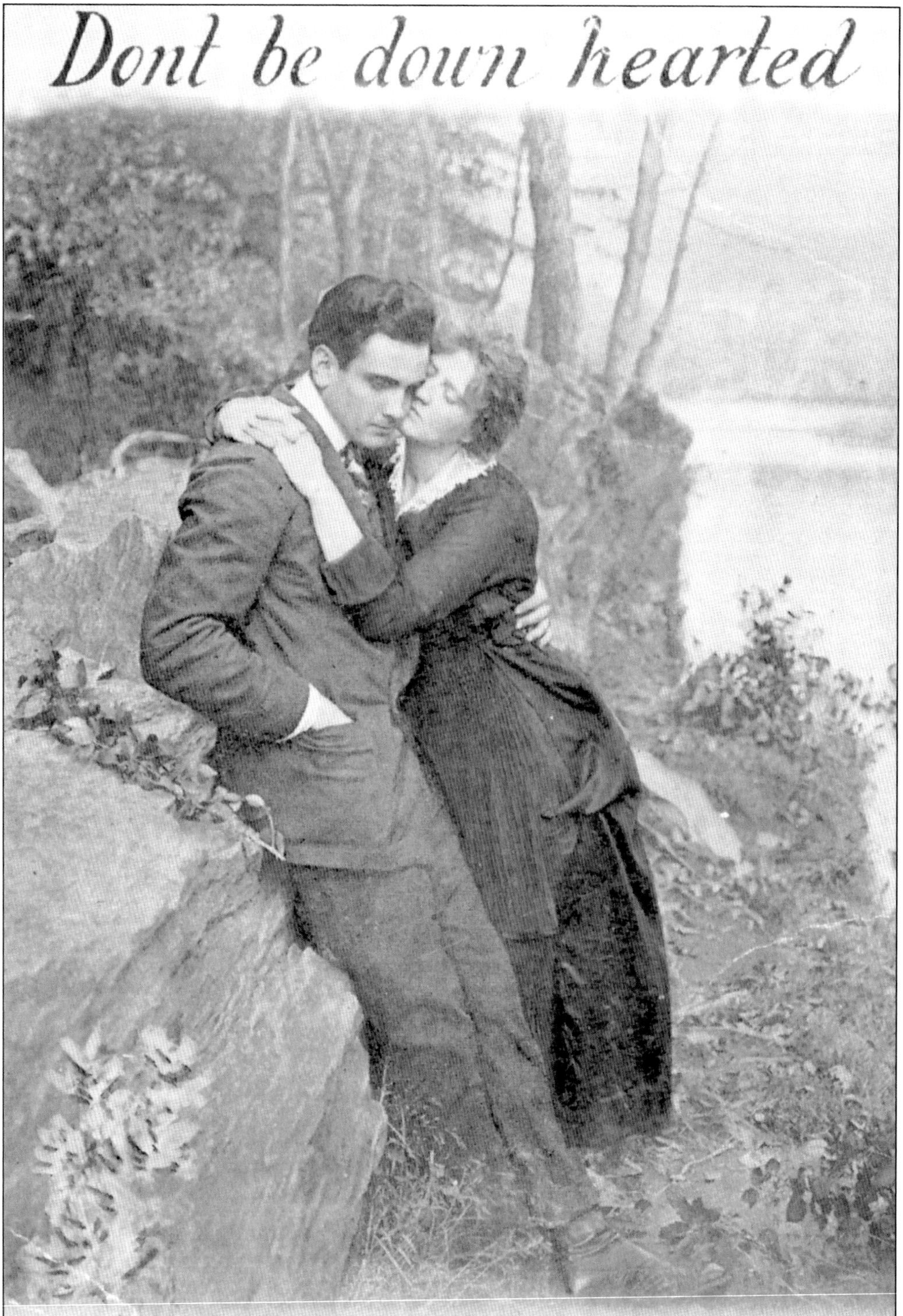

DID SHE SUCCEED IN CHEERING HIM UP? We'll never know!

BIBLIOGRAPHY

Blackman, Dee. *Fifty Famous Favorites*. Luther Burbank Home & Gardens, 1989.

Collins, Lynne. *Luther Burbank, A Biographical Sketch*. Luther Burbank Home & Gardens, 1992.

Gilbert, George. *Photography: The Early Years*. Harper and Row, 1980.

LeBaron, Gaye, Dee Blackman, Joann Mitchell, and Harvey Hansen. *Santa Rosa, A Nineteenth Century Town*. Historia, Ltd., 1985.

LeBaron, Gaye and Joann Mitchell. *Santa Rosa, A Twentieth Century Town*. Historia, Ltd., 1993.

Peterson, Geraldine and Dan. *Santa Rosa's Architectural Heritage*. Sonoma County Historical Society, 1982.

Slater, Lillian Burger. *Rose Carnivals of Santa Rosa in Review 1894–1932*. Press Democrat, 1932.

Stindt, Fred A. and Guy L. Dunscomb. *The Northwestern Pacific Railroad—Redwood Empire Route*. Stindt and Dunscomb, 1964.

Vanderwood, Paul J. and Frank N. Samponaro. *Border Fury*. University of New Mexico Press, 1988.

City Directories and Maps, Sonoma County Library.

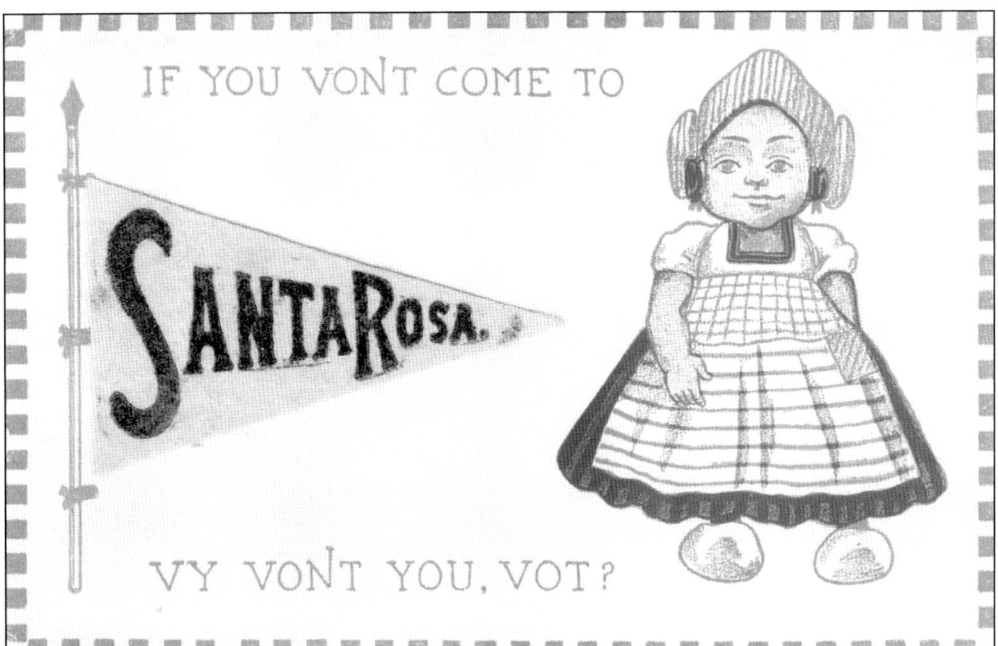

HOMETOWN POSTCARD. This comical postcard flew a felt pennant imprinted with the name of your hometown.

INDEX